Contents

A CRIME
OF
SELF-DEFENSE

Bernhard Goetz and the Law on Trial

George P. Fletcher

The University of Chicago Press

This edition is reprinted by arrangement with
The Free Press, a division of Macmillan, Inc.

The University of Chicago Press, Chicago 60637
Paperback edition published 1990
Printed in the United States of America

99 98 97 96 95 94 93 92   6 5 4 3

Library of Congress Cataloging-in-Publication Data

Fletcher, George P.
    A crime of self-defense : Bernhard Goetz and the law
on trial / George P. Fletcher.
        p.   cm.
    Includes bibliographical references.
    ISBN 0-226-25334-1 (paperback)
    1. Goetz, Bernhard Hugo, 1947-   —Trials,
litigation, etc.   2. Trials (Assault and battery)—New
York (N.Y.)   3. Self-defense (Law)—United States.
I. Title.
KF224.G63F54   1990
345.73'04—dc20
[347.3054]   90-35781
                                                  CIP

⊗ The paper used in this publication meets the minimum
requirements of the American National Standard for
Information Sciences—Permanence of Paper for Printed
Library Materials, ANSI Z39.48-1984

_____ Preface _____

MANY portions of this book were written in places where people could look over my shoulder at the manuscript. Whenever anyone noticed that the subject was the Goetz case, I could count on a pointed and often passionate comment. Whether a stranger on an airplane or a passerby in a café, everyone had an opinion about the rights and wrongs of Goetz's shooting. Doormen and cab drivers became instant social philosophers. Nurses, dentists, shopkeepers, waiters—no one was at a loss for an opinion about what should be done in a case that touched our instinct to survive in an America ridden by violence and poverty.

While the facts of the Goetz case are clear in their basic outline, the social and moral implications of Goetz's shooting invite argument. The problems of crime and racial bigotry stand out in the foreground, but as the discussion deepens, we pass beyond these signposts of urban malaise and come upon troublesome questions of moral and legal responsibility. When and under what circumstances should individuals be able to defend themselves? Should the race of the feared assailants be relevant? Who is in a position to judge whether acting in self-defense should be punished as a crime?

These questions are not new to law teachers, who meet with students and colleagues in commodious university rooms to ponder the foundations of the legal system. I have written about these questions many times for audiences of academic lawyers and philosophers. It is rare, however, that the philosophical inquiries of the academic world have such a strong and direct bearing on the morality of interaction in the oppressive world of a filthy, graffiti-marred subway car. As the prosecution of Bernhard Goetz unfolded, it became clear to me that this was a case in which the theory of criminal law was indispensable to a proper understanding of what was going on. For many, the pending trial of Bernhard Goetz loomed as a struggle between black and white, between crime victims and the law-enforcement establishment. For me, the trial presented itself rather as a gripping realization of moral and theoretical questions that have long been on my agenda.

When the prescreening of the jurors began in December 1986, Acting Justice Stephen G. Crane graciously welcomed me as an academic observer to the small group that would sit around a seminar table and talk privately to prospective jurors about their knowledge of the case and their possible biases. Gregory Waples, for the prosecution, and Barry Slotnick and Mark Baker, for the defense, also kindly consented to my presence in these often personal conversations with the candidates for the jury. As the jury selection progressed and the trial began, I developed admiration for these men who would seek, in the ritual of legal debate, to domesticate urban conflict within the bounds of civilized discourse. Of course, each of them made tactical and legal mistakes, and I point these out in this book. But given the pressures under which they were acting, given the number of tormenting decisions that had to be made every day of the trial, the performances of Crane, Waples, Slotnick, and Baker were of historical moment. Whatever their task—judging, prosecuting, or defending—they demonstrated how much lawyers have to offer in society's quest for the orderly resolution of fundamental conflict.

I have been aided in my observations and writing by research assistants whose passionate interest in the case paralleled my own. Charles C. Hwang observed portions of the prescreening and made useful observations. Suzanne D. Malmgren was in court every day during the public portion of jury selection. Her nonlegal wisdom and sensitivity proved to be invaluable. I am indebted to her, as well, for laboring as my secretary on various phases of the manuscript. Adam R. Kasanof came to the project after the trial was over, but having been a New York city peace officer before coming to law school, he was able to supplement my theoretical work with insights from the law of the streets.

Several of my colleagues, Bruce Ackerman and H. Richard Uviller, read portions of the manuscript and gave me encouragement and criticism. Gerard E. Lynch read it all and responded with detailed comments worthy of publication in their own right.

My editor, Joyce Seltzer, sustained this effort with encouragement at the right moments and taught me to appreciate the beauty of the law as understood by the lay reader.

As I could not possibly satisfy all those who joined the discussion along the way, I am sure that this printed final version of my thoughts will provoke disagreement. The Goetz case has become a cultural monument precisely because it is so difficult to reduce the meaning of the case to a few words and determine, definitively, whether justice was done.

New York City
January 1988

1

A Shooting
in the Subway

DECEMBER 22, 1984, the Saturday before Christmas, about 1:00 P.M., Bernhard Goetz leaves his apartment at 55 West 14th Street and walks to the subway station at the corner of Seventh Avenue and 14th Street. He enters a car on the number 2 line, the IRT express running downtown, and sits down close to four black youths. The youths, seeming drifters on the landscape of the city, are noisy and boisterous, and the 15 to 20 other passengers have moved to the other end of the car. Goetz is white, 37 years old, slightly built, and dressed in dungarees and a windbreaker. Something about his appearance beckons. One of the four, Troy Canty, lying nearly prone on the long bench next to the door, asks Goetz as he enters, "How are ya?" Canty and possibly a second youth, Barry Allen, then approach Goetz, and Canty asks him for five dollars. Goetz asks him what he wants. Canty repeats: "Give me five dollars."[1] Suddenly, the moving car resounds with gunshots, one aimed at each of the young blacks.

At this point the story becomes uncertain. According to Goetz's subsequent confession, he pauses, goes over to a youth sitting in the two-seater by the conductor's cab at the end of the car, looks at him, and says, "You seem to be [doing] all right; here's another,"[2] and fires a fifth shot that empties his five-shot Smith & Wesson .38 revolver. The bullet enters Darrell Cabey's body on his left side, traverses the back, and severs his spinal cord. There are other interpretations of these events, particularly an argument that Goetz hit Cabey on the fourth rather than the fifth shot, but in the early days after

1

the shooting these alternative accounts are not widely disseminated.

Someone pulls the emergency brake and the train screeches to a halt. The passengers flee the car, but two women remain, immobilized by fear. Goetz says some soothing words to the fearful women, and then a conductor approaches and asks him whether he is a cop. The gunman replies, "They tried to rip me off." He refuses to hand over his gun and quietly walks to the front of the car, enters the platform between cars, patiently unfastens the safety chain, jumps to the tracks below, and disappears into the dark of the subway tunnel. Three young black kids lie bleeding on the floor of the train; Darrell Cabey sits wounded and paralyzed in the end seat.

A mythical figure is born—an unlikely avenger for the fear that both unites and levels all urban dwellers in the United States. If the four kids had mugged a passenger, newspaper reporters would have sighed in boredom. There are, on the average, 38 crimes a day on the New York subways. If a police officer had intervened and shot four kids who were hassling a rider for money, protests of racism and police brutality would have been the call of the day. This was different. A common man had emerged from the shadows of fear. He shot back when others only fantasize their responses to shakedowns on the New York subways.

Like the Lone Ranger, the mysterious gunman subdues the criminals and disappears into the night. If he had been apprehended immediately, the scars and flaws of his own personality might have checked the public's tendency to romanticize him. The analogy to Charles Bronson's avenging crime in *Death Wish* is on everyone's lips. The *Times* remains cautious, but the *Post,* from the beginning, dubs the unknown gunman the "subway vigilante." The police participate in this posturing of the case by setting up an "avenger hotline." They expect to receive tips leading to an arrest and eventually they get one, but at first they are swamped with calls supporting the "avenger." Though Mayor Ed Koch condemns the violence, he too inflates the incident by describing it as the act of a vigilante. No common criminal, this one. An everyman had come out of the crowd and etched his actions, right or wrong, in the public imagination.

With no offender to bear down on, the press has only the four black kids to portray in the news; the picture they present is not attractive. Uneducated, with criminal records, on the prowl for a few dollars, they exemplify the underclass of teenage criminals feared by both blacks and whites. In October of the same year, Darrell Cabey, age 19, had been arrested in the Bronx on charges of armed robbery. In 1983, James Ramseur, age 18, and Troy Canty, age 19, had both served short sentences for petty thievery. Barry Allen, age 18, had twice pled guilty to charges of disorderly conduct. James Ramseur and Darrell Cabey are found with a total of three screwdrivers in their pockets—the tools of their petty thievery. The few witnesses who come forward describe the behavior of the four youths before Goetz entered the car as "boisterous."

The emerging information supports the picture that frustrated New Yorkers want to believe in. Four stereotypical muggers who harass and hound a frail-looking middle-class "whitey." That he should turn out, against all odds, to be armed confirms the extraordinary nature of true, spontaneous justice. It is not often that things turn out right, and here in the season of religious miracles comes an event in which good triumphs over evil.

A willingness to accept a rumor of "sharpened screwdrivers" testifies to the widespread bias in favor of the romanticized gunman. The *Times* reported the day after the shooting that two of the victims were found with screwdrivers in their jackets. There was no suggestion that they were "sharpened." Somehow, however, the story got abroad that the screwdrivers were sharpened weapons rather than merely tools for opening sealed metal boxes. On the "Donahue" show, a week after the event, the discussion was of "sharpened" screwdrivers. In an article in the *Times* surveying the first week's events, the writer reports the supposed fact: "three of the youths were found to be carrying sharpened screwdrivers."[3] Some journalists resist the popular rumor that the screwdrivers were specially prepared weapons of assault.[4] On the whole, however, the press and the public want to believe the worst about the subway victims.

Goetz makes an effort to go underground. On the day of the shooting he rents a car and drives north to Vermont and New Hampshire. As he later describes it, "heading north, is the way to go if there's a problem."[5] The countryside in New England may remind him reassuringly of his early years in rural upstate New York.[6] He thinks "the system would interpret it as one more crime. I just figured I'd get away for two days, I wanted to come back."[7] When he does come back to New York a few days later, he learns that the police, acting on a tip that Goetz meets the description of the slight blond gunman, left notes for him in his mailbox and on his door. They want to talk to him, but they are far from having singled him out as a serious suspect. Nonetheless, he fears apprehension and returns to Vermont and New Hampshire. He agonizes for almost two days and then walks into the police station in Concord, New Hampshire, shortly after noon on December 31.

He delivers several lengthy confessions. One two-hour interview with the New Hampshire police is recorded on audiotape; another of equal length, with New York authorities, is videotaped. Neither of these is fully disclosed to the public until after the trial begins. Goetz is turned over to the New York authorities on January 3, 1985, and spends a few days at Rikers Island prison. When he is released January 7 on $50,000 bail, his popular support is at its peak.

From the very beginning, the Goetz proceedings are caught in a political dialectic between the rush of popular support for the "subway vigilante" and the official attitude of outrage that anyone would dare usurp the state's task of keeping law and order. While the public calls into the newly established police hotline to express support for the wanted man, public officials, ranging from President Reagan to black leaders to Mayor Koch, come out strongly against "vigilantism" on the streets. The general public might applaud a little man's striking back against uncontrolled violence, but the President speaks of the "breakdown of civilization" when people like Bernhard Goetz "take the law into their own hands." Hazel Dukes of the NAACP calls Goetz a 21st-century version of a Ku Klux Klan "nightrider."

These pitted, hostile forces eventually find their way into well-prepared channels of legal argument and customary patterns of legal maneuvering. The legal system converts our ill-understood rage into a stylized mode of debate about broader issues of criminal responsibility and fair procedure. The "breakdown of civilization" never comes to pass, precisely because the issue of defending oneself against a threat in the subway can be formulated as a question beyond passion and instinctual conflict.

The tension in these background forces causes Goetz's public image and legal position to fluctuate wildly. On January 25, a first grand jury convenes and hears the taped confessions and the few witnesses that have come forward. None of the victims testifies against Goetz. The grand jury refuses to indict Goetz for anything more serious than three counts of illegal gun possession.[8] Apparently, the 23 laypeople on the grand jury assume that Goetz has such a persuasive claim of self-defense that there is no point in indicting him for assault, attempted murder, or even reckless endangerment.

Goetz's legal team celebrates. The mayor pronounces the judgment "Solomonic" (forgetting, presumably, that Solomon did not actually compromise and slash the baby in two). But the relief proves to be premature. Goetz becomes a media celebrity, and every appearance seems to generate more skepticism about New York's "folk hero." He urges distribution of an additional 25,000 guns to properly trained private citizens. His lawyer says on "Face the Nation" that the subway gunman feels no remorse about the near killings.

In February 1985 Goetz's fortunes begin to turn. His neighbor Myra Friedman publishes an article in *New York* magazine which attributes to him overtly racist views about cleaning up the "spics and niggers" on 14th Street. Two of the victims, Troy Canty and Darrell Cabey, file lawsuits for tort damages against him. Backed by civil rights lawyer William Kunstler, Cabey demands $50 million in damages. The N.Y. District Attorney, Robert Morgenthau, comes under increasing criticism for not having made a better case to the first grand jury. He could, after all, have offered immunity to the four youths, thereby securing testimony that they intended merely to panhandle, not to molest or mug.

On February 26, Rudolph W. Giuliani, U.S. Attorney in Manhattan, makes it clear that he will not take the pressure off the local prosecutors. There will be no federal prosecution against Goetz for having deprived the four youths of their civil rights (the only basis for federal intervention); apparently, there is insufficient evidence that the shooting expressed a racial motive. Significantly, of the two women that Goetz sought to soothe with his comments after the shooting, one was black.

The following day, Morgenthau's office releases a police report from New Hampshire that creates a new and far more incriminating scenario of the fifth shot that paralyzed Darrell Cabey. For the first time the public learns of the line that would resonate through the case: "You seem to be [doing] all right; here's another."[9] The defense protests that the disclosure makes its client look like the aggressor, but the judge presiding over the trial, Acting Justice Stephen Crane, makes the police report part of the public record.

A week later the District Attorney petitions the judge for permission to resubmit the assault and attempted murder charges to a second grand jury. Crane concurs.[10] When the grand jury convenes, Morgenthau makes a maximum effort. He appoints a top assistant, Gregory Waples, to present the case. He grants immunity to two of the four victims, Troy Canty and James Ramseur. Neither could be prosecuted for any crimes he might concede in reporting his behavior leading up to the shooting. Both reportedly testify that Goetz picked the fight. This time the 23 laypeople are less convinced of Goetz's claim of self-defense. On March 27, 1985, they indict him on every possible charge of aggressive violence in shooting the four.[11] The 10 new charges join the 3 gun-possession counts from the first indictment for a composite indictment of 13 counts.

For the next year and a half, Goetz's fortunes continue to fluctuate. Waples's explanation of self-defense to the second grand jury prompts Justice Crane, in April 1985, to disclose relevant portions of the otherwise secret grand jury minutes to the defense, which thereupon petitions Crane to dismiss all charges affected by the allegedly improper stand on the theory of self-defense. On January 16, 1986, Crane dismisses nine counts of the indictment, leaving only the charges of gun possession and reckless endangerment of the other passengers on the train. An appellate battle ensues, resulting finally in a decision by the Court of Appeals in July 1986 that Waples's theory of self-defense was correct after all.* The remaining nine counts of the indictment are reinstated and the path cleared for the long-awaited trial on the rights and wrongs of the subway shooting.

After these highs and lows of 1985 and 1986, one can imagine the relief of Goetz and his lawyers when Justice Crane declares the trial officially opened on December 12, 1986. But this proves to be a beginning in name only. The first several months are devoted to "prescreening" the jurors, namely filtering out potential jurors who are able to serve and who are not obviously biased for or against Goetz. After the screening of over 300 Manhattanites, the public *voir dire* (or formal phase of the jury selection) begins on March 23, 1987. After both sides agree on the 12 who will serve, the jury is impaneled on April 6, and finally on April 27, after a two-week break for the Easter and Passover holidays, in a packed courtroom at 111 Centre Street, the moment arrives. Gregory Waples approaches the jury box and, shaking nervously after over two years of preparation, begins his opening argument in the case of the People of the State of New York versus Bernhard Hugo Goetz.

The adversary system of trial, sometimes called the sporting approach to the truth, recalls our commitment to democracy as the least corruptible form of government. The system requires that two equally matched lawyers, a prosecutor and a defense counsel, joust

* This debate is discussed in detail in Chapter Three.

in open court. Each lawyer makes the best case and fights as hard as he can for his client, whether he thinks his client is morally right or wrong. The fight that the lawyers undertake encompasses not only the questions of guilt and innocence, but the range of evidence that the jury should be allowed to hear. The adversary system differs radically from the neutral, objective inquiry of scientists and historians, who consider all the evidence and who come to a decision only when they are convinced that the evidence supports their hypothesis.

In a criminal trial, two pitted advocates urge contradictory perspectives on the truth, and a neutral judge presides over the battle; the 12 members of the jury must come to a verdict one way or another. Unlike scientific investigators, the jury cannot postpone its decision and request additional research that would clarify unresolved factual questions. A trial leads to a day of judgment. The defendant must be found guilty or not guilty—for all time. The pressure of reaching a decision skews the scales of justice toward the defense; if the prosecution fails to prove guilt beyond a reasonable doubt, at least on most issues,[12] the jury is supposed to decide for the defense.

This preference for the defense is expressed in the maxim that it is far better than ten (some say a hundred) guilty defendants go free than that one innocent person be convicted. If Goetz were falsely convicted, his case would probably be forgotten as he disappeared behind bars. There would be no ongoing process of inquiry about his guilt as there would be about the validity of a scientific claim. And even if the error were subsequently discovered, there would be no way to replace the lost years in prison and to correct the insult of having treated him as a criminal. Trial and error may be a salutary way of refining our sense about what works in the world, but in resolving accusations of crime, our greatest fear is a trial ending in error.

The adversary system may not be ideal, but our experience teaches us that it poses the fewest risks of error. The opposition between prosecutor and defense counsel insures that both sides of the story are aired. Another distinctive feature of the system, separating the jury's function of deciding the facts from the judge's role of resolving questions of law, minimizes bias in the jury room as well as on the bench. Vesting the final power of judgment in laypeople, whose careers are not affected by their rejecting the state's position, contributes to an independent decision on guilt or innocence.

Further, if the jury and not the judge makes the decision about guilt or innocence, the lawyers remain free to argue to the judge as zealously as they like about issues of law without fear that if they alienate the judge, they will thereby influence a determination on the ultimate issue of guilt or innocence. The adversary system has resulted, therefore, in a practice of criminal defense that is characteristically more vigorous than that displayed by lawyers in European legal systems that function without vesting final authority in a jury of laypersons. No one likes the thought that justice for the People or for the defendant depends, in part, on the skill of combative lawyers. But the distortions of competition are less serious than the potential for corruption when the power of judgment is concentrated in a judge who, like the inquisitorial judge of the European past,[13] claims the final word on the accusation, the facts, and the law. If, as Lord Acton said, power corrupts and absolute power corrupts absolutely, the safest way to run a criminal trial is to bifurcate the power of presenting the evidence between prosecution and defense and to divide the power of decision between judge and jury.

The functioning of the adversary system depends obviously on the people who take up these shares of power. No two lawyers would prosecute or defend Goetz exactly the same way. District Attorney Morgenthau replaced Susan Braver with Gregory Waples because he expected Waples would bring to the case the high level of competence that he displayed in securing a conviction in the complicated CBS murder case. Goetz replaced his first lawyer, Frank Brenner, appointed by the court to insure representation in the early stages of the case, with Barry Slotnick because Goetz apparently preferred Slotnick's commitment to try the case on the issue of self-defense. The perspectives on the truth that would emerge from the Goetz trial depended in large part on the styles as well as the strengths and weaknesses of Waples and Slotnick.

It is hard to imagine two gifted lawyers with a greater divergence of personal and rhetorical style than the two adversaries. Their personal styles would invariably have an impact on the jury. Waples generated an image of modesty in dress and insouciant casualness. He almost made a point of showing off his orange backpack that he used to carry legal materials as he jogged from the Upper West Side of Manhattan to the courthouse downtown in Foley Square. Slotnick presented himself in impeccably tailored, expensive suits, and even on the warm days of early summer, the jury would never see him without his vest buttoned beneath his dark blue wool jacket.

Slotnick arrived at court every morning in his long black, chauffeur-driven limousine from suburban Westchester. With the press already assembled at the judge's entrance, he would step out of his private carriage, with Goetz and the rest of the defense team,[14] confront the sea of live microphones and clicking cameras, and offer comments on the progress of the defense. Though Slotnick never missed an opportunity to explain and justify the defense's position to the press, Waples zealously avoided publicity. Largely as a matter of personal style, he avoided the contemporary practice of trying the case in the media as well as in the courtroom.

Waples maintained an argumentative posture of taut, pointed remarks, and he seemed to have no time or patience for little ingratiating gestures. He remained sitting as the entire defense table stood every time the jury entered the room. He spoke to Justice Crane crisply and directly. Slotnick and his assistant on legal questions, Mark Baker, could hardly utter a remark to the bench without adding "respectfully" at every grammatically appropriate point.[15] For Waples, Justice Crane was simply "Judge." For Slotnick and Baker, he was almost always "Your Honor."

Waples sat alone at the prosecution table, his assistants remaining incognito in the audience of the courtroom. Slotnick sat with his team of three or four assistants as well as with his client Goetz.[16] Waples sought to avoid giving the impression of overweening state power, expressed in a battery of prosecutors bearing down on the defendant. It made sense not to trigger sympathy for a defendant by casting him as the underdog against the full force of the District Attorney's office. But Waples seemed also to enjoy his isolation in the well of the court. He was there to bring justice to the City of New York, and with his modest, taciturn style and lean good looks, he called to mind Jimmy Stewart as the solitary lawyer fighting for the truth in *Anatomy of a Murder*.

Waples is a loner—curiously like his prey, the intense, thin, taciturn man sitting at the defense table. Neither Goetz nor his prosecutor chatted much with others in the course of the trial; neither had wife nor children who would come to court to wish him well.[17] Both whiled away waiting time in private pleasures like reading. Goetz too must have sensed his kinship with Waples, for in the early days of screening the jurors, in one of the most ironic, private remarks of the trial, he turned to the person next to him and said, "Don't you think that Gregory Waples is a very intense young man?"

The bearded, imposing, religiously observant[18] Slotnick had the air of an Old Testament prophet. But he surely was not a prophet

ignored in his own land. He was constantly surrounded by his follow-
ers, by the press, by his colleagues on the defense, by his wife and
children, who often came to court.

The dozen or so artists at the trial had a relatively easy time
capturing Goetz's meek and passive look, Waples's sincere and
straight intensity, and Slotnick's elegant and assertive figure. The
one personality they never seemed to get right was Stephen Crane,
the judge at the center of the storm. A learned and patient man,
always correct in the way he speaks to his staff and to litigants in
his court, Crane comes across as a professional spokesman of the
law. As he runs his courtroom, his own needs and his own personality
recede into the background. His gentle style and the softly curved
lines of his face eluded the artists.

As the presiding judge in the trial, Justice Crane was the only
major figure in the drama who was not supposed to have a perspective
on the truth. Waples could believe that Canty's demand for money
was not a veiled threat and that Goetz overreacted by shooting.
Slotnick and Baker could believe firmly in their client's moral as
well as legal innocence. And their client, of course, could maintain
his silent conviction that he had triumphed over his aggressors. The
jury too would eventually generate its decisive perspective on the
truth of what happened. Justice Crane, however, had to stay above
the fray. His task combined moving the trial along and resolving
the legal debates that surrounded the admissibility of evidence. He
was at once traffic manager and oracle of the law.

The man at the center of attention, Bernhard Goetz, remained
an enigma to trial observers. Born of a Jewish mother and a German
father, Lutheran by practice but regarded as Jewish by his childhood
friends,[19] reared in the small upstate New York town of Rhinebeck
but living in the dense urban mosaic of 14th Street in Manhattan,
Goetz eludes conventional categories. He has always sought in fact
to be his own person, speaking out against authority when others
would be silent. As a nuclear engineer working on submarines, he
would point out design and manufacturing defects to the Navy that
his bosses in private industry allegedly preferred to suppress. As an
individualist who could not readily surrender to corporate authority,
Goetz eventually gravitated to running his own electronic repair
service out of his 14th Street apartment.

If we were looking for a psychological account of Goetz's shooting, we might focus on his tumultuous relationship with his father.
That he bought a heavy-duty gun, a 9-mm semiautomatic pistol,

on September 4, 1984, during the week of his father's funeral, should be enough to rivet our attention on that relationship. That Goetz's father was known for his authoritarian tendencies and that Goetz displays a clear resistance to authority might invite further inquiry, and so might the elder Goetz's being accused and tried for allegedly abusing two young boys when Bernie was 13 years old.[20] In view of the family's persistent faith in the elder Goetz's innocence, the torment of witnessing his father's prosecution may have contributed to the younger Goetz's later contempt for the legal system. These intriguing facts are critical to understanding Bernhard Goetz as a human being.

Goetz resists interviews that probe the foundation of his actions on December 22, 1984, but his four hours of taped confession provide a strikingly revealing glimpse into the way he, nine days after the event, explained the events to himself. As his own rambling free associations teach us, Goetz came to think of street mugging in New York as a game with fixed rules and reciprocal expectations. As he says, "they know the rules of the game and they're serious about the rules."[22] Among the most basic are these: "you can't carry a gun and you can't kill somebody."[23] Before the ritual collapsed into a spasm of violence, Ramseur tried to call Goetz's attention to a bulge in his pocket. Goetz had no doubt that Ramseur was bluffing. Undoubtedly, some muggers carry guns, but in this case Goetz's insouciant confidence that the bulge was "bullshit" turned out to be well founded.

Goetz's judgment of Canty's opener "How are ya?" also reveals his sense for the ritual of mugging. This was an ambiguous move by Canty. It obviously did not have the crisp, hard edge of "Okay, motherfucker, give it up." That was the standard opening line of an ex-mugger, one of Goetz's acquaintances who, as he says, "taught me a little about taking care of myself."[24] Canty did not use this code language, and therefore Goetz did not take his opener to be a "threat," though "in certain circumstances that [line] can be a real threat."[25]

The innocent-sounding "How are you doing?" rings with associations for Goetz: "And a question like that, 'how are you doing,' it normally means nothing. But in a certain frame of reference, there's an implication."[26] And his mind turns to the brutal mugging of Al, his doorman at Courtney House on West 14th Street, whose travail began with an innocent-sounding "How are you doing?"[27] On the videotape he describes a potential mugger's opening with

"How are you?" or "How are you doing?" as "legally . . . a nothing statement and . . . an everyday statement."[28] The curious use of "legally" in this context reflects Goetz's understanding of the rules of the game: for an opening line to count "legally," it had to be an unequivocal declaration that the game was on.

At the point that Canty was standing next to him asking for money, and Goetz saw him smiling—"his eyes were shiny, and he was enjoying himself . . . he had a big smile on his face"[29]—fear took over and Goetz prepared himself quickly for action. He laid down his pattern of fire from left to right. But still in the mode of move and countermove, he needed "verification" that the game had reached the point of no return. Thus he asked Canty again, "What did you say?" When Canty responded with another demand for money,[30] Goetz seized the initiative and the game dissolved into pools of blood.

In Goetz's thinking about what he did, the game metaphor is critical to his sense of rectitude. He was attacked, he waited for verification, and then he gained the upper hand. Those are the critical facts. As he states the "correct" rule of law, a rule he incorrectly attributes to English law of several decades ago, "if a person is attacked and then gains the upper hand, he should not be answerable in law."[31]

Goetz played by the rules as he understood them, but he did not expect the New York system of criminal justice to understand and sympathize with him. His two previous encounters with the criminal justice system left him bruised and cynical. He was mugged in 1981 when three youths jumped him as he was carrying electronic equipment in the subway. They threw him to the ground and injured his knees; he collided with a glass door and the handle went into his chest. An off-duty sanitation officer helped Goetz subdue Fred Clark, the leader of the group. It seemed to Goetz fundamentally unjust that he was kept in the station under interrogation for over six hours and that the police let Clark go, Goetz thinks, in less than half that time. Worse than that, the female prosecutor[32] handling the case did not charge the assailants with robbery, but only with what Goetz called "mischievous mischief."[33] Apparently, there was no evidence that they were after his money or his property, without which an assault does not amount to the more serious crime of robbery. According to Goetz, the significant fact in the minds of the officials was that the muggers had ripped his jacket (and thus a charge of criminal mischief).[34] It is not clear why the police and prosecutor chose this charge instead of assault, but in any event, Goetz found unbearable the legalistic concern about the details of what seemed to him an obviously serious crime.

He adjusted quickly to what he perceived to be another game. He was so frustrated that the police would not file charges of attempted robbery that in what seems to be a follow-up telephone interview with the Manhattan police, he said:

> Look, whatever you want me to say, I'll say, if you want me to lie, I'll lie. . . . I'll say whatever it takes to, you know to arrest these guys, or to get these guys, or whatever it is.[35]

He was surprised that the police rebuked him for his willingness to falsify evidence.

His second encounter with the police followed immediately thereafter. Though he admits that he started carrying a gun right after the mugging, he tried to follow the rules for obtaining a pistol permit. He claims to have spent $2,000 on preparing the papers and filing an application for a license. The license division of the city police turned him down with a flippant explanation to the effect that they could not give a license to everyone who applied for one. These two experiences with the NYPD left Goetz with a constant irritation that the city was concerned only about "technicalities."

Goetz's fears of being beaten and maimed come repeatedly to the surface of his confession. In the audiotape, he is almost reluctant to admit that he was afraid. He rationalizes away his fear as one of the necessities of "combat." Fear "makes you think and analyze . . . and speeds up your mind. . . . it builds up your adrenalin. . . ."[36] Anticipating the testimony of a defense expert, Dr. Bernard Yudwitz, on his behalf, he says that when the fear takes over, "the upper level of your mind . . . just turn[s] off . . . and you react."[37] On the videotape, visibly more agitated by the probing of Assistant District Attorney Susan Braver, he concedes terror without linking it to its combat utility: he felt that he "was about to be beaten into a pulp."[38] And he elaborates an extended metaphor of himself as akin to a cornered "rat":

> you start poking it with . . . red hot needles and . . . you wind up doing it again . . . [and if the] rat turns viciously on you and just becomes a vicious killer, which is . . . really what I was, then don't go passing statements of morality. . . .[39]

A broader view of Bernhard Goetz reveals another perspective on his fateful confrontation with four black youths that Saturday afternoon. A strong suggestion of deliberately courting danger runs through Goetz's personal history. His behavior on several occasions suggests that when given a choice, he would expose himself to risk rather than seek safety. When he mistakenly took a train to the edge of Harlem, he did not simply cross over and catch the first train running in the opposite direction. He went for a walk along the northern edge of Central Park. An attempted mugging ensued that he frustrated by pulling his gun. At the time of his 1981 mugging he was riding on the subway carrying electronic equipment (including an oscilloscope that resembled a television set) that could only have been an attraction to potential muggers. On the day of the shooting, he entered the subway car and sat down right next to the four youths, who by their dress and boisterous conduct could be quickly identified as "trouble." This pattern of behavior suggests what sociologists would call a propensity toward victimization. He was riskprone. He chose not to avoid danger, but to expose himself to it.

The biggest psychological issue of all is why Goetz remained in New York City, particularly after his mugging in 1981. He despised the city. His confession is one long tirade against the misery that New Yorkers are forced to endure. His business did not require him to be in an urban environment. He could easily have operated his electronic repair business from somewhere like New Hampshire, where he felt safe among "decent people."[40]

It might be prudent to avoid danger, but Goetz was not obligated to do so. He had every right to live on 14th Street, to walk at night on Central Park North, to carry electronic equipment on the subway, and to sit amidst rambunctious young teens that Saturday afternoon on the subway. His psychological disposition and his lack of vigilance hardly undercut his basic rights as a citizen in the city. A psychological analysis of what triggered the shooting may be important from some points of view, but it hardly controls the legal or moral analysis of Goetz's right to defend himself.

The purpose of a trial is neither to explain nor to diagnose, but to judge the act as right or wrong, to determine whether Goetz himself is personally to blame for what he did. However unique an individual Goetz may be, the law starts on the dignifying assumption that, absent evidence of insanity, we are all essentially alike. When Goetz went down into the subway on December 22, 1984, he was everyman. He became a hero because the public identified with him, and he would have to be judged on the assumption that when he fired those damaging shots, he had the same capacity as the rest of us to judge whether it was right or wrong, reasonable or unreasonable, to respond to the apparent threat as he did.

Goetz says, "Don't go passing [judgments] of morality. . . ." But the law cannot avoid judgments of morality. Goetz had given his lawyers materials from which they could craft a theory of self-defense based on his need to strike back with deadly force in order to save himself. If the jury agreed with him that his fear was sufficient to excuse him, that would be one moral judgment; if it imposed a rigorous standard of reasonableness and concluded that he over-reacted in shooting, that would be another moral judgment. In either case, moral judgment was inescapable.

The distinctive feature of the law is not its rules and its commands, but the opportunity offered by legal debate and criminal trials to articulate and refine our views about the issues that divide us. It is not easy to think through and express our feelings about Goetz's shooting four black youths on the subway. It is not easy even to formulate the conflict between those who side with the victims and those who side with the gunman who thought himself in danger. We know that the conflict must be more profound than a conflict between black and white, between criminals and decent people, between the unemployed lower class and the established working and middle classes. The law helps us see what is at stake when a confrontation erupts into violence. It provides us with words and concepts for refining our reactions, expressing our judgments, and engaging in debate with those who disagree with us.

The law should be understood, therefore, as a stylized form of discourse. The boundaries of this discourse have been "fined and refined," as Thomas Hobbes wrote,[41] by generations of learned lawyers. By the common understanding of the tradition, lawyers do not speak of love and friendship, of God or the angels, of salvation or the afterlife, of beauty and ultimate moral worth. These are the concerns that shape our lives, but it would be improper for an advocate to appeal to them in search of advantage for his client. Lawyers have agreed to argue not about what people are, but about what they do. The focus is not on why we do what we do, but on the moral qualities of our actions.

As poets have refined sensibilities about human yearning, lawyers have sharpened insights into the ways in which human actions disturb the social order. Their idiom speaks of harm and causation, obligation and responsibility, fault and excuse. These concepts and others like them are the filters that enable us to see what happened when Goetz pulled his gun and shot Canty, Allen, Ramseur, and Cabey. Of course, we may disagree about what we see. Some may see the red of aggression; others, the blue of fear; still others, the yellow of irrational overreaction. If we argue about these shades and hues, we can be certain, at least, that the picture is not simply black and white.

Legal argument is rooted in a shared faith in reason. The law moves forward by comparing one case with another, judging whether they are alike or different, whether the solution for one applies as well to the next. None of these judgments would be possible without the guidance of reason. Our passions divide us, but reason unites us in the quest for answers that all can accept. The clearest manifestation of reason in legal argument is the fact of argument itself. We know that appealing to another's reason differs from appealing to his or her prejudice or self-interest. An appeal to reason testifies to respect for the person to be persuaded. An appeal to prejudice or passion expresses contempt; it denigrates the other from a person to be persuaded by argument to an object to be manipulated by playing on emotional forces.

As Maimonides said about God, however, it is easier to postulate what reason is not than to conclude what it is. Reason is not passion, not prejudice, not the drive for pleasure. As God transcends the material world, reason transcends these impulses of the human condition. The analogy with the divine dignifies human reason, but as we can never be sure that we know whether God exists and in what form, we can readily slip into skepticism about both the existence and the dictates of our reason.

Doubts about the clarity of reason's call lead lawyers to take refuge in the authority of those who, by the conventions of the profession, provide the guideposts to decisions under the law. Rather than debate private visions of what is right and good, lawyers proceed by mustering on their side of the case authoritative legal materials that point to the result they advocate. In a criminal case, these materials include the text of our federal and state constitutions, the criminal code and the code of criminal procedure, and the voluminous body of judicial opinions that seek to justify decisions in specific appellate cases. This library of written materials is typically sufficient to indicate an answer to routine legal problems. But in an unusual case like the prosecution of Bernhard Goetz, the written law is but the beginning of the argument.

Lawyers begin their arguments with citations of statutes and cases and, if they are true advocates, quickly move beyond these anchors of authority with their own reasoned vision of justice in the particular case. Significantly, lawyers in the Anglo-American legal tradition prefer to invoke cases rather than to rely squarely on the words of a statute. Case law comes closer to the law of reason. When a decision departs from the received principles of the tradition, lawyers and judges tend to disregard it. Cases become influential precedents only when they capture the more refined sentiments of justice that have crystallized in our tradition.

The agony of Bernhard Goetz illustrates in one tangled life both the promise and the despair of the legal system. Unlike modern skeptics, Goetz has a strong vision of right and wrong. In his four-hour taped confession in New Hampshire, he repeatedly says that it is up to others to decide whether he was right or wrong. He does not want to be let off on grounds of mental illness. As he says:[42]

> You decide. I became a vicious animal and if you think that is so terrible, I just wish anyone could have been there in my place. Anyone who is going to judge me, fine, I was vicious. My intent was to kill 'em, and, and you just decide what's right and wrong.

In his own moral vision, he had rightfully done everything possible to comply with the law, but it was clear that the law was wrongfully unresponsive to his fears of a repeat mugging. His contempt for the legal system generated a sense of justified self-reliance in carrying a loaded gun in public, whether he had bureaucratic approval or not. Yet his rebellion against the system went further than satisfying his immediate needs. Though never charged with gunrunning, he admits in his confession that he frequently bought guns and sold them to friends at cost.

Goetz's rage at the legal system, of course, does not control our judgment of what he did. His conception of right and wrong cannot displace the necessity of a community judgment about the rights and wrongs of carrying unlicensed weapons and shooting four youths on the subway. The problem of our judging Goetz is most acute in the tangle of passionate and reasoned arguments that run through the law of self-defense. If he is guilty of a crime of self-defense, it would be by virtue of our judgment that his beliefs do not prevail over the rule of reason in the law. Yet to have confidence in our judgment about whether Goetz acted criminally, though in perceived self-defense, we need to understand the complicated moral sentiments triggered by an argument of self-defense.

2

Passion and Reason in Self-Defense

SELF-DEFENSE was always the central issue in the Goetz case—from the decision of the first grand jury not to indict on the shooting charges to the final verdict in June 1987. A legal system is possible only if the state enjoys a monopoly of force. When private individuals appeal to force and decide who shall enjoy the right to "life, liberty and the pursuit of happiness," there can be no pretense of the rule of law. Yet the state's monopoly also entails an obligation to secure its citizens against violence. When individuals are threatened with immediate aggression, when the police cannot protect them, the monopoly of the state gives way. The individual right of survival reasserts itself. No inquiry could be more important than probing this boundary between the state's obligation to protect us and the individual's right to use force, even deadly force, to repel and disarm an aggressor. There is no simple rule that traces this boundary between the authority of the state and the right of individuals to protect themselves. The inquiry itself generates an ongoing debate about the values that lie at the foundation of the legal system.

As the Goetz case wound its way through the courts, the lawyers and judges proceeded on a general set of assumptions about the contours of self-defense. Merely examining these general points of law, however, will not be sufficient to understand the fierce, continuing debate about the legitimacy of Goetz's shooting Troy Canty, Barry Allen, James Ramseur, and Darrell Cabey. Behind the general principles of self-defense swirl conflicting moral and ideological theories about when and why self-defense is legitimate. Some of these theories appeal to our passions; others, to our reason. Our passions pull us in the direction of seeing the act of defense as punitive, as the vengeful response of a private citizen against those who deserve to suffer. The passionate response is captured in the refrain heard throughout the Goetz trial: "These kids got what they deserved." Our reason pulls toward understanding self-defense not as an act of punitive justice, but as a necessary means for vindicating a stable social order. By examining these conflicting theories, we can begin to understand why, from the outset, blacks and whites, liberals and conservatives, have disagreed so vehemently about the Goetz case.

The New York Penal Law (NYPL), under which Goetz was tried, identifies self-defense as one of several justifications for crimes of violence.[1] Other examples of justification are the provisions on necessity (choosing the lesser evil under the circumstances),[2] and the use of force in law enforcement.[3] Consent is also a justification for physical intrusions and taking the property of another, even though the New York statute does not discuss consent as a distinct defense. The point of a *justification* is that it renders a nominal violation lawful—in conformity with the *jus,* or higher, unwritten law of legitimate conduct.

Claims of justification are distinguishable from other claims that bar conviction for crime, such as the claims of duress ("Someone forced me to do it") and insanity ("My disease forced me to do it").[4] These claims do not render conduct lawful and proper. No one would say that an insane man has a right to kill, or that his killing conforms with higher principles of rightful conduct. These other claims of defense, often called excuses, merely negate the actor's personal responsibility for the violation. It is unquestionably wrong for an insane man to kill, but his mental condition undercuts his responsibility for his wicked deed.

The struggle between passion and reason in the law of self-defense is played out against a background of shared, albeit vague, assumptions about the contours of the defense. First, in order to be properly resisted, an attack must be *imminent.* Further, the defender's response must be both *necessary* and *proportional* to the feared attack. And finally, the defender must act with the *intention* not of hurting the victim per se, but of thwarting the attack. There is no statute or authoritative legal source that expresses this consensus, but lawyers all over the world would readily concur that these are the basic, structural elements of a valid claim of self-defense.

The requirement of *imminence* means that the time for defense is now! The defender cannot wait any longer. This requirement distinguishes self-defense from the illegal use of force in two temporally related ways. A preemptive strike against a feared aggressor is illegal force used too soon; and retaliation against a successful aggressor is illegal force used too late. Legitimate self-defense must be neither too soon nor too late.

In the case of a preemptive strike, the defender calculates that the enemy is planning an attack or surely is likely to attack in the future, and therefore it is wiser to strike first than to wait until the actual aggression. Preemptive strikes are illegal in international law as they are illegal internally in every legal system of the world. They are illegal because they are not based on a visible manifestation of aggression; they are grounded in a prediction of how the feared enemy is likely to behave in the future.

The line between lawful self-defense and an unlawful preemptive strike is not so easily staked out, but there are some clear instances of both categories. Because the general principles of international law are the same as those of domestic legal systems, we can ponder some dramatic examples among current international events.

Think about the various military moves that Israel has made against Arab forces in the last 20 years. The strike against the Iraqi nuclear reactor in 1981 was clearly preemptive, for the supposition that the Iraqis would use the reactor for military purposes was based on an inference from private Israeli military intelligence. Even if it is true that the Iraqis intended to manufacture a nuclear bomb, that activity hardly constitutes an attack against Israel. Israel has its own nuclear weapons, and its government would hotly contest the inference that this fact alone establishes its intention to bomb Arab territory.

Preemptive strikes are always based on assumptions, more or less rational, that the enemy is likely to engage in hostile behavior. Israel could well argue that it did not wish to take the chance that Iraq would use nuclear weapons against the Jewish state as well as against Iran and other opponents of the Baghdad regime. Be that as it may, there is no doubt that the air attacks on the reactor constituted a preemptive strike. The possible attack by Iraq was not sufficiently imminent to justify a response in self-defense.

More controversial is Israel's attack against Egypt in June 1967, initiating the spectacular Israeli victory in the Six-Day War. Egypt closed the Straits of Tiran to Israeli shipping, amassed its troops on Israel's border, and secured command control over the armies of Jordan and Iraq. In the two weeks preceding the Israeli response on June 5, Nasser had repeatedly made bellicose threats, including the total destruction of Israel. The question is whether Egypt's threat was sufficiently imminent to justify Israel's response under international law. Perhaps Egypt was merely bluffing; perhaps its leaders did not know whether they intended to attack or not. There is no doubt, however, that Egypt was attempting to intimidate Israel by behaving as though it were about to attack (unlike Iraq in the reactor incident). Israel took the Egyptians at face value; it responded to what appeared to be an attack in the offing. Could Israel have waited longer? Of course it could have. But the requirement of imminence does not require that guns actually fire, that bombs be in the air. And if anything short of letting the missiles fly constitutes an imminent attack, then that requirement was fulfilled in the June 1967 conflict between Egypt and Israel.

The distinction between a preemptive strike and a response to an imminent attack haunts our analysis of the Goetz case. We know that Canty asked Goetz for five dollars. But we don't know his tone of voice and his body language. The request for five dollars could be understood as panhandling, as harassment, as intimidation (hand it over or else!), or as a prelude to a violent assault whatever Goetz did. If Canty was merely begging, with no threat implicit in his request, there was no imminent attack. If the request was a veiled threat of violence, the circumstances are much closer to an imminent attack.

In cases of interpersonal as well as international violence, the outbreak might be neither defensive nor preemptive. It could be simply a passionate retaliation for past wrongs suffered by the person resorting to violence. Retaliatory acts seek to even the score—to inflict harm because harm has been suffered in the past.

Retaliation, as opposed to defense, is a common problem in cases arising from wife battering and domestic violence. The injured wife waits for the first possibility of striking against a distracted or unarmed husband.[5] The man may even be asleep when the wife finally reacts. Goetz's response to the four young blacks was retaliatory so far as he perceived them as "four young muggers" rather than as individuals; he was striking back for having been mugged by the "same type of guys" in 1981 and suffering lasting injuries to his knee and chest.

Retaliation is the standard case of "taking the law into one's own hands." There is no way, under the law, to justify killing a wife batterer or a rapist as retaliation or revenge, however much sympathy there may be for the wife wreaking retaliation. Private citizens cannot function as judge and jury toward each other. They have no authority to pass judgment and to punish each other for past wrongs.

Those who defend the use of violence rarely admit that their purpose is retaliation for a past wrong. The argument typically is that the actor feared a recurrence of the past violence, thus the focus shifts from past to future violence, from retaliation to an argument of defending against an imminent attack. This is the standard maneuver in battered-wife cases. In view of her prior abuse, the wife arguably has reason to fear renewed violence. Killing the husband while he is asleep then comes into focus as an arguably legitimate defensive response rather than an illegitimate act of vengeance for past wrongs.

The New York statute on self-defense recognizes two distinct forms of imminent attack on which Goetz could and did ground his claim of self-defense. The first is that one is subject to the "imminent use of deadly physical force"; the second, making New York more favorable than many states to claims of self-defense, is that a robbery is about to be committed.* In both cases, provided that other conditions of self-defense are satisfied, Goetz would be entitled to respond with deadly force.

In the latter case of robbery, the requirement of an imminent attack finds expression in the question whether the aggressor is about to commit or attempting to commit a robbery. How do we know and how should Goetz know whether Canty's behavior amounted to an attempted robbery? In a case of self-defense, there is obviously no time to confer with a lawyer.

Whether Canty was in fact engaged in an attempted robbery is far from obvious, both as a matter of fact and a matter of law. Of course, if his intention was merely to beg for five dollars, there was no attempt to rob. But let us assume that Canty was bent on mischief. If Goetz had not given him the five dollars, he might have demanded the whole wallet. If Goetz had refused, Canty and his three companions might have begun to abuse him, with the risk that the abuse would lead to a brawl and a beating on the floor of the subway car. Does the implicit threat of physical violence render Canty's demand for money an attempted robbery?

---

* The requirement of "imminence" is expressed in the statutory reference to a robbery's being "about" to be committed.

Robbery is defined at common law and in the New York statute as "forcible stealing."[6] Simple stealing, such as picking pockets, is not robbery and therefore there would certainly be no right to use deadly force to prevent a thief from getting away with a pilfered wallet. The additional element for robbery is that the thief must threaten to use force "upon a person" in order either to overcome resistance or to compel the owner "to deliver up" the property. The threatened force must be both immediate and to a person. If Canty had said, "Give me five dollars or I'll beat you up the next time I see you," that act would have supported a conviction for larceny by extortion[7] but not for robbery.

In order to think of Canty's act as an incipient robbery, therefore, one has to read into his demand an implicit threat to use force against Goetz and to use it immediately if Goetz should refuse to cooperate. This is precisely the picture of the subway encounter that the defense sought to portray.

If we assume that the requirement of an imminent attack is satisfied, the question remains whether the other elements of justifiable self-defense are present in his subway shooting. Goetz's firing each of the five shots must have been *necessary* under the circumstances.[8] Was there an effective response less drastic than firing the gun at the four feared assailants? Was it necessary to shoot? Would it not have been enough merely to show the gun in its holster? Or to draw and point the weapon without firing? Goetz had twice scared off muggers on the street merely by drawing the gun.

But the uneven grind of the accelerating train made Goetz's footing uncertain. During his initial exchange with Canty he rose to his feet and was standing in close quarters with his feared assailants. Showing the gun in the holster or drawing it would have risked one of the four young men's taking the gun away and shooting him. Gauging necessity under the circumstances turns, in the end, on an elusive prediction of what would have happened if Goetz had tried this or that maneuver short of shooting. There is no objective way of knowing for sure what indeed was necessary under the circumstances.*

The requirement of *proportionality* adds a problem beyond the necessity of the defensive response. To understand the distinction between proportionality and necessity, think about the ratio between the means of resistance and the gravity of the attack. Necessity speaks

---

* On the problem of whether Goetz "reasonably perceived" that it was necessary to shoot, see the discussion on pages 26–27.

to the question whether some less costly means of defense, such as merely showing the gun or firing a warning shot into the air, might be sufficient to ward off the attack. The requirement of proportionality addresses the ratio of harms emanating from both the attack and the defense. The harm done in disabling the aggressor must not be excessive or disproportionate relative to the harm threatened and likely to result from the attack.

Some examples will illuminate the distinction. Suppose that a liquor store owner has no means of preventing a thief from escaping with a few bottles of scotch except to shoot him. Most people would recoil from the notion that protecting property justifies shooting and risking the death of escaping thieves. It is better from a social point of view to suffer the theft of a few bottles of liquor than to inflict serious physical harm on a fellow human being.

It is not simply that property rights must sometimes give way to our concern for the lives and well-being even of aggressors. Suppose that the only way for a woman to avoid being touched by a man harassing her is to respond with deadly force—by, say, cutting him with a razor blade. May she engage in this act necessary for her defense rather than suffer the personal indignity of being touched? It is not so clear. Of course, if she were threatened with rape, she could use every necessary means at her disposal to protect herself. No legal system in the Western world would expect a woman to endure a rape if her only means of defense required that she risk the death of her aggressor.

Proportionality in self-defense requires a balancing of competing interests, the interests of the defender and those of the aggressor. As the innocent party in the fray, a woman defending against rape has interests that weigh more than those of the aggressor. She may kill to ward off a threat to her sexual autonomy, but she has no license to take life in order to avoid every petty interference with her autonomy. If the only way she can avoid being touched is to kill, that response seems clearly excessive relative to the interests at stake. Even if our thumb is on the scale in favor of the defender, there comes a point at which the aggressor's basic human interests will outweigh those of an innocent victim, thumb and all. There is obviously no way to determine the breaking point, even theoretically. At a certain point our sensibilities are triggered, our compassion for the human being behind the mask of the evil aggressor is engaged, and we have to say "Stop! That's enough."

The New York Penal Law has a rough principle of proportionality built into it. The provision on self-defense distinguishes between two levels of defensive response: the use of "physical force" and the use of "deadly physical force." The former is permissible to prevent the "imminent use of physical force" against oneself or against a third person;[9] the more serious response, the use of deadly force, is permissible in specified cases where the threatened force is more serious. Of the cases enumerated in the provision on self-defense, the threats relevant to the justification of Goetz's conduct are (1) the threat to "use deadly physical force," and (2) the attempt to commit a robbery.[10]

Admittedly, the provision on attempted robbery is a peculiarity of New York law. It seems paradoxical for the statute to demand in its first part that the defender face the imminent use of "deadly physical force" and then in its second part to lower the threshold of deadly defensive force to protecting oneself against a robbery that might entail a minimal threat of assault. Even more curiously, deadly force is permissible against an imminent attack of deadly physical force only if the defender first retreats whenever he knows that he can do so safely,[11] but he may use deadly force against an imminent robbery without first retreating. But paradoxical or not,[12] this is the New York statute and Justice Crane and the Goetz jury had to apply it as is.[13]

The preceding three characteristics of self-defense—imminence, necessity, and proportionality—speak to the objective characteristics of the attack and the defense in response. In order to establish that these requirements are satisfied, we need not ask any questions about what Goetz himself knew and thought as he shot the four youths. But suppose that while being attacked without knowing it, he started shooting with the aim of inflicting harm on the four black youths. In this hypothetical situation, could he invoke self-defense on the ground that his act in fact frustrated the attack? It would be a de facto act of self-defense, even though Goetz had his own reasons for shooting.

The consensus among Western legal systems is that in order to invoke a sound claim of self-defense, the defender must know about the attack and act with the *intention* of repelling it. Why should Goetz receive the benefit of a justification if he acted maliciously, without fear of attack? Surprisingly, some leading scholars think that in a case of criminal homicide, the accused should be able to invoke self-defense even if he does not know about the attack.[14] Their argument is that if you cannot be guilty of homicide by killing someone who is already dead (no matter what your intent), you should not be guilty of homicide by killing an aggressor (no matter what your intent). No harm, no crime. And there is arguably no harm in killing an aggressor.

Yet there is an important moral difference between pumping lead into a dead body and killing an aggressor in self-defense. We can comfortably say that there is no harm in the former case (except perhaps interference with a dead body), but injuring or killing a human being remains a harm, even if the harm is inflicted in self-defense. Troy Canty, Barry Allen, James Ramseur, and Darrell Cabey are victims even if it turns out that Goetz's shooting them is justified under the law. If they are victims of self-defense (unlike dead bodies that are not harmed), the least the law can demand is that the defender inflict harm only when he has a good reason to act. If he does not know that he is being attacked, he cannot have a good reason for claiming four human beings as his victims.

Think about the screwdrivers that Ramseur and Cabey were carrying when they were shot. In the first few weeks after the shooting, some circles in the press reported, in blatant disregard of the available facts, that the screwdrivers were sharpened. The screwdrivers, sharpened or not, confirmed what many people wanted to believe: that these four kids were about to mug Goetz and that therefore his response was justified as self-defense. Yet there was no evidence that Goetz knew of the three screwdrivers. Not one of the four victims pulled a screwdriver from his pocket, either before or during the shooting. If Goetz did not know of the screwdrivers, however, they could not contribute to his justification. They had no more legal relevance than a secret, undisclosed plan to kill Goetz because he was white.

These four elements, then—imminence, necessity, proportionality, and intention—provide the general framework for the law of self-defense. The first three elements bear on the objective reality of the circumstances of using force; the fourth element of intention speaks to what the actor knows and his reasons for acting. The actor's subjective perceptions of reality introduce an additional element in the analysis that goes beyond his intention to repel the attack. If Goetz was mistaken about whether an attack was imminent and whether his defensive response was necessary and proportional, he might well be excused for acting under circumstances that do not meet the objective requirements of self-defense. In most legal systems of the world, the case of mistaken or putative self-defense is clearly distinguished, in terminology and legal consequences, from real self-defense based upon the criteria of imminence, necessity, and proportionality. The essential difference is that real self-defense justifies the use of force, while putative self-defense merely excuses it.[15]

Under American law, and in particular New York law, there is no distinction between mistaken and real self-defense. Indeed the law is geared to the case of mistaken self-defense, the assumption being that whatever is true about the case of a subjective but mistaken perception of reality would be true about a correct perception of imminence, necessity, and proportionality. The New York statute applies, therefore, whenever the defendant "reasonably believes" that the conditions of self-defense are present. Of this phrase and its problematic meaning, there will be more to say later.[16]

The requirements of imminence, necessity, and proportionality, expressed in different terms in different languages, are found in virtually every legal system in the world. Yet these basic structural elements account only for the surface language of the law. Beneath the surface there surge conflicting moral and ideological forces that drive the interpretation of the law in particular directions. We may all be united in the terms in which we discuss self-defense, but we are divided in our loyalties to unarticulated theories that account for our willingness now to stretch the law broadly, now to interpret it narrowly. These deeper forces shaping our interpretation reflect the confrontation between passion and reason in the law.

On the surface, the doctrine of self-defense purports to be a unified whole. New York has a single statutory provision on the subject, and Justice Crane tried to give a single explanation of self-defense to the jury.[17] Beneath the surface, however, there are at least four theories, four models of the defense, that run through New York law and that interweave in the debate about Goetz's shooting, pulling our sentiments in at least four different directions. Terms like imminence, necessity, and proportionality take on differing connotations, depending on the theory in which they are anchored. In presenting evidence, cross-examining witnesses, and making arguments to the jury, Waples and Slotnick sought to tap the jury's underlying and unexamined sentiments about self-defense. By articulating these conflicting value systems, we come to understand the larger issues at stake in the rhetoric of the Goetz case.

Our passion for justice and for the symbolic expiation of evil pulls us in the direction of thinking of self-defense as a form of just punishment. The individual acts in place of the state in inflicting on wrongdoers their just deserts. If Troy Canty, Barry Allen, James Ramseur, and Darrell Cabey were in fact muggers, then this rough principle of justice holds that "they got what they deserved." These are the exact words of a black witness, Andrea Reid. Present with her baby in the subway car at the time of shooting, she was also afraid of the four "punks who were bothering the white man." Barry Slotnick referred to her words "they got what they deserved" dozens of times in the course of the trial. Sometimes he paraphrased the comment in a more respectable legal idiom: "They got what the law allowed."

Goetz became a folk hero because, as the folk saw it, his shooting brought these arrogant predators to their knees. Yet even under a punitive theory of giving criminals what they deserve, there remain questions of fact. Did these kids have records long enough to support the judgment that they were criminals and predators? Or is the public perception of Canty, Cabey, Ramseur, and Allen as criminal types largely a function of their race and youth? When our passions seek gratification, when our lust to avenge evil gains the upper hand, we don't always ponder the facts and weigh the gradations of evil and its fitting punishment.

That people should be rewarded and punished on the basis of their character and their lifelong behavior expresses a principle of justice, but it is a principle better suited for infallible divine punishment than the imperfect institutions of the law. In fairy tales, the witch may receive her comeuppance at the end. But surely it is not the business of human institutions—not to mention a loner riding the subway—to determine who is a witch, or a wicked person or a habitual criminal.

The law wisely limits itself to the question whether a particular act constitutes a crime and merits punishment or whether, in the context of self-defense, a particular aggressive attack properly triggers a defensive response. The general character of suspects is important neither for human punishment nor for the assessment whether defensive force was permissible in a particular situation. Some people who passionately sided with Goetz's victims may think that when Goetz's lawyer Slotnick was jumped and assaulted a few weeks after the trial was over, he too got what he deserved. They are entitled to their opinion. But their passion for justice on the streets should not be heard in court. Nor should Slotnick's repeated reiteration of Andrea Reid's words "they got what they deserved" have been heard as a persuasive argument about the proper scope of self-defense.

But a persuasive argument it may have been. And therefore we have to ask the question, If a juror thinks about self-defense as a form of punishment, how would he or she be inclined to interpret the requirements of imminence, necessity, and proportionality? First, he would probably loosen up on the requirements both of imminence and necessity; further, he would blur the line between legitimate defense and a preemptive attack. He would probably see Canty's demand for five dollars as sufficiently close to a real attack to warrant a defensive response. An actual, unavoidable attack is simply not important to someone whose thinking is geared to the punitive theory. What counts is the justice of the response, given the generally evil character of the aggressor.

Thinking about the proportionality of Goetz's punitive response requires that we distinguish between punishing the four kids for what they were and punishing them for their specific acts on December 22, 1984. Perhaps if they were being punished for what they were and one believed they were the embodiment of our urban ills, one might—in the irrationality of hatred—think they received what they deserved. But there is no way that one could think of Goetz's shooting them as fair punishment for their specific acts in the subway car.

Proportionality in punishment—making the punishment fit the crime—is more rigorous than proportionality in self-defense. Using the death penalty for rape, for example, violates the principles of proportional punishment as expressed in the Eighth Amendment, which prohibits cruel and unusual punishment.[18] Yet if a woman is threatened by rape, she may legally resist by killing the aggressor. Even legal systems that have abolished the death penalty permit the use of deadly force in the defense of vital interests. While proportionality in punishment requires that the sentence fit the crime, clearly more is permitted in self-defense.

Thinking of self-defense as a form of punishment, then, should strengthen the requirement of proportionality. The defensive response would have to fit the "crime" committed by Goetz's four adversaries. So far as their crime on that day is at issue, we can only wonder what people might mean when they say that those "punks"—Troy Canty, Barry Allen, James Ramseur and Darrell Cabey—got what they deserved. What, after all, was their crime? Even if they were about to subject Goetz to a fierce beating, they would hardly deserve a punishment of being shot, paralyzed, being brought to the edge of death. No modern legal system would countenance a penalty of maiming or death for the crime of mugging.

Another significant approach to self-defense shifts our focus away from our anger toward the aggressor and our passion to punish and directs our attention instead to the personal plight of the defender. In the closing portions of his summation to the jury, Barry Slotnick played on this theme. He stressed Goetz's fear, his back to the steel wall of the subway car, with no choice but to strike back.

The theme of fear invokes the primordial form of self-defense in English law. From roughly the 13th to the 16th century, the plea of self-defense, called *se defendendo,* came into consideration whenever a fight broke out and one party retreated as far as he could go before resorting to defensive force. His back had to be literally against the wall.

If he then killed the aggressor, *se defendendo* had the effect of saving the defendant from execution, but it left intact the other stigmatizing effects of the criminal law. The defendant forfeited his goods as expiation of his having taken human life. The murder weapon was also forfeited to the crown as a deodand, a tainted object. Killing *se defendendo* was called excusable homicide, for though the wrong of homicide had occurred, the circumstances generated a personal excuse that saved the manslayer from execution. The defense of *se defendendo* springs more from compassion for the predicament of the trapped defender than from a passion for justice or the dictates of reason. If we would all act the same way if caught in the same circumstances, we can hardly condemn and execute the manslayer who had no choice.

Conceiving of self-defense as an excuse, based on the defender's uncontrollable reaction to the specter of death, leads, it would seem, to tightening the screws on the issues of imminence and necessity, but loosening them on proportionality. The former two must be strictly applied in order to assure that the defense is indeed an involuntary response to the terror of the situation. Yet if the reaction is indeed involuntary, greater tolerance should be allowed for the defender's overreacting and inflicting disproportionate harm.

The punitive theory of self-defense loosens the imminence and necessity requirements and should lead to a stricter application of proportionality as a value. Conceiving of self-defense as an excuse based on fear has the opposite effect in all three dimensions. Ingeniously, the defense brought both of these theories into play on behalf of Goetz's shooting the four youths.

Most legal systems today think of self-defense neither as a form of punishment nor as an excuse based on the defender's involuntary response to an overwhelming threat. We have come to think of acting to ward off aggression as the exercise of a basic right—an act, grounded in the dictates of reason, that justifies inflicting injuries and even killing the aggressor. To understand this emergence of self-defense as a justification, we must first consider the shortcoming in the law left by the defense of *se defendendo*. The only way for the defendant to avoid the harsh consequence of forfeiting his property on a successful plea of *se defendendo* was to argue that the death of the victim was not his act at all. If the killing was not his act, there was no blot on his escutcheon, nothing for him to expiate. The jury would acquit him outright and he would retain his goods.

The line between killing and passively being the instrument of death is, of course, a fine one. Sir Mathew Hale distinguishes between a defender's stabbing a victim (*se defendendo*) and a victim's impaling himself on the defender's motionless sword.[19] Like many other poets in history, Shakespeare had little patience for this kind of legal hair-splitting. His satire in *Hamlet* is worth recalling.

If Ophelia killed herself by her own hand, she was not entitled to a Christian burial. She appears to have done just that. When the Clown's partner tells him that Ophelia is entitled to a Christian burial, he is dumbfounded:[20]

CLOWN: How can that be, unless she drowned herself in her own defense?

OTHER: Why, 'tis found so.

CLOWN: It must be *se offendendo;* it cannot be else. For here lies the point: If I drown myself wittingly, it argues an act, and an act hath three branches; it is to act, to do, to perform: argal, she drowned herself wittingly.

OTHER: Nay, but hear you, goodman deliver.

CLOWN: Give me leave. Here lies the water; good: here stands the man; good: if the man go to the water and drowns himself, it is, will he, nill he, he goes; mark you that? But if the water comes to him and drown him, he drowns not himself: argal he that is not guilty of his own death shortens not his own life.

The Clown's mockery of lawyers and their reasoning is so effective precisely because he understands the legal relevance of action and the rationale for *se defendendo*. It all depends, as he says, on whether Ophelia comes to the water or the water comes to Ophelia. Of course, if she throws herself into the river, there would seem to be little doubt about who comes to what. But the view that she "shortens not [her] own life" turns on the whimsical view that the stream comes to her. The Clown's colleague sees through the play on the logical distinction with the kind of comment that today would be regarded as an insight into the class struggle: he claims that if she were not of aristocratic birth, "she should have been buried out of Christian burial."

The common law was obviously incomplete. Could it be the case that killing to save one's life always left a taint on the defender? At early stages of the common law, as in Roman law, there was no offense in killing a thief caught in the act—a *fur manifestus*. Why should not the defense against an apparent murderer be treated in the same way? Lawyers of the 15th and 16th centuries paid close attention to the jurisprudence of the Bible; in Exodus 22 we read that there is no bloodguilt, no taint, in killing a thief who seeks at night to break into one's home. Why should the common law suppose, in opposition to Exodus, that there is a taint requiring forfeiture of goods? Why should the only escape from this conclusion be the whimsical argument that the thief came to the knife, rather than the knife to the thief?

Even before Shakespeare's wit conceived of "se offendendo," Parliament came center stage and filled the role left vacant in the common law. Significantly, Parliament's statute enacted in 1532 licenses the killing, without any taint whatsoever, of robbers and other assailants on the public highway. The modern analogue to these highwaymen feared in the 16th century is muggers on our underground public highways—subways. This statutory defense came to be called justifiable as opposed to excusable homicide. The defense is not based on compassion for someone with his back to the wall, but rather it expresses a right to hold one's ground against wrongful aggressors. The claim is not "I could not do otherwise," but rather "Don't tread on me!" As the leading scholar of the 17th century Sir Edward Coke said of this defense, "no man shall ever give way to a thief, etc. neither shall he forfeit anything."[21] The consequence of justifiable homicide, as the 1532 statute prescribes, is total acquittal. There was no forfeiture of goods, no need to ponder whether the killer was really acting.

This version of self-defense is appropriately called "individualist," for it takes the vindication of individual autonomy as its fundamental imperative. Its philosophical champions were John Locke and Immanuel Kant. Locke insisted that yielding even an inch to an aggressor would put one on the path to submission and slavery.[22] Kant conceived of an unqualified right of self-defense as the foundation of a liberal legal system in which each citizen recognized and willed maximum freedom for himself as well as for his fellow citizens. That the legal system should be organized on the basis of maximum freedom was, for Kant, the implication of pure reason in human affairs.

Relying implicitly on this tradition, Slotnick invoked the individualist theory in his opening statement:[23]

> [N]o one can ever take away your inalienable right to protect your property or your life or your family. No one can walk up to me and say, "give me that watch," "give me your ring," "give me five dollars." And if they do, heaven help them if I'm armed, because I know what the law allows.

The "individualist" stands in contrast to the "social" variation of justifiable self-defense. The difference between the two is expressed in a very loose as opposed to a very strict approach to proportionality. The extreme version of the individualist defense rejects proportionality altogether. Any encroachment on an individual's rights represents an intolerable violation of personal autonomy. The affected individual can do everything in his power, deploy all necessary means to end the encroachment and vindicate his autonomy. The expansive attitude toward self-defense in the individualist theory leads, as well, to more generous interpretations of imminence and necessity.

The individualist theory has always expressed itself most strongly in the protection of one's home. Any intrusion against one's castle, against one's refuge from the heartless world, seems intolerable. The individualist theory would vindicate the use of all necessary means to defend one's home against an attempted intrusion. Perhaps, as Kant would say, our moral concern for the welfare of others would lead us not to exercise our right of defense,[24] but liberal writings leave no doubt that freedom entails the option to resist all forms of encroachment.

The social variation of the same defense rejects absolutes like the imperative to secure one's rights, one's autonomy, or one's private physical space. The individualist treats every person as an island, entitled to full sovereignty in his own domain. This theory, which treats human beings as though they were nation-states, ignores our interdependence, both in shaping our sense of self and in cooperating in society for mutual advantage. The aggressor is another member of the same society of interdependent selves. He has interests that we cannot ignore even if he acts wrongfully in aggressing against someone else. These interests are expressed in the obligation of the defender to consider the aggressor not merely as an intrusive force, but as a human being.

Recognizing the humanity of the aggressor implies that in some situations the defender must absorb an encroachment on his autonomy rather than inflict an excessive cost on the aggressor. If the only way to prevent an intrusion and nonviolent theft in one's home is to kill the aggressor, the defender may voluntarily have to forgo the defense and risk losing his property. He must suffer a minor invasion and hope that the police will recover his goods; the alternative of killing the aggressor is too costly and too callous a disregard of the human interests of the aggressor.

Blackstone's influential argument for the social interpretation of justifiable self-defense harks back to the punitive theory that we considered at the beginning of this discussion. As he puts it, if the courts do not execute a petty thief for his crime, neither the police nor a private citizen should be able to kill him to prevent his theft.[25] The analogy is powerful. If punishment is limited by the principle of proportionality, it makes sense to limit self-defense by a version of the same principle.

Yet self-defense is not punishment. The purpose of a defensive act is not to inflict harm according to the desert of the aggressor. Its purpose is to repel the attack. And if there is a principle of proportionality that restricts self-defense, it cannot be the same principle of justice that governs sentencing after trial and conviction.[26] As the example of repelling rape by deadly force demonstrates, the right to subject an aggressor to a risk of death attaches even when capital punishment would be unacceptable.

In the 1950s and the 1960s a strong defense of the social theory emerged from the general and seemingly uncontroversial view that the purpose of the criminal law was to further the public good. After all, who could be against the public good? The consequence of this view in the thinking of criminal law reformers was that the purpose of punishment was primarily to encourage people to act in a socially desirable way, and the determination of socially desirable conduct turned largely on the assessment of the costs and benefits of acting in particular ways.

The consequence of thinking about self-defense as a measure

furthering the public welfare led courts and legislatures, for a time, to eschew all absolutist thinking about the right of people to defend their autonomy against aggressive attacks. In cases of burglary, for example, the lawmakers demanded that for a homeowner to use deadly force against an intruder, he must fear violence to himself or the other occupants; the fear of theft would not be sufficient to justify fighting off the burglar with force endangering his life.

An illustrative case is the decision of the California Supreme Court in *People v. Ceballos,*[27] which held that injuring a burglar with a spring gun could not be justified. Since no one was home at the time of the intrusion, the burglary did not subject an occupant to the risk of violence, and therefore the only interest at stake on the side of the homeowner was his property. Defending property alone did not justify the use of deadly force against the burglar.

The social theory of self-defense says, in short, that burglars and muggers also have rights, and the rights of the victims must therefore be restricted when their exercise inflicts an excessive cost on those who attack them. It would be fair to say that if the public at large supported this philosophy a generation ago, their feelings about crime and the rights of criminals have shifted dramatically since then.

There is little sympathy today for the welfare of those who aggress against others. We are witnessing a return to absolutist thinking about self-defense, a return to the individualist philosophy that ignores the costs of a necessary defense to the aggressor. This is evident in legislative changes. When Illinois adopted its criminal code in 1962, it restricted the use of deadly force in burglary cases "to prevent the commission of *forcible* felonies in the dwelling."[28] In 1967 the legislature dropped the word "forcible," making it clear that deadly force would also be permissible merely to prevent larceny—a felony that does not require the use of force. The same pattern is evident in New York. In 1968, the New York legislature amended the new Penal Law, just three years old, to make the commission of a burglary a sufficient ground, in itself, for resistance with deadly force.[29]

Some changes in the last few years have been even more dramatic. Colorado enacted a statute in 1985 that begins with the bold declaration that "the citizens of Colorado have a right to expect absolute safety in their homes." The statute goes on to postulate that self-defense should be applicable if an intruder in one's home is "committing or intends to commit a crime . . . [even] against property" and "the occupant reasonably believes that [the intruder] might use any physical force, no matter how slight, against any occupant."[30]

The problem faced by Bernhard Goetz is not the exactly the same as that faced by a homeowner confronted by an unlawful intruder, but there is an important analogy. Goetz also felt that his rightful space was being intruded upon by a stranger confronting him and demanding money. As a homeowner does not know for sure that an intruder will injure him or his family, Goetz did not know for sure that had he said, "No, I have no money," Canty and his friends would have assaulted him. The social theory of self-defense requires the victim to suffer a loss of property rather than fight back with deadly force.

There is no doubt that from a social point of view, life and limb are more important than property rights. What the social theory of self-defense ignores, however, is the ever-present risk that a burglar or an intruder into your space on the subway will do much more than merely take your money or your watch. The individualist theory acknowledges that risk as real and holds that it is wrong to force innocent, law-abiding individuals to suffer a risk of personal violence. As the Colorado statute endorses deadly force whenever there is a risk that an intruder "might use physical force, no matter how slight," many who sympathize with Goetz would argue that he too should have been able to use deadly force to counteract the risk of "physical force, no matter how slight."

What, then, is the balance that we can draw from all these conflicting theories of self-defense? Several of these perspectives support an expansive interpretation of Goetz's right to use deadly force. The theory of self-defense as an excuse generates an acquittal for virtually any degree of force that Goetz, in his state of fear, with his back against the wall, felt compelled to use. The individualist theory of self-defense as a justification also vindicates the use of deadly force, when necessary, to uphold the defender's rights to his personal security, his autonomy, and his liberty of movement.

Strains of all but the social theory of self-defense interweave in the defense's appeals to the jury in the Goetz trial. When the focus fell on Goetz's fear, the argument implicitly invoked the theory of self-defense as an excuse. When the emphasis was directed to a subway passenger's right not to surrender his money or his watch, the argument rested on the individualist theory of self-defense as a justification.

The defense also relied heavily on the punitive theory, although a careful analysis of "what those punks deserved" could hardly support a finding that they were rightly subject to a potentially fatal shooting. If they were convicted for what they did, both on that day and in the past, their legal punishment would not even approach the suffering of Darrell Cabey.

The only perspective that uneqivocally stood for a narrow interpretation of Goetz's right of self-defense was the social variation of self-defense as a justification. It is only by thinking of the alleged aggressors as people with interests to be balanced against those of the defender Goetz that a jury could be led to think of Goetz's response as excessive and illegitimate. The more Troy Canty, Barry Allen, James Ramseur, and Darrell Cabey come into focus as human beings worthy of our compassion, the more we might expect Goetz to have taken some risks that he could exit from the confrontation on the train without inflicting the human costs that he did.

From the perspective of our efforts to understand the rhetoric of the Goetz case, the four theories of self-defense provide an invaluable matrix of interpretation. Rhetorical gambits like "they got what they deserved" make sense as an appeal to a particular conception of self-defense. Emphasizing Goetz's fears draws on a different strain in the accretions of the legal tradition, and appealing to Goetz's right to be free of harassment invokes yet another perspective. Understanding the rhetoric of the Goetz case requires, above all, that we grasp the theoretical forces driving the debate.

Passion and reason interact in the law of self-defense, then, by generating conflicting theories that nag at our loyalties when we seek to interpret the vague contours of the defense. Passions impel us to think of defensive force as punitive and vengeful, inflicting deserved harm on wrongdoers. Reason invites us to think of self-defense as a means of maintaining order and harmony among independent, autonomous persons. The historic struggle of the law has been from passion to reason, from inflicting just deserts to the vindication of the defender's autonomy. Other theories, such as self-defense as an excuse based on an involuntary response and the social theory of justifiable self-defense, complicate the task of reason.

Could it be the case that reason requires a single theory of self-defense? Or is reason tolerant of diverse theories within the same legal system? The question whether reason tolerates diversity invites us to think about diverse perceptions of an ambiguous situation like Troy Canty's approaching Bernhard Goetz and asking for five dollars. As there are many approaches to self-defense, there are potentially many plausible interpretations of what might have happened in that subway encounter. In the end, the inquiry must turn to Goetz's subjective perception of what was about to happen to him. His claim of self-defense resolved into an inquiry whether his perception of the events was consistent with reason. Reason in the law drives us toward the truth, but it can also be tolerant of sensible error.

3

Tolerant Reason

IN the 17th and 18th centuries, the leading scholars of English law assumed that the common law, as it evolved in the courts, was the embodiment of reason. Sir Edward Coke, the quintessential lawyer of the 17th century, argued in his scholarly commentaries that reason is the soul of the law. As a leading judge of the time, Coke acted on his commitment to the common law as a set of truths born of refined reason. So confident was he that reason could tolerate only one law that he struck down a statute duly passed by Parliament as violative of "common right and reason."[1] If a statute violated the dictates of reason, it could not be the law of England. Writing a century later, William Blackstone, whose *Commentaries* became the basic work for generations of lawyers in the American colonies, identified the common law of England with the enduring law of nature.

In the course of the 19th century, reason made its impact on the language of the common law, both in England and in the United States. The term "reasonable" came into the lexicon of lawyers as a daily reminder of Coke's teachings on reason as the soul of the law. The term "reasonable" quickly became ubiquitous in the arguments of Anglophone lawyers, distinguishing their speech from that of lawyers who plead in French, German, or indeed any other European language. Listen to English-speaking lawyers today and you will hear them talk about reasonable time, reasonable price, reasonable mistake, reasonable care—just to name a few of the expressions testifying to our commitment to reasonableness. In none of these legal contexts will you find a French, German, or Soviet lawyer using a term that derives from the indigenous linguistic root for "reason." It is not that these lawyers could not say *raisonnable,* *vernünftig,* or *razumnyi* if they wanted to. They do not. Only lawyers in the English-speaking world are wedded to the term.

The centerpiece of this preoccupation with reasonableness is the reasonable man—or, as we say today, the reasonable person. The conventional way of determining what is reasonable is to inquire what a reasonable man would do. For example, in negligent accident cases, juries all over the Anglophone world are instructed, "If you find that the defendant did not act as would a reasonable person under the circumstances, then you should find that he or she acted negligently." The term "reasonable" is so common in lawyerly discourse that a student who failed to master use of the term would hardly belong to the special linguistic community that constitutes the American bar.

The pervasive use of "reasonableness" by American lawyers bears witness to the ongoing influence of Coke's faith in reason as the foundation of the law, but it also departs from the pretension of reason to a single truth. Acting reasonably does not require that one be right. The reasonable person can be wrong. Today American lawyers assume that there is more than one reasonable answer to any given problem in the law. This point is captured in the standard that judges use for deciding when to submit a disputed question of fact to a jury. The question goes to the jury if it is the kind of dispute on which "reasonable men might disagree."

The range of reasonable decision is like the middle of a football field, say the distance from the 20-yard line on one side to the 20-yard line on the other side. If the evidence is so clear that the matter lies below the plaintiff's 20-yard line, then the judge himself will find for the defendant; if it lies below the defendant's 20-yard line, the judge will find for the plaintiff.[2] The jury decides only if the evidence lies in the middle of the field, where reasonable people may disagree. Reason is never at war with itself, but reasonable people are often at odds with each other. Some of them turn out to be right and others, wrong.

Reasonableness lies at the center of American legal thought, and as our pivotal concept, it distinguishes us from our European brethren, who are still committed, at least nominally, to the singular truth of the law as the Right and the True. For Americans, the voice of reason has become the spirit of tolerance. Others may be wrong, but their wrong path might still be on the map of reasonable alternatives. And even in an age when we are inclined to believe that right and wrong exist in the eyes of the beholder, the law must defend the core of reason against the extremes of unreasonable behavior.

This is the central issue that taxed the lawyers and the courts in the Goetz case from the time of the second grand jury in March 1985 until the resolution of the dispute by the New York Court of Appeals in July 1986. What does the rule of reason require in self-defense cases? Could it be the case that every time someone believes that he is being attacked and that he must shoot to defend himself, he acts reasonably under the law? Or do we as a society, represented by the 12 men and women of the jury, have to decide whether some fears and some reactions are so extreme as to be labeled unreasonable and unacceptable?

Technically, the argument was about the proper reading of the statutory requirement that the defendant "reasonably believed" both that he was about to be killed or robbed and that it was necessary to respond with deadly force. The defense took the position that any belief should qualify as reasonable under the law. All that should matter was that the defendant sincerely held the belief. They referred to their position as "subjective," for they wanted the legal decision to turn exclusively on the defendant's subjective state of mind. Their opponents held the "objective" theory, for they believed that the standard of reasonableness entails an objective standard set by the hypothetical behavior of a reasonable person under the circumstances. Beliefs, fears, and reactions that fall below this standard are unreasonable and unacceptable; they merit blame and condemnation.

One would think that there would be little dispute about jurors' applying an objective standard of acceptable behavior. How could the statutory phrase "reasonably believe" possibly refer to a subjective standard, to what the defendant actually believed, regardless of whether it was objectively reasonable or not? Even apart from the dictates of the statutory language, it is hard to make a case for a subjective standard that enthrones the private judgments of every person. A sensible legislature or judge would not choose a rule that allowed people to escape liability for homicide or attempted homicide simply because they believed in good faith that they were about to be robbed.

Yet there is a version of the objective standard that makes it seem unjust and indifferent to the situation of the defendant. If appealing to the conduct of a "reasonable person under the circumstances" means that the actual beliefs of the defendant are irrelevant, then it seems that not the defendant, but a hypothetical reasonable defendant is on trial. Yet no one has ever seriously proposed that the objective standard dispenses with a need to establish that the defendant himself believed that he was under attack and it was necessary to respond. The briefs of the District Attorney distanced themselves from this extreme version of the objective standard (one that disregards the beliefs of the defendant) by referring to their version of the objective test as the "two-pronged" or "hybrid" test. This test requires in its first prong that the defendant actually believes in the necessity of deadly force, and in its second, that this belief corresponds to what a reasonable person would believe under the circumstances. They called the test a "hybrid" because it combined a purely subjective requirement of belief with an objective standard of reasonableness.

Surprisingly, the subjective standard began in 1981 to slip into the decisions of the New York Appellate Division—the appellate courts standing between the trial courts in the Supreme Court and the Court of Appeals in Albany. The change came about not with a bang, but with a whimper. In the first case, *People v. Gonzalez*,[3] the prosecution needlessly and inexplicably[4] conceded that the trial court had erred in charging the jury to evaluate the accused's claim of self-defense according to the behavior of the "ordinary prudent man."[5] The court affirmed the conviction, but the published opinion referred to the objective standard for assessing self-defense as "error."

As curious as this planting of the seed of the subjective standard in New York may be, the nourishing of its growth in subsequent decisions is even more surprising. *Gonzalez* originated in the First Department of the Appellate Division, the panel of judges that hears appeals from Manhattan criminal courts. The Second Department of the same court, with jurisdiction primarily over the trial courts in Brooklyn, then adopted *Gonzalez* as though it were a thoughtful ruling and not simply a reflection of the prosecution's gratuitous concession. In a 1983 decision citing *Gonzalez,* the Second Department reversed a manslaughter conviction because the trial "court had erred in enunciating an 'ordinary prudent man' standard for the evaluation of the defendant's behavior." The correct standard, as the 1983 case held, was "what the defendant must have thought."[6] The court's opinion, which is less than a page long, is written in a summary style, with no reasoning other than the citation of authority[7] to support its conclusions.

In 1984 several other decisions in the Second Department confirmed this apparent shift in the meaning of "reasonable belief."[8]

When the second grand jury considering the Goetz indictment met in late February 1985, none of these decisions had received confirmation from the high court in Albany. Nor had the First Department— the appellate court that mattered[8]—accepted the questionable progeny of its gratuitous dictum in *Gonzalez*.

In light of the precedents in the Appellate Division, Assistant District Attorney Gregory Waples, who had taken over the case from Susan Braver, faced a difficult strategic situation.[10] Should he instruct the grand jury that the standard of decision was "what the defendant must have thought" and thereby reduce his chance of securing an indictment? Or should he instruct the grand jury in what he took to be the correct view of the law—the view that incidentally helped the prosecution? If he misstated the law, he might subject the entire indictment to later attack.

Waples tried to avoid committing himself to either the subjective or objective standard by instructing the grand jury in the language of the statute: the defendant had a valid claim of self-defense only if he "reasonably believed" in the factual basis for the defense. When a grand juror seized the initiative and asked for clarification of the standard of "reasonable belief," particularly as applied to irrational fears and beliefs, Waples himself was against the wall, with little room to avoid taking a stand on the law. Arguably, his duty as an official of the state was to state the law as authoritatively interpreted by the Appellate Division—even if there was no authoritative decision by the high court in Albany. Thus he was duty-bound to instruct the grand jury in the subjective standard. He confronted not only a strategic problem, but an ethical quandary about his duty as a prosecutor.

Beneath Waples's quandary simmers one of the deepest unresolved jurisprudential debates of our time. What is the New York "law" that he was bound to communicate to the jurors? One view holds that the law is whatever the legislatures and courts say it is. Another position is that the law consists of enduring principles that the courts (and even the legislatures) sometimes get wrong. If Waples was convinced that the Appellate Division was wrong about the law of self-defense, was he bound nonetheless to instruct the grand jury in the law laid down in these cursorily reasoned precedents? The question reflects tension between the two opposing theories of law, between law as enduring principles of right and wrong, on the one hand, and law as the collected decisions of the courts on the other. The former view maintains our faith in law as the embodiment of principle.

The latter view anchors flights of reason in a stable system of legal decision making that provides continuity and insulation from shifting political tides, each claiming reason on its side.

When the grand juror asked for clarification, Waples decided he would instruct on the correct principles of law. He responded with strong support for precisely the view that the Appellate Division had rejected:[11]

> [A]nd in determining whether [his response] was reasonable under the circumstances you should consider whether the *defendant's conduct was that of a reasonable man in the defendant's situation.*
> . . . whether that was the action—the response was the action that he—that a reasonable man who found himself in the defendant's situation. . . . [A]nd if it was unreasonably excessive or—otherwise unjustifiable it—then the defense would not be made out. . . . [italics added.]

The statutory standard of "reasonable belief" should turn not solely on what the defendant believed, but on the "conduct. . . of a reasonable man in the defendant's situation." The objective standard increased the likelihood that the grand jury would reject Goetz's claim of self-defense as unreasonable and thus improved the prosecution's chances of securing an indictment for attempted murder. Yet Waples also risked infecting that indictment with legal error. He risked a legal crisis in the hope of overcoming the Appellate Division precedents that stood in the way of the prosecution.

His move turned out to be a tactical failure but a strategic victory—probably more successful in the long run than he anticipated. The grand jury, motivated in part by his instruction on the objective standard, rejected the claim of self-defense and indicted Goetz on charges of assault and attempted murder.[12] At about the same time the second grand jury was deliberating, however, the First Department of the Appellate Division confirmed its opposition to the objective standard. It rendered a decision bringing the germ sown in *Gonzalez* to fruition in a precedent of its own. In *Santiago,*[13] for the first time, the appellate court hearing appeals from Manhattan trials reversed a conviction on the ground that the trial judge had improperly instructed the jury to apply the standard of the "ordinary reasonable man."[14] That this was error, the court concluded, was "beyond dispute."[15]

One clear implication of this decision was that Justice Crane would apply the subjective standard at the trial. Even if Goetz was indicted on the objective standard, the trial judge would unhesitatingly follow the law of the Appellate Division, and particularly of the judges with the power to reverse his decisions.

Waples faced a trial on the subjective standard. Goetz's chances on the critical issue of self-defense would be much stronger at trial than they were before the second grand jury. There was no way the prosecution could get a petition to the Court of Appeals to clarify the law of self-defense in its favor. But if the defense appealed the grand jury's issuing the indictment on the basis of Waples's arguably erroneous instruction, Waples could argue his position to the appellate courts, and perhaps he would prevail. Thus he might secure a change in the law prevailing in the courts before the Goetz trial began.

Ironically, the defense did not initially know that Waples had instructed the jury to rely on the objective standard of the reasonable man. They were not present. Goetz was not present. Who was supposed to tell them? Gregory Waples was the only lawyer in the room.[16]

As a throwback to the inquisitorial mode of trial, the grand jury is totally in the hands of the prosecutor, who functions both as judge and advocate. As part of this combined function, the prosecutor instructs the grand jury on the law they should apply to the facts. The only check on the prosecutor's plenary powers over the grand jury resides in the power of the supervising judge, in this case Justice Crane, to review the minutes of the proceedings for possible legal error.

At the very moment that Justice Crane was reading the minutes, he noticed a *New York Law Journal* report of the decision in *Santiago*. Greg Waples's comments stood out as an obvious challenge to the established law of the Appellate Division. Accordingly, Justice Crane released relevant portions of the minutes to the defense, and in October they petitioned him to dismiss all the charges allegedly infected by the incorrect instruction on self-defense.

It was almost as though Waples had carefully designed this trap and the defense could not resist the bait. Slotnick and Baker thought they had a victory for the asking. Indeed they had. In view of *Santiago* and the other precedents, Crane had little choice but to dismiss all the charges that turned on the erroneous instruction. What matters to well-trained men and women on the front line of trial justice is not political vision, but whether they can comply with the precedents of the courts that sit immediately above them.[17] The law as laid down in the precedents required that Justice Crane dismiss nine counts[18] of the indictment returned by the grand jury, and he did so on January 16, 1986.[19]

True, the dismissal was a tactical victory for the defense. At the same time, however, the defense exposed itself to a major strategic defeat by opening up the standard of self-defense to an appellate argument, including an appeal to the Court of Appeals, which would not regard itself as bound by *Santiago* and the other Appellate Division cases.

If the defense had not moved to dismiss the indictment, it would have gone to trial on the subjective standard of self-defense; without explicit guidance from Albany, Justice Crane would never have deviated from the rule laid down in *Santiago*. And if Goetz had been acquitted on the subjective standard, which was far more likely than an acquittal on the objective standard, the prosecution could not have appealed. The prosecution can appeal the dismissal of an indictment, but once a case goes to the jury and the jury renders an acquittal, the defendant is a free man or woman. The principle of double jeopardy prevents further appeals or accusations based on the same alleged events.

The opportunity of the prosecution, therefore, to appeal Justice Crane's dismissal came as an unsought blessing. Before conferring this advantage on the prosecution, before giving them this unique opportunity to secure a more favorable appellate ruling on the standard of self-defense, the defense should have thought more seriously whether they could prevail on an appeal to the Court of Appeals. Perhaps they could not have anticipated the unanimous ruling that the high court rendered against them, but they should have realized that they were betting their chips on cards that were easily trumped by serious reflection on the law.

The appellate argument engendered by Justice Crane's ruling provides an extraordinary opportunity to examine the way in which lawyers work with authoritative sources—statutes, case decisions, and scholarly opinion—in order to craft a persuasive interpretation of the law. The argument takes shape first in Justice Crane's lengthy and thoughtful opinion, then in the briefs of the lawyers on appeal to the Appellate Division, in the three opinions written by the judges of the Appellate Division, in briefs to the Court of Appeals in Albany, and finally in the high court's opinion concluding that Gregory Waples's instruction on self-defense to the second grand jury was right after all. Procedurally, the Court of Appeals reversed the Appellate Division's upholding Justice Crane's decision and reinstated the indictment. More profoundly, they came to a conclusion about a basic principle of New York law—a principle that was law not only in July 1986 when they reached their decision, but in March 1985 when Gregory Waples decided to express his vision of the law in the face of contrary authority. The story of this argument about the proper standard of self-defense should engage all those interested in the Goetz case and the law of self-defense, but more significantly, the pitched battle on the theory of reasonableness in self-defense illuminates the struggle of tolerant reason against the forces of moral relativism in modern legal theory.

The debate about the standard of self-defense in *People v. Goetz* probed the teachings of various conflicting sources of law. The decisions of the Appellate Division were relatively clear in their endorsement of the subjective standard; they were persuasive simply because they emanated from an authoritative body—a court with the power to reverse decisions they didn't like. The decisions of the Court of Appeals were less to the point, but they contained suggestive language and intimations that lent themselves to interpretation on both sides of the argument.

Alongside the cases and precedents stood the 1965 Penal Law itself. What did the legislature intend when they enacted the problematic § 35.15 on self-defense? The debate about legislative intent turned out to be a struggle between two sources of influence on the new law. There was the influence of history. Did the new law simply carry forward the prior law on the standard of self-defense, or did the new statute change the law under the influence of the prestigious Model Penal Code,* which urged legislators to adopt a version of the subjective standard? It was not so easy for New York lawyers, who rarely delve into the intricacies of the Model Penal Code, to understand the theory of that code and to cope with its impact on the new Penal Law provision on self-defense. Legislative intent, it turns out, is not so readily fathomed.

Beyond the debate about how to read authoritative legal sources, the advocates and deciding judges had to struggle with the ultimate

---

* The Model Penal Code was drafted by the American Law Institute in Philadelphia, a distinguished group of academics, judges, and practicing lawyers devoted to research and law reform. The code was designed as a model for state legislatures; it has no official legal authority of its own. Since the adoption of the Proposed Official Draft in 1962, the Model Penal Code has had an impact on law reform in at least 35 states.

questions of theory and value that shape the criminal law. These are the factors that impel us toward particular readings of the legal sources. We should confront these arguments of value as openly as possible, for then we are less likely to adopt them unthinkingly as the conventional wisdom of the time.

For Justice Crane, the holdings of the precedents in the Appellate Division were clear. They all stood for the rejection of an "[extreme] objective test to determine the justification of a defendant's reaction."[20] In his view, these cases also stood for the rejection of the "hybrid" view urged by the District Attorney. In his opinion explaining the dismissal of the indictment, he wrote that "the hybrid concept embraced by the People . . . is virtually repudiated by . . . e.g. *Santiago, Wagman, Desmond.*"[21]

The prosecution embarked on the road to Albany by petitioning the Appellate Division, a few blocks north in Manhattan, to reverse Justice Crane's decision. They had every reason, however, to anticipate that they would not receive satisfaction from this court near home. It was the local decision in *Santiago* that provided the primary authority for Justice Crane's decision. If Robert Pittler, arguing for the District Attorney's office, was to win in the Appellate Division, he had to undermine the authority of *Santiago* and the earlier precedents in the series. He tried to do this by arguing not only that these decisions were inconsistent with the precedents of the Court of Appeals, but that the first case in the Appellate Division series, *Gonzalez,* was an aberration, a deviation based on a needless concession by the Bronx District Attorney. It should follow, he reasoned, that all of *Gonzalez*'s progeny in the Appellate Division lacked proper paternity in the law. Most seriously, he attacked these cursorily reasoned cases as the product of a "jurisprudential vacuum"—a lack of reflective thought on the basic issues of self-defense.[22]

Mark Baker, who argued for the defense, had little to add to the discussion of these cases, except to ridicule Pittler's argument that the Appellate Division cases "were forged in a jurisprudential vacuum." In his brief and in the oral argument, Baker tried to convert Pittler's critique of the Appellate Division decisions into a personal affront to the court.

Writing an unusually thorough opinion for the Appellate Division,[23] Justice Bentley Kassal hints that Baker's appeal to personal pride succeeded. The opinion reflects pique about the suggestion of a "jurisprudential vacuum" and maintains that the "precise issue here was specifically and fully presented in each of those cases[24] and was carefully considered." Convincing a court to abandon one of its own decisions requires advocacy sensitive to the pride of the judges. The task is not eased by a critique of the judges' process of decision making.

Justice Kassal's opinion reveals the moral and philosophical implications of equating the statutory phrase "reasonable belief" with actual, good-faith belief. According to the majority of the Appellate Division, someone reasonably believes that he is being attacked or that deadly force is necessary to avert an attack if his belief "is reasonable to him."[25] This is but a variation of the popular moral relativism that reduces right and wrong to what is right and wrong for each of us. A standard of reasonableness in which each person decides what is reasonable is obviously no standard at all. And if there are no standards for judging whether Goetz overreacted and exceeded the bounds of reasonableness, the law gives way to each person's deciding for himself whether the circumstances warrant the use of deadly defensive force.

The meaning of "reasonable belief" is a question of principle, but by the convention of their profession, lawyers shy away from grand questions of principle and spend most of their rhetorical energies mustering "authorities" on their side of their argument. Even if reason supports their position, they prefer to ground their argument in the words and decisions of others. In the debate for and against the objective standard, the most important sources of authority were the decisions rendered (or "handed down," as lawyers say) by the Court of Appeals. In this case, the debate was fueled by suggestive but nondecisive precedents on both sides of the question. If in any of these cases, the court had squarely decided that a trial judge must instruct the injury on some version either of the subjective or objective theory of self-defense, there would not have been an appellate controversy. Greg Waples would presumably have followed the ruling in instructing the grand jury. Had he slipped and misinstructed the jury in the face of a clear ruling by the high court and had Justice Crane, as a consequence, dismissed the indictment, the District Attorney would most likely have abided by that result.

According to the defense, the Court of Appeals had spoken on the issue. As early as Justice Crane's opinion supporting dismissal of the indictment, the leading case for Goetz's position was *People v. Miller*,[26] decided in 1976. The defendant in *Miller*, relying on self-defense in a prosecution for murder, sought to introduce evidence of specific violent acts committed by the victim, which acts were known to the defendant at the time of their confrontation. There might be two reasons for introducing this sort of evidence, one bad and one good. The bad reason is that the victim's record of violence tends to make him look morally less worthy and therefore generates sympathy for the defendant, precisely as the criminal records of Goetz's four victims put them in a bad light. The good reason is that if the defendant knows of his adversary's propensity for violence, he is likely to react differently in a physical confrontation. His knowledge bears, therefore, on the reasonableness of his perception of danger and of his judgment of the force necessary under the circumstances.

Overcoming their qualms about prejudice to the interests of the victim, the Court of Appeals held that the evidence was, in principle, admissible. The judges hastened to add "that this evidence may only be considered with respect to the issue of the reasonableness of defendant's apprehensions. . . ."[27] This reference to the issue of reasonableness seems to put the case in the prosecution's column, but there are other passages in the opinion that lend themselves to interpretation for the defense. The Court of Appeals also wrote:[28]

> [T]he crucial fact at issue, where a claim of justification is presented, is not the character of the victim, but, rather, the state of mind of the defendant.

Justice Crane seized upon the reference to the defendant's "state of mind" to support his claim that "the modern day Court of Appeals has put any controversy to rest in People v. Miller."[29] Justice Kassal's opinion for the Appellate Division confirms this reading of *Miller* as an endorsement of a subjective theory of self-defense.[30]

The leading case for the prosecution was *People v. Collice*, decided in 1977.[31] In the brief opinion in this case, the Court of Appeals affirmed a conviction for reckless endangerment, among other offenses, based on an incident in which the defendant fired a gun from his car at another car that followed him home. The defendant claimed self-defense, presumably on the theory that the complaining witness's following him home put him in fear of imminent aggression. The trial judge refused to instruct the jury on the defense, a decision a judge may take when there is virtually no evidence to support the assertion of a defense.

The defendant appealed to the Court of Appeals on the ground that the trial judge should have instructed the jury on the alleged defense of self-defense. The high court summarily affirmed the conviction, and reasoned:[32]

> Even if defendant had actually believed that he had been threatened with the imminent use of deadly physical force, and there is no evidence that he had so believed, his reactions were not those of a reasonable man acting in self-defense . . . defendant's conduct could not be reasonably perceived to have been useful in evading danger, let alone "necessary to defend himself."

This language seems unequivocally to put the court on the side of the objective standard. The judges admit that the defendant himself may have thought he was in danger, but if so, "his reactions were not those of a reasonable man." In the face of this case, decided after *Miller,* it would seem difficult to take the ambiguous language in *Miller* as testimony to the high court's commitment to a subjective theory of self-defense.

Nonetheless, Justice Crane sidestepped *Collice* and sided with *Miller.* He justified his stand with this argument:[33]

> In *Collice,* the court was in no way receding from the subjective—defendant's state of mind—test of *Miller.* It was applying the well-settled guide to appellate review, urged in the prosecutor's brief to that court, that under no view of the evidence, considered in a light most favorable to defendant, was he entitled to a justification [i.e., self-defense] charge.

Justice Kassal, writing for the majority in the Appellate Division, takes a similar line, but he also finds it necessary to misstate the holding in *Collice:* "[C]ontrary to the suggestion of the dissent, [*Collice*] does not authorize the substitution of the mind of the ordinary reasonable person."[34] *Collice* says nothing about "substituting the mind" of the reasonable person; it merely requires that the subjective beliefs and reactions of the defendant meet the standard of reasonableness.

This is a good example of the way in which the adversaries in this debate tends to attribute extreme positions to their opponents; here the subjectivist Justice Kassal implied that objectivists treated the standard of the reasonable person as a "substitute" for the beliefs of the defendant. In fact, the objectivist position holds that the actual beliefs of the defendant be tested for moral acceptability against the objective, community standard of reasonableness.

We have, then, these two cases, *Miller* and *Collice*. One seems to favor the defense; the other, the prosecution. In the argument before the Court of Appeals, the challenge for each side was to latch onto the favorable case and argue away the contrary case.

Arguing against the decisions of both the trial court and the Appellate Division, Robert Pittler, for the prosecution, insisted that *Collice* "reiterated that the reasonable person standard remains the law of this state, as it has for 150 years."[35] The plurality of three in the Appellate Division had engaged in "serious misreading of [the Court of Appeals] opinion in *Miller*."[36] The misreading consisted of taking the reference to "state of mind" as "the only principle upon which all justification claims hinge."[37] That the actor know of the prior acts of violence may be a *necessary* condition for the defense, but it does not follow that mere knowledge, whether reasonable or unreasonable, suffices for a good claim of self-defense.

As a general matter, the strategy of both advocates was to rely upon the explicit language of the case that favored them and to limit the language in the opposing case to the context of the specific question under decision. The way to contextualize the references to "state of mind" in *Miller* was to focus on the particular problem of admitting evidence of prior violent deeds by the alleged assailant. The analogous technique in coping with *Collice* was to stress that the question there decided was not the standard for self-defense, but simply whether there was sufficient evidence to warrant an instruction on self-defense.

Advocates on the Continent typically rely on statutory sources, and if there is no statute right on point, they will cite scholarly commentary on the law as their leading source. But lawyers in the common law tradition have always felt more comfortable arguing from precedent than from other sources of authority. This is true even in the criminal law, which is ostensibly governed not by cases, but by statutory definitions of crimes and defenses. The working assumption of lawyers seems to be that the true meaning of statutory provisions is reflected in appellate cases that clothe, as it were, the naked words of the legislature.

New York enacted a new Penal Law in 1965, and sooner or later in the appellate debate about the standard for self-defense, the lawyers had to take up the statutory definition of the defense. The relationship between statutory and case law remains a bit of a mystery in all legal systems descended from the English system of judge-crafted law. In the early stages of the English common law, the power of Parliament to intervene and change the common law was cloaked in ambiguity; like the law of nature, the common law was regarded by many as beyond manipulation by legislative fiat. Now it is assumed that legislatures can change the law at will— any law, anytime. Yet as definitive acts of will rather than tentative acts of reason, statutes call for a reading different from that given to the often learned and thoughtful opinions that explain judicial decisions. A statute gets its force from the will, not from the wisdom, of the legislature. The aim of lawyers in reading statutes is to discern this will, sometimes called the "intent" or "purpose," of the authoritative lawgiver.

Lawyers do not read cases this way. Cases, once decided, live not in the unexpressed intentions of the deciding judges, but in the opinions justifying the decision. These opinions embellish the living law. Judges interpret past decisions as expressions of a consistent and coherent system of principles. Whether a decision becomes an influential precedent depends on the wisdom of the decision and the rhetorical elegance of the opinion supporting the decision. The decisions of Justices Cardozo, Brandeis, and Holmes live on, not because they had any special authority as judges, but because they reached wise decisions under the law, persuasively explained in the language of the tradition.

The essential difference between statutes and cases, then, is that if a case deviates from traditional principles of law, it will be quickly forgotten. It will become, as Justice Frankfurter predicted of one decision by the Supreme Court, "a derelict on the waters of the law."[38] Statutes cannot be forgotten, even if they deviate from tradition, even if they explicitly repeal tradition. By common consent of the lawyers who live under statutory rule, legislatures can do what they want with the law—within the bounds of the Constitution. The job of lawyers and judges is to listen to the voice of democratic authority.

The problem of interpreting statutes, therefore, is much more difficult than interpreting cases. First, there is no opinion explaining the decision. The most one can hope for is records of the legislative debate, but as we know, legislators need not explain their votes. The statutory resolution may represent the lowest common denominator of conflicting political forces. Furthermore, a strong presumption favors the reading of cases within the traditional body of accepted principles. Revolutionary precedents are rarities. But those who read statutes are never quite sure whether the statute carries forward the prior law or is designed to break sharply with the past.

The reading of the critical phrase "reasonably believe" in the

New York provision on self-defense illustrates the special problem of fathoming the legislative will. Did the assembled group in Albany mean to carry forward the prior law of self-defense that had been in force since the first New York statute in 1829? Or did they mean to change the law in line with the Model Penal Code, which the legislators took as their blueprint for the 1965 Penal Law? Roughly speaking, if they followed prior law, they can be read as having intended the objective standard; if they followed the Model Penal Code, they can be treated as having incorporated a subjective standard at least, as we shall see, on the charge of attempted murder. These are the basic contours of the debate.

In 1965, when the legislature enacted the new Penal Law, the legislators were obviously ambivalent about the prior law. If they had wished to preserve it intact, they would have had little interest in a new code. The very process of "law reform" implies partial rejection of the old law. Yet legislators can never completely reject the past, as much as they might try. The question raised by the appeal in *People v. Goetz* is whether they implicitly retained the prevailing objective standard of self-defense or abandoned it for something new and more fashionable.

The Model Penal Code represents a new and, as some maintain, a better approach to the problem of mistake in self-defense cases. The drafters identified a problem with the traditional approach. In case of mistaken self-defense, the defender either got the whole defense or no defense. If his mistake was reasonable, he was acquitted on grounds of self-defense; if his mistake was unreasonable, he forfeited the defense and subjected himself to conviction as though he were an intentional killer. The advocates of the objective standard in the Goetz case endorsed this all-or-nothing approach. If Goetz's act was not that of a reasonable person under the circumstances, he merited no defense at all; he was to be treated as though he had gone out with the purpose of shooting the first four street kids he could find.

The drafters of the Model Penal Code argued that it was irrational to equate self-defense induced by an unreasonable mistake with an intentional killing in which the conditions of self-defense are wholly absent. When everyone agrees that a distinction is irrational, reason demands a change in the law. And in this context everyone concurred that reason was offended by the all-or-nothing approach implicit in the objective standard. Some compromise was necessary.

A ground for compromise was found in the insight that an unreasonable mistake was conceptually equivalent to a negligent accident or mistake; after all, someone who negligently caused death, say in a hunting accident, also falls short of the standard set by the reasonable person. It would follow that someone who killed after having made a negligent mistake about the factual basis for self-defense should be treated like someone who killed having made a negligent mistake about whether his gun was loaded or the object he spied in the distance was a deer and not a human being. In these latter cases, the negligent mistake would support a conviction for negligent homicide, and therefore a negligent mistake about the necessity to shoot in the subway should also support a conviction for negligent homicide (in a case in which someone was killed).

The compromise is ingenious. It is unquestionably one of the proud achievements of the drafters of the Model Penal Code. German theorists, working independently from the Americans, have come upon the same solution. Their rationale, which the drafters of the Model Penal Code might accept as well, is that a mistake about the factual basis for self-defense negates the intention required for liability. If the actor mistakenly thinks that someone is attacking him and he responds with the intent to defend himself, it cannot be said that he intends to kill (and certainly not to murder) the perceived aggressor.

This solution bears a serious flaw in a case like that of Bernhard Goetz, in which the shooting is at most an attempted homicide. The approach of the Model Penal Code presupposes that as there is negligent as well as intentional homicide, any act in mistaken self-defense could generate liability for a negligent offense. Yet only a very few crimes are punished if committed negligently.[39] And attempted homicide is not one of them. Neither the Model Penal Code nor New York law recognizes a crime of negligent attempt. Attempts, everyone agrees, are by their nature intentional efforts to commit a crime.

The implications of the Model Penal Code solution, therefore, are the following: If Goetz had killed someone under an unreasonable (negligent) mistake about the necessity of self-defense, he would have been liable, at most, for negligent homicide. But the victims did not die, which means that he could be liable, at most, for negligent attempted homicide. But the code does not recognize a crime of negligent attempted homicide. Either the attempt is intentional or it is not a crime at all. It follows that, under the Model Penal Code, if Goetz had believed, in good faith but unreasonably, in the necessity of defensive force, he would not be liable for any form of attempted homicide.[40]

The entire approach of the code depends on whether the victim dies. The code puts us in a comical position that its drafters would surely disown: in a case of shooting with an intent to kill, under an unreasonable mistake about the necessity of self-defense, we have to watch the hospital charts in order to decide whether Goetz might be liable for the consequences. If Cabey died two years after the shooting and it was determined that the death was a consequence of the original shooting, Goetz would then become liable for negligent homicide. Putting this much weight on consequences beyond the actor's control requires an argument that the code never gives us. It appears, in fact, that the drafters simply did not think through the implications of their proposal to treat all mistakes alike.*

The solutions generated by the subjective and Model Penal Code approaches coincide in cases of attempted murder: there is no liability in a case of good-faith but mistaken belief in the conditions of self-defense, regardless whether the mistaken belief is reasonable or unreasonable. It is not surprising, then, that the lawyers in the Goetz debate described the Model Penal Code as having adopted the subjective standard. This confusion is encouraged by the complex structure of the Model Penal Code, which first prescribes that anyone who "believes" in the conditions of self-defense has a good defense[41] and then, in a later provision, imposes liability in cases of unreasonable mistake about these conditions.[42] Most of the participants in the appellate debate read the first part of the model code and forgot the second part.[43] The proponents of the subjective standard, then, could rely on the supposed influence of the Model Penal Code in reshaping New York law.

The most telling argument against the influence of the Model Penal Code, pushed relentlessly by the prosecution, was that the legislature had in fact introduced the word "reasonably" after the word "believes" in the provision on self-defense, and this signaled an undeniable intent to reject a subjective standard.[44]

The situation, it has to be admitted, is rather amusing. Here we have a bunch of lawyers and judges trying to figure out whether a group of legislators in Albany passed a law in 1965 with an intent to retain the law then in force or to change it in line with the Model Penal Code. You would think the legislature would tell us what they were doing on so basic a point. Yet we have no clear evidence one way or the other. Some scholarly articles on the law reform came out at the time, including an interview with the head of the

---

* This theme is developed in Chapter Four.

legislative commission that proposed the change.[45] Yet these scholars are silent on the conflict between the subjective and the objective standard. The lawyers in this debate were trying to figure out what happened in 1965 with about as much evidence as they would have for debating a legal innovation in ancient Greece. The matter was undoubtedly complicated by the sorry failure of the lawyers to grasp the theory behind the Model Penal Code. The defense had little to say on the subject; the prosecution, perhaps because it was losing, did a bit more research and finally discovered that the Model Penal Code did not really endorse a subjective standard. Thus the lawyers were arguing in the dark about the shape of a legislative intent they could never see anyway; they were searching with lanterns they had not figured out how to turn on.

Without much assistance from the lawyers, the Court of Appeals managed to display a remarkably sound grasp of the philosophy behind the Model Penal Code. The issue is not subjective versus objective, but whether in cases of self-defense,[46]

> any culpability which arises from a mistaken belief in the need to use such force should be no greater than the culpability such a mistake would give rise to if it were made with respect to an element of a crime.

This point requires clarification. Lawyers are accustomed to dividing the issues of criminal liability into elements of the offense and elements of defenses. Homicide is an offense, and two of its elements are that the actor (1) kill a (2) living person. Self-defense as well as other claims of justification are defenses; they are so named because they are characteristically asserted and sometimes proved by the defense. The approach of the Model Penal Code derives from an elementary logical point about the wording of defenses: every defense could be reworded so that it appeared to an element of the offense. Consent is a general defense, but there is no reason why the defense could not be reworded so that nonconsent became an element of offenses like assault and rape. Similarly, the *absence* of self-defense could be viewed as an element of homicide. For convenience we may refer to the absence of defenses as negative elements of the offense.

The gist of the Model Penal Code approach is that mistakes about negative elements of the offense (i.e., defenses like self-defense) should be treated the same as mistakes about the positive elements of the offense. A mistake about whether self-defense is necessary under the circumstances should be analyzed the same as a mistake about whether the object of one's shooting is a human being or an inert object. If it results in death, a negligent mistake about the object of one's aim generates liability, at most, for negligent homicide. Similarly, a negligent mistake about the factual basis of self-defense should generate liability, at most, for negligent homicide.

Having perceived what was at stake in the Model Penal Code proposal, the Court of Appeals rejected it. The court adhered to the traditional view that claims of justification really are different from elements of the offense. According to the traditional view, the defendant can claim a defense like self-defense only if he acts reasonably in making judgments about the facts that drive him to a violent act like shooting. If he makes an unreasonable mistake about these factual conditions, he forfeits the defense entirely.

The opinion by Judge Sol Wachtler for a unanimous Court of Appeals hardly gives us evidence for the judges' conclusion that the New York legislature followed the Model Penal Code but implicitly disavowed the code's theoretical commitment to treat mistakes about defenses like mistakes about elements of the offense. Nonetheless, the judges may have made the right decision in imputing to the 1965 legislature an intent to retain the traditional approach to mistaken beliefs about justifying circumstances. In the final analysis, trying to fathom what the New York legislature intended in 1965 brings us to the questions: What is the most sensible reading of the language the legislature adopted in the new Penal Law? What would a reasonable legislature have intended with the language we find in the provision on self-defense?

Putting the question of statutory interpretation this way invites consideration of the ultimate principles governing self-defense. How should we go about thinking about the right approach to subjective and objective standards? In every effective brief, the advocate must buttress his arguments about what the law says with persuasive claims that it is right and good for the law to say what it does. Appealing to authority must give way, sooner or later, to arguments of reason and moral value.

Unfortunately, the lawyers arguing the appeal in the Goetz case did not deal with the issues of policy and principle that lay beneath the surface of the legal materials. The defense had little to say about these matters; and the most the prosecution could muster was the obvious point that the subjective standard would lead to intolerable results. It would, in effect, grant:[47]

a license to kill to any subway rider like [Goetz] who is asked for money—or the time—by black youths, simply because he honestly, but totally unreasonably believes that every such encounter with young members of a racial minority is potentially life-threatening.

This point is well taken, but it fails to come to grips with the reasons that might tempt someone to adopt either the subjective standard or the Model Penal Code approach which, in the case of attempted murder, has the same effect as the subjective standard.[48] It is not that anyone would argue that it is good for subway riders to indulge their fears of minority youth. The concern of those who advocate the subjective standard is rather that it is simply unjust to punish someone who thinks—however fancifully—that the circumstances warrant his using deadly force. The controversy about the subjective standard points to uncertainty and confusion about when it is just to condemn and punish someone as a criminal.

Shortly after Justice Crane made his decision in January 1986, a law professor, Richard Singer, entered the debate with a widely noticed article in the *New York Law Journal*.[49] Singer made a good case, not for the Model Penal Code test, but for the subjective standard, pure and simple. He sidestepped the problem of interpreting the phrase "reasonably believes" in the Penal Law and addressed himself exclusively to the philosophical question whether the objective or subjective standard is more desirable as a matter of principle. It is worth noting his arguments carefully, for though they never received full attention in the appellate argument, they bespeak the concern for justice that makes some judges and law reformers receptive to the subjective standard.

Singer concedes that the objective standard prevailed in New York from the mid-19th century until the recodification of the criminal law in 1965. The objective standard, he claims, distorts traditional legal principles which, in his view, put primary emphasis on the moral culpability of the actor. He interprets the Model Penal Code as[50]

> reflect[ing] a mounting movement among both criminal law academics and others to refocus the criminal law on the subjective mental culpability of the defendant, and to remove from the criminal law a long-standing fictional standard—the "reasonable person."

Reliance upon the "fictional standard" of the reasonable person distracts us from the true question, which is the "mental culpability" of the concrete defendant. Returning to the subjective standard is the only way, in Singer's view, to realize the unique function of the criminal law, which he says is "to punish morally culpable actors on the basis of their culpability and of their act."[51]

It makes good sense to insist that we only blame and punish those violators of the law whose actions are worthy of blame. Lawyers use a number of interchangeable expressions to signal the same requirement of blameworthiness. They may prefer "culpability" or "fault" or the Latin expression *mens rea* that is now falling out of favor after centuries of prominence. The point of these general moral terms is the same: criminal punishment has a condemnatory function, and it can serve this aim only if the persons convicted under law are worthy of condemnation.

Why should Bernhard Goetz not warrant condemnation and blame if he unreasonably believed that the circumstances warranted his shooting? The response would be that in his mind he was doing the right thing. How can he deserve blame for that? True blameworthiness consists in a state of consciousness, in a state of mind, in choosing to do evil, in knowingly pitting oneself against the interests and rights of others.

Theorists of the criminal law have had persistent qualms about treating negligence—or deviating from the standard of the reasonable person—as a form of culpability. The negligent actor does not choose to harm; he merely fails to take heed of the likelihood that his action will produce harm. If Goetz acted unreasonably, if he was negligent in judging the intentions of the four youths, we cannot say that he chose to use unnecessary force. How can he be blamed for that? And indeed, if people can be blamed only for what they choose to do, Goetz could not be blamed for failing to meet a standard of reasonable care.

Yet in daily life, we routinely blame ourselves and others for failing to meet conventional standards of attentiveness. Failing to remember an appointment or an important occasion invites blame from others, just as failing to keep track of our belongings or our investments can lead to self-censure. We are always setting standards of attentiveness and faulting those who could have met the standards but did not.

Now suppose that Goetz deviated from the standard of the reasonable person when he concluded that he was being physically attacked or robbed. The assumption would be that there was insufficient evidence in the demand for five dollars for a reasonable person to infer an imminent attack. The fault would lie in too hastily inferring the attack. The problem would not be *what* he thought, but allowing himself to think as he did. Had he been more sensitive, say, to the inhibiting effect of a crowded subway, he might not have perceived the same degree of danger in the situation.

There is no difficulty perceiving fault in failing to meet the common standards of human interdependence. We make these expectations of each other every day, and there is no reason why the criminal law should not enforce conventional expectations of reasonable behavior. When this way of thinking comes into proper focus, it seems very curious that anyone would argue, as do Singer and all the proponents of the subjective standard, that one must choose to do wrong in order to be properly subject to blame.

The subjectivists have become confused about the nature of blameworthiness in the criminal law. They seem to think that guilt and blame must be mirrored in the offender's thoughts. If he is not thinking guilty thoughts, if his mind is pure, they can find no way to blame him for his actions.

This misconstrues the foundation of criminal responsibility. The basis for all blaming is not the offender's thoughts, but our judgment about whether he could and should have acted otherwise under the circumstances. This judgment about "could" and "should" applies to cases in which offenders have wicked thoughts as well as cases of innocent mistake. If the actor cannot control his actions, we cannot blame him for his wicked thoughts. But if he could have been more attentive to his situation and avoided a mistake that resulted in harm to others, we can blame him for not having tried harder.

That this confusion exists in the academy as well as in the courts tells us something about our cultural condition. We have lost confidence in the very notion of guilt based on self-control (or "free will"). It is hard for us to understand individuals' having the capacity to act other than they have acted. If someone makes a mistake, then the mistake "must have been in the cards." If he acts wrongly, then it must have been the case that he would act wrongly. In most of us, there lurks the suspicion that humans have no more control of their actions than do animals driven by instinct and reflex. And if that is what we are, there is no room left in moral discourse for guilt, blaming, and condemnation. Training for future conformity will then take the place of punishing for past disobedience.

This uncertainty about the very possibility of guilt drives theorists of the criminal law to locate fault, not in a failure to have acted otherwise, but in a state of mind that accompanies a wrongful deed. If fault consists in a state of mind, then there is no need to speculate about counterfactual conditional situations, about what would have happened had the actor desired to do otherwise. In an age in which psychology has nearly displaced moral philosophy, this is a tempting way out. It fills the old moral vessels of guilt and blameworthiness with psychological surrogates. It enables us to continue deploying the apparatus of condemnation and punishment when we are radically uncertain about whether its foundational ideas are still coherent.

These are the ideas, then, that lay at the base of the debate between the subjective and objective standards of self-defense. The Court of Appeals decision for the objective standard lends itself to interpretation on many different levels. On one level, the judges decided that *Collice* was a more persuasive precedent than was *Miller*. One level deeper, they concluded that the 1965 recodification of New York law retained the prior commitment to the objective standard and rejected the teachings of the Model Penal Code. At a deeper level underlying these readings of legal authorities and legislative history, the judges recommitted themselves to a criminal law that made sense. What made sense to them, as it should to us, is that individuals can be at fault, they can properly be subjected to blame, for failing to meet the standards of a reasonable person.

But fault and unreasonable behavior matter only if one has done something to others that warrants being called a crime. At first blush, it seems clear what Goetz did: he shot four young men on the subway. Upon closer examination, however, the analysis of his wrong and his crime requires that we think about whether the core of his alleged crime was his harmful intention alone or his actually having made the victims suffer.

4

The Significance of Suffering

THE second grand jury concluded that the prosectuion had a sound basis for bringing Goetz to trial and convincing the jury beyond a reasonable doubt that Goetz's responses in the subway were unreasonable under the circumstances. Thus they indicted Goetz for a variety of crimes, 10 distinct offenses in all, based not only on the possession of the gun but on shooting the four youths without justification. If there was no self-defense, Goetz committed a crime by pulling his gun and firing five shots, injuring each of the youths once. But precisely what was the crime? There is no crime called "shooting in a subway" nor even a crime of shooting a gun. The criminal law seeks to specify particular aspects of violent and aggressive behavior that make the conduct wrongful and worthy of punishment.

In a single act of shooting at Troy Canty, Goetz might have committed three distinct offenses, each offense focusing on a different aspect of the violent outburst. The crime of attempted murder stresses Goetz's allegedly murderous intent in shooting. The crime of assault zeroes in on the actual suffering inflicted on Troy Canty. The newly devised crime of "reckless endangerment" consists exclusively in creating a risk of harm to Canty as well as the other passengers on the train. These three perspectives are hardly consistent. If the essence of the crime is Goetz's shooting with murderous intent, why should it matter whether the bullet rips through Canty's flesh? And if the crime inheres in wounding Canty, why should we inquire whether, in addition, Goetz endangered him by creating a risk of wounding him?

A single volley of shots generated nine felony charges, one count of attempted murder and of assault against each of the four victims and an additional charge of endangering others. It makes good sense to distinguish among the four victims, to recognize the humanity of each and thus to hinge distinct offenses on each of the wounding shots. It is far more questionable to apply three overlapping offenses to each of these shots.

The multiplicity of charges camouflages basic uncertainty in the legal system about why an act of shooting should be treated as a crime. Two conflicting schools of thought have emerged about the essential nature of criminal wrongdoing. A traditional approach emphasizes the victim's suffering and the actor's responsibility for bringing about irreversible damage. A modern approach to crime takes the act—the range of the actor's control over what happens—as the core of the crime. It is a matter of chance, the modernists say, whether a shot intended to kill actually hits its target. It is purely fortuitous, as the argument goes, that Goetz failed to kill one of his four intended victims. It is a matter of providence, as Gregory Waples later argued to the jury, that the volley of shots did not injure an innocent bystander on the train.

The traditionalists root their case in the way we feel about crime and suffering. Modernists hold to arguments of rational and meaningful punishment. Despite what we might feel, the modernist insists, reason demands that we limit the criminal law to those factors that are within the control of the actor. The occurrence of harm is beyond his control and therefore ought not to have weight in the definition of crime and fitting punishment. The tension between these conflicting schools infects virtually all of our decisions in designing a system of crime and punishment.

Historically, it is hard to deny the relevance of actual harm and suffering in our thinking about crime. The criminal law would never have come into being unless people actually harmed each other. Our thinking about sin and crime begins with a change in the natural order, a human act that leaves a stain on the world. The sin of Eden was not looking at the apple, not possessing it, but eating it. Oedipus's offense against the gods was not lusting, but actually fornicating with his mother. Cain's crime was not endangering Abel, but spilling his blood. The notions of sin and crime are rooted in the harms that humans inflict on each other.[1]

The classical conception of retributive punishment, the *lex talionis,* reenacts the crime on the person of the offender. This is expressed metaphorically in the biblical injunction to take an eye for an eye, a tooth for a tooth, and life for a life. In *Discipline and Punish*, the philosopher Michel Foucault argues that classically, punishment symbolically *expiated* the crime by replicating on the body of the criminal the harm he inflicted on another. It is hard even to think about punishment without perceiving the relationship between the harm wrought by the criminal and the harm he suffers in return.

From this perspective the salient fact in Goetz's crime, then, is his actually injuring the four youths. And the greater the injury, the greater the crime. If one of the four youths had died, even a year later, the crime would have fallen into a different category. Causing death is the ultimate evil, at least in the prevailing secular worldview. Homicide is the only crime for which, in some of its variations, capital punishment is still constitutional. The feature of homicide that makes it so heinous is not only the intention, not only the risk implicit in the defendant's act, but the inescapable fact of death. We no longer speak about the victim's blood crying out for revenge. But sensitivity to death and other irreversible harms represents an enduring afterglow of the biblical passion for punishing violations of the natural order.

This is not the way many or perhaps most policy makers think about crime in the modern world. Sometime in the last two or three centuries, our scientific thinking about crime began to shift from the harm done to the act that brings about the harm. The fortuitous connection between acts and their consequences did not trouble the great jurists of the past, but today, in the thinking of the moderns, a great divide separates the actor and his deed from the impact of his act on others. "There is many a slip 'twixt the cup and the lip."[2] And all those slips, all those matters of chance, have undermined the unity we once felt between a homicidal act and the death of the victim.

The notions of risk, probability, and chance circumscribe the modern way of thinking about action and harm. Instead of seeing harm first and the action as the means for bringing about the harm, we are now inclined to see the action first and the harm as a contingent consequence of the action. And if we see the action first and the harm second, we invite the question, Why should we consider the harm at all in assessing the criminal evil of shooting someone in the subway? Many radical reformers hold that indeed the harm is totally irrelevant. If you shoot and miss, you should be punished as though you had killed someone. All that matter are the acts that you can control. And you cannot control the bullet after it leaves the barrel. Power may come from the barrel of a gun, as Chairman Mao said, but according to the modernists, you exhaust your power as soon as you fire the gun.

Modernists pride themselves on the rationality of their theory. If the purpose of punishment is *either* to punish wickedness *or* to influence and guide human behavior, the criminal law should limit its sights to conduct and circumstances within human control. There is nothing wicked about the way things fortuitously turn out. The actor's personal culpability is expressed in his actions—not in the accidents of nature that determine the consequences of his actions. And so far as the purpose of punishment is to set an example and deter future offenders, the only conduct that can be deterred is that within our control. The arguments of reason seem almost unbeatable.

The shift toward arresting and prosecuting those who merely attempt crimes reflects a practical concern as well. The legal system should arguably not only react to crimes already committed, but should intervene before the harm is done. The police should arrest the would-be offender before he has a chance to realize the harm his conduct bespeaks. Crimes should be defined and jail sentences inflicted not only to expiate previous wrongs and deter future offenders, but to prevent harm from occurring. This makes a good deal of sense in a world in which we try to manage the resources of government in order to maximize the welfare of all. This approach to punishment is typically called "preventive" as opposed to the traditional "retributive" practice of punishing past crimes, measure for measure.

The rationalists have held sway over English and American criminal law for most of the period since World War II. The prevailing view is that criminal law should serve social goals, rationally determined and efficiently pursued. Punishment should serve the goal of control either by rehabilitating offenders or, when we despair of changing criminals with doses of therapy, by deterring people in the future from choosing crime as a profitable career. The modern approach to crime dismisses as subrational the argument that people simply *feel* that actually killing someone is far worse than trying to kill. The Model Penal Code, a rationalist document that reflects the attitudes of reform-minded lawyers in the 1950s, goes so far as to recommend punishing attempted murder the same way we punish murder.[3] Yet the concern for the suffering of victims is too deep-seated to be rejected simply because the reformers have so limited a conception of fair and decent punishment.

We punish convicted criminals not only because as social planners we see a need to deter crime in the future, but because we recognize the irrepressible need of victims to restore their faith in themselves and in the society in which they live. The imperative to do justice requires that we heed the suffering of the victims, that we inquire at trial whether the defendant is responsible for that suffering, and we adjudge him guilty, if the facts warrant it, not for antiseptically violating the rules of the system, but for inflicting a wrong on the body and to the dignity of the victim. If Goetz was guilty for having shot at Troy Canty, Barry Allen, James Ramseur, and Darrell Cabey, his guilt consisted primarily in having brought these young men to their knees in pain, in leaving lead in their flesh and scars on their bodies, and, in Darrell Cabey's case, in severing his spinal cord, causing him to be paralyzed and to suffer brain damage for the rest of his life.

Whether the defendant actually causes the harm to the victim becomes, therefore, a pivotal question in every trial responding to the fact of suffering. Usually there is no particular problem in establishing the toll a gunshot takes on its victim, but unexpectedly, the question whether Goetz's shooting Cabey actually caused Cabey's brain damage became a hotly contested issue in the Goetz trial.

The prosecutor, Gregory Waples, returned repeatedly to the theme of the permanent disabilities that Goetz inflicted on Cabey. As Waples stressed in his opening statement, as a result of the cold-blooded fifth shot when Cabey was sitting defenseless in his seat, Cabey could "look forward to the rest of his life . . . living in a wheel chair."[4] It would be hard to deny that Goetz's shot severed Cabey's spinal cord, but did the same shot also produce the brain damage? Cabey incurred damage to his brain because, as Waples explained:[5]

> while he was in the hospital struggling, fighting for his life, struggling to recover from the gunshot wound the defendant inflicted which paralyzed him for life . . . medical complications set in and . . . three weeks after he was shot, [as a result of] these medical complications, he suffered a respiratory arrest. Darrell Cabey actually stopped breathing while in the hospital and was deprived of oxygen . . . [and he] plunged into a deep coma . . . a persistent vegetating state.

When Waples called the doctor who ministered to Cabey, one Claude Macaluso, and questioned the doctor about the coma, the defense protested vigorously. It is clear why Slotnick would want to avoid burdening his client with the stigma of having caused this misery. Goetz may not have killed anyone, but his actions allegedly reduced Cabey to a "vegetating state" even worse than suffering paralysis from the waist down. If Waples's accusation proved to be correct, Goetz's shooting Cabey would appear in the worst possible light, worse even than swiftly and painlessly killing. Whatever the legal implications of this responsibility, portraying Goetz as someone who wreaked this human damage would obviously weigh heavily in the jury's mind.

The defense's objection generated an arcane but significant legal debate, out of the presence of the jury, in which both lawyers questioned Dr. Macaluso about the details of the treatment afforded Cabey in the hospital. Slotnick tried to elicit an admission from the doctor that the coma occurred because the doctors waited too long to put Cabey on an artificial respirator. Perhaps they did. Dr. Macaluso conceded that they could have prevented the coma if they had intervened sooner, but in response to Waples's follow-up question, he insisted that there was nothing irregular or improper about the procedures followed in Cabey's treatment.

The thrust of the defense was that Cabey suffered the brain-damaging coma not because Goetz shot him, but because the hospital doctors were negligent in not putting him on a respirator sooner and thereby preventing the coma. The case was analogous, in the defense's theory, to a hypothetical situation in which Cabey lay recuperating in the hospital and someone came along and hurt him for reasons totally unconnected to the subway shooting. Slotnick and Baker maintained that if the doctors were at fault, Goetz was not causally responsible and therefore not to blame for Cabey's brain damage. This aspect of Cabey's suffering should not, the defense reasoned, be presented to the jury as a consequence of the shooting.

The defense's maneuver foundered on Dr. Macaluso's testimony that there was nothing out of the ordinary about the treatment accorded Cabey. Even if, in theory, the doctors might have intervened sooner, his vital signs did not indicate the use of a respirator; there was nothing negligent about the procedures used. If there was nothing unusual in the hospital treatment, Goetz had to stand responsible for the consequences. His shooting Cabey triggered the treatment, which in turn resulted in the coma and the brain damage. He initiated a foreseeable chain of consequences, and these consequences were to be reckoned as part of his deed. As the matter was resolved, Waples could question Dr. Macaluso in front of the jury about the details of the coma and the resulting brain damage.

An analogous debate ran through the trial about whether Goetz hit Cabey and severed his spinal cord with the fourth or fifth shot fired. The prosecution argued that the fifth shot, fired after the pause and the comment "You seem to be [doing] all right; here's another,"[6] did the damage. The defense developed the countertheory that the fourth shot was the one that hit home. The reason for this maneuver is apparent: Goetz had a better claim of self-defense on the fourth shot than he had on the fifth shot. Therefore, the defense wanted the jury to think that the fourth shot, following immediately after the first three, caused the permanent injuries. Even if the fifth was fired in cold blood, against a sitting, defenseless Cabey, the act of firing that bullet would be seen as less heinous if the bullet missed Cabey and careened into the cab wall.

The question that united these two debates is why consequences should matter at all in defining a criminal offense. The traditional approach to crime, stressing the consequences more than the actor's intention, still shapes the law of New York, and even more significantly, it controls the way ordinary people sitting as jurors make decisions about how wrong, how criminal, a shooting should be regarded. A shooting that results in brain damage is worse than one that merely wounds. And a shot that inflicts permanent injuries is harder to justify on grounds of self-defense than one that misses altogether.

Each of the two competing theories, the traditional and modern, generated one of the primary charges levied against Goetz. The traditional theory expresses itself in the crime of assault, which is hinged to the harm, the serious physical injury, suffered by each of the victims. The modern theory comes to the fore in the charge of attempted murder, a crime that inheres in an unsuccessful effort to bring about an intended harm. The attempter is liable even if he has not caused harm to anyone. He can stab and miss, put poison in food that is never eaten, point a gun that unbeknownst to him is unloaded—in all of these cases he can be guilty of attempted murder. The charge of attempted murder against Goetz did not require proof that his bullets struck anyone.

The crime of assault, traditionally called assault and battery, dates back to the earliest stages of the common law of crimes. The core of the crime is the physical injury inflicted on the victim. The actor must act in some way to bring about this injury, and it cannot be the case that the injury is purely accidental. In a general way, we can say that the injury must be intentional.*

The crime of attempt is an innovation of the early 19th century. It comes into the law in the same period that the preventive theory of crime takes hold in the minds of reformers and the use of the modern prison replaces forms of punishment like flogging and modes of execution that reenacted the crime on the body of the criminal. As homicide and assault embody the old order, the crime of attempt is the flagship of modern, rational penology.

The external aspects of both assault and attempted murder—apart from the questions of Goetz's intention, motive, and subjective state—lent themselves to easy proof. Assault merely requires that the actor cause physical harm to the victim. It is true the New York statute distinguishes among levels of injury. Reflecting the influence of the traditional school, the statute requires a "serious physical injury" for the crime of assault in the first degree.[7] Causing mere "physical injury" can never be worse than assault in the third degree.[8] There is not much learning about the difference between regular and serious physical injury, but presumably, a gunshot would be serious under anyone's definition.

The external side of attempted murder was equally easy to prove. The New York statute defines a criminal attempt in general terms suitable to any offense. All that is required is "any conduct which tends to effect the commission"[9] of the crime. There is no doubt that shooting represents some conduct tending to "to effect the commission" of homicide.

Generally we can determine when particular crimes occur. An assault occurs when injury sets in—in Goetz's case, when the bullet strikes the flesh of each of the victims. Attempted crimes are different, for there is no way, in theory or in fact, to know when the actor crosses the threshold of punishable, criminal conduct. Let us suppose that Goetz decided in 1981, after being mugged and beaten, that he would arm himself and shoot the first group of black kids who made any move at all toward harassing him. That act of arming himself would not, everyone would agree, be sufficient to constitute attempted murder. But then let us consider the events of December 22, 1984. At what point did Goetz commit the crime of attempt—

---

* But see the discussion on page 79 of reckless assault, a recent innovation.

when did he complete the act that "tended to effect the commission" of homicide? When he entered the subway car? When he sat down amid the four youths? When he stood up in response to Cabey's asking him for five dollars? When he pulled the gun? When he aimed it? There is simply no way of drawing the line, even in theory. Unmoored from the traditional anchor of criminality—the suffering of the victim—the boundaries of attempted crime have remained hopelessly vague.

Legal discomfort with this vagueness has spawned a whole new set of offenses that are seemingly more precise in their contours. The most notable are the possession offenses. Instead of trying to prosecute the attempted use of narcotics, we punish the act of possessing narcotics. Possession, at least in theory, is well defined. When you pick up an object, you possess it. When you sell it, give it away, or otherwise dispose of it, you cease possessing it. Of course, there may be problems at the boundaries of possession, but compared with the vagaries of criminal attempts, the contours of criminal possession are positively rigorous.

Possession offenses do not prohibit wrongful deeds. Rather they regulate behavior so that people never reach the stage of using the prohibited article in a harmful or wrongful way. There is nothing per se immoral or wicked about a single instance of possessing narcotics, guns, or counterfeit plates. But it might be better for society as a whole to eliminate these articles from circulation. Possession offenses are addressed not to the single incident, but to the entire class of problematic events. When extrapolated over a large class of acts, the practice of possessing guns is arguably harmful. Lawyers express the regulatory purpose of possession offenses by referring to them as "prophylactic" offenses. They seek to insulate society from the presence of articles—like narcotics, guns, and counterfeiting materials—that are likely to be misused in particular cases.

In addition to charges of assault and attempted murder based on his shooting the four youths, Goetz faced an array of possession charges based on his possession of weapons prior to the shooting. The first grand jury returned charges against Goetz only for two possession offenses—two counts of possessing guns at home and one count of possessing a loaded gun in public. The charge of possessing guns at home, a misdemeanor,[10] was based on two guns that, according to the testimony of Myra Friedman, he gave her for safekeeping on December 30, the day before he turned himself in. She turned them over to her lawyer on January 2, the first business day after Goetz's surrender. The evidence showed clearly that Goetz purchased the guns legally, a .38 Smith & Wesson pistol in Connecticut in 1970 and a 9-mm black semiautomatic in Florida in September 1984, when he returned home for his father's funeral.

The more serious charge of carrying a loaded gun in public,[11] punishable by a maximum term of seven years in prison, was based on Goetz's use of a Smith & Wesson .38 in the subway shootings. The police never recovered this gun after Goetz disassembled it and threw it away in the Vermont woods during his nine-day flight from the police, but there was no dispute about whether he carried a loaded gun in public on December 22, 1984.

In addition to these charges returned by the first grand jury, the second grand jury, which indicted Goetz on charges of assault, attempted murder, and reckless endangerment, added another possession charge: possessing a loaded gun with the intent to use it unlawfully. This crime could have been committed at any moment prior to the shooting. If the prosecution could establish this intent beyond a reasonable doubt, it could claim a penalty as serious as that threatened for assault in the first degree: a maximum of 15 years in prison.

A license to possess a gun in the City of New York would have been a good defense to any of these possession charges. The New York Penal Law recognizes the possibility that a "licensing officer" in a police department may grant a license even to someone like Goetz who wishes to carry the weapon in public and who has no special occupational claim—like being a messenger for Brink's—to justify his application. The language of the statute requires vaguely that "proper cause"[12] be shown in support of the application; if the application is denied, the licensing officer must give his reasons "specifically and concisely stated in writing."[13] After he was mugged in 1981, Goetz tried to get a license, and apparently he spent $2,000 in the effort. He was turned down, with no explanation beyond "we can't give everyone a license."[14]

The provisions defining these possession offenses say nothing about whether self-defense and other defenses might fend off a prosecution for keeping a gun without a license. The Penal Law defines offenses and defenses and leaves it to the reader to figure out, in reliance on reason alone, which defenses work to defeat which offenses. For example, if we suppose that someone feels threatened and keeps guns solely for purposes of self-defense, does it follow that he can invoke self-defense as a justification at trial? How do we reason our way through a problem like this—one that is obviously pivotal in the prosecution of Bernhard Goetz?

The principles and criteria of self-defense are a response to the problem of justifying an active response to an imminent attack. But there is no way that passively possessing a weapon can repel an attack. Perhaps showing a weapon might deter an aggressor, but showing is more than possessing: it is a form of acting. The gears of self-defense simply do not engage the formal problem posed by violating a regulatory prohibition against possession. The proper task of self-defense is not to generate an exception to a prohibited passive state, but rather to justify aggressive and harmful behavior.

It is not surprising, then, that the New York Court of Appeals held in a recent case, *People v. Pons*,[15] that self-defense could not serve to justify a charge of criminal possession in the second degree, namely possession of a weapon with the intent to use it unlawfully. The defendant in *Pons* shot and killed another man in a fight. In the middle of an altercation, he went home, got a shotgun, and returned to the scene. Charged with various grades of criminal homicide as well as criminal possession of the shotgun, the defendant understandably relied on self-defense. He had to arm himself, even illegally, for fear of the attack that in fact ensued. The trial judge advised the jury to consider self-defense as a justification for homicide, but held that self-defense was irrelevant to his possessory acts leading up to the moment of attack and necessary defense. The jury had sufficient faith in his claim of self-defense to acquit him of homicide, but following the judge's instructions, they convicted Pons of the criminal possession committed prior to the actual attack.

Affirming the trial judge's decision not to apply self-defense to the charge of criminal possession of the gun, the Court of Appeals reasoned that self-defense justifies only the actual use and not the mere possession of the weapon. This part of the holding was to be expected. What surprised many observers is that the court also held that self-defense had no bearing on the intent to use the gun unlawfully. The judges' bottom line: "there are no circumstances when justification [i.e., self-defense] can be a defense to the crime of criminal possession of a weapon."[16]

The best explanation of this decision is that the court was concerned about clarifying the difference between having a gun and using it, between the status of possession prior to the defensive act and the defensive act itself. In a case like *Pons* or indeed *Goetz*, where the prosecution charges both criminal possession and criminal shooting, it is important to regard the possession as complete at some moment of time prior to the moment of shooting. That is the only way to explain why self-defense in the shooting does not justify the prior passive possession of the pistol.

Once that time gap is acknowledged, the possibility arises that someone like Goetz acted justifiably in shooting but nonetheless had a criminal intent as a passive possessor. As the court reasoned:[17]

> [I]t does not follow that because defendant was justified in the actual shooting of the weapon under the particular circumstances existing at that moment, he lacked the intent to use the weapon unlawfully during the continuum of time that he possessed it prior to the shooting.

In other words, a possessor may simply be lucky that after he arms himself with the intent to use the gun unlawfully, his intended victim attacks him first. When that happens, he may be justified in repelling the attack but nonetheless guilty of arming himself illegally. The jury concluded, it seems, that Pons had this mixed fortune, and Goetz might have had the same fate of his jury's concluding that he was justified in acting but criminal in his antecedent possession of the gun.

The *Pons* decision came down just as the Goetz case reached the phase of pretrial screening of the jury. The lawyers and Justice Crane's law secretary, Leon Schechter, talked about the decision candidly in the screening room. Everyone seemed to think the decision was badly reasoned and wrong as an interpretation of the law. It seems that they thought of possessing a weapon with intent to use it as analogous to a criminal attempt. Indeed, as the law of attempts is generally interpreted, possession of a gun with the intent to commit a crime could be prosecuted as an attempt to commit the crime intended. If self-defense applies to the behavior when it is called an "attempt," why should self-defense not extend to the same behavior when labeled as a possession offense? The answer lies in the deep difference felt by the courts between action offenses and possession offenses.

Everyone agreed that *Pons* posed a danger for the Goetz defense. The charge of criminal possession in the second degree carried a maximum penalty of 15 years, with an absolute unwaivable minimum jail sentence of a year and a half. The jury would not be informed of this grave penalty, and they might think that criminal possession in the second degree was just another gun possession charge, a charge that they might agree on in a compromise verdict. Also, there was the danger that Justice Crane would say nothing about self-defense in his charge—not even make the simple definitional statement "If Goetz intended to use the gun in self-defense, he would not have had the intent to use it unlawfully." Justice Crane would probably follow the admonition of *Pons* to avoid linking self-defense with criminal possession in the second degree. As a result the jury might think that intending to possess the gun without a license, i.e., unlawfully, was sufficient evidence of an intent to use it unlawfully.

Even more dangerous for the defense, Justice Crane might instruct the jury in an anachronistic statutory presumption that those who possess certain weapons intend to use them unlawfully.[18] Guns are not mentioned in the statute along with the possession of any "dagger, dirk, stiletto, dangerous knife,"[19] but the catchall phrase at the end of this list "or any other weapon, instrument, appliance or substance designed, made or adapted for use primarily as a weapon"[20] looks like it would include guns. A better reading of this statute would restrict it to those weapons where the presumption made sense. The other weapons mentioned in the list are not subject to licensed possession. That would suggest that they are never possessed for a good reason. But many people, including those licensed to carry guns, possess pistols like Goetz's .38 revolver without the intent to use them illegally. There is no reason, therefore, to infer an unlawful intent from the mere fact of possession (the statute says nothing about possession without a license). Yet this is a subtle reading of the statute, one that might not succeed in the criminal courts. All in all, this charge could easily ensnare Goetz even if the defense managed to overcome every charge of violent shooting. Second-degree possession, with its supportive presumption and the concealed gravity of the offense, is a booby trap for the unwary.

If the jury was not confused by the instructions, however, the defense could probably prevail on the factual question whether Goetz had an "intent to use [the gun] unlawfully." There was no evidence that Goetz left his apartment with the intent to kill the first kids who harassed him on the subway. If the prosecution wished to argue that he had that malicious intent on that particular day, Waples would have to explain why December 22 differed from every other day (though we don't know how often) Goetz left his apartment with a loaded gun concealed in his quick-draw holster. Why had he not shot before? The confrontation on the train was a critical factor triggering the shooting; if the jury concurred in this way of thinking, the prosecution could hardly prevail beyond a reasonable doubt on its claim that Goetz had a malicious intent at the time that he left his apartment.

The charge that would be difficult for the defense to counter on the facts was criminal possession in the third degree, for this offense required proof only of knowing possession of a loaded gun in public.[21] If Goetz fired the gun, he must have had a loaded gun in public, and if he wasn't insane, he must have known that he had it. From the beginning of the case, this looked like an unbeatable charge. Self-defense was not available here any more than it was to any other charge of possessory status.

These possession offenses, then, provided backup for the prosecution's seeking convictions on the shooting charges. The offenses themselves are a response to the vagueness of the crime of attempted homicide. Penalizing the offense of possession permits early intervention in potentially harmful conduct on the basis of a seemingly precise definition of prohibited behavior. And the logic of possession offenses gave the prosecution an additional boon: self-defense could not defeat these charges as it could defeat the allegations of assault, attempted murder, and reckless endangerment.

The vague contours of attempted murder also trigger increased attention to the intention required for it to be said that someone attempts to kill. Both the traditional crime of assault and the modern offense of attempted murder require intentional conduct, but the requirement is construed more narrowly for the latter. The difference between the narrow view and broad view of intention emerges from reflecting about the intention of Lee Harvey Oswald in firing two shots in the apparent aim of assassinating President Kennedy. One shot hit Governor Connally, who was sitting in front of Kennedy. Oswald knew that it was likely that he would hit Connally as well as the President. Did he intend to kill, or at least to injure, Connally as well as to kill Kennedy? Many lawyers would say yes. Others would insist that Oswald was, at most, reckless in hitting Connally, that he did not intend to injure him.

The moral doctrine of double effect distinguishes between two results of an action—the conscious object of the action and an expected side effect on the basis of what is important to the actor. The actor *intends* only the result in which his desires and personality are invested. Expected but undesired side effects are therefore not within the scope of the actor's intention. Accordingly, killing a fetus as an undesired side effect of removing it from a fallopian tube would not be an intentional killing. Destroying a schoolhouse and killing children as the by-product of bombing a railroad depot would not qualify as an intentional killing. Nor would injuring Connally be regarded as intentional. Oswald had neither an interest in injuring Connally nor a desire to injure him; in this strict sense he did not intentionally hit him with the shot intended for Kennedy.

The intention required for common law assault and battery has always been more expansive than this narrow linking of intention with the desired end of one's action. Intentional assault includes knowingly causing harm as a side effect. If the required intent is understood in this broader sense, Oswald was guilty of an intentional assault against Connally. Lawyers capture this point by saying that the intent required for assault need not be specific or purposeful, but may be general.

In contrast, the intention required for attempted murder is narrowly construed. Because attempted murder lacks the element of harm inflicted on a specific victim, the burden of the wrong is expressed in a pointed, narrowly construed intent to kill. The required intention is so demanding because that is all there is to the crime. Accordingly, few lawyers would say that Oswald intended to kill Connally. The notion of an assault is compatible with lesser degrees of focus on causing harm, such as the element of recklessness sufficient for assault in the second degree.* But the law of attempts remains linked to intended wrongdoing, narrowly understood.

This restrictive approach to liability makes sense, for the crime of attempted murder has already gone far toward an innovative, atypical form of liability. It insists neither on the suffering of a specific victim nor on a precisely defined boundary as a fair warning to those who might trespass on the interests of others. The least that the law can require is a precisely defined intention.

From a moral perspective as well, the crime of attempted murder demands a more rigorous intention than does the traditional crime of assault. Assault requires an intent to injure; murder officially requires an intent to kill. Jurors might well be inclined, however, to take the name of the attempted crime—murder—as the object of the required intent. A critical conceptual difference divides killing from murder. The sixth commandment does not say: thou shalt

---

* See the discussion on pages 78–80.

not kill. It says: thou shalt not murder. Killing in self-defense under-scores the difference. If justified by self-defense, a killing is not murder, but it is a killing nonetheless.

If the jurors thought about attempted murder as turning on an intent to murder, they might well think that Goetz's claim of self-defense precluded his having this vicious intent. If, in his own view of what was going on, he was motivated by a desire to save himself, then one could not say that he desired to kill as an end in itself. His end would not be to murder, but to save himself from a threatened attack. If his intent was morally sound and not evil in itself, jurors might balk at treating it as an intent to murder or even to kill.

This way of thinking about attempted murder makes perfectly good sense, even though New York judges would be loath to instruct a jury to integrate the issue of self-defense with the analysis of inten-tion.* The standard instruction in New York defines intention, dryly, as merely the "conscious end or object" of the act. Even a killing in self-defense is the conscious end of the defense act, and therefore the killing is intended—even if thought to be necessary to personal survival. Yet, in the final analysis, lay jurors invariably follow their commonsense understanding of an intent to murder. If the jurors thought of this intent as necessarily vicious, they might well take any belief in the necessity of self-defense as logically incompatible with the required intent.

The irony of this logic would be that they would, in effect, bring in the subjective standard of self-defense by the back door. The prolonged pretrial appeal in the Goetz case rejected the subjective standard in favor of the standard of reasonableness, but conceptualiz-ing viciousness as an element of the required intent to kill turns out to have the same logical implications as the subjective standard of self-defense. Both imply that a good faith belief in self-defense precludes liability for attempted murder, in one case because the intent is not vicious and in the other because the claim of self-defense is subjectively sound.

The charges levied against Bernhard Goetz reflect the traditional harm-oriented as well as the modern act-oriented approaches to crime. The grand jury faulted him both for causing suffering (assault in the first degree) and for acting with the potential of causing even greater intended suffering (attempted murder).

---

* But note that this is the way the jurors in fact thought about the requirement of an intent to kill; see pages 186–188.

The tension between these two philosophical positions reappears in the field of reckless conduct. As intentional conduct can be considered criminal, with or without resulting harm, so reckless conduct can be faulted, apart from the harm that may eventuate. When harm occurs, the proper charges are reckless homicide[22] or reckless assault[23]—depending, of course, on the victim's fate. If no one is hurt, the reckless act itself might support a charge of reckless endangerment.

Intentional crimes are admittedly more serious than reckless offenses; in the former case, the offender identifies himself with the evil he tries to bring about. He chooses it; he wants it. The evil is his. But in a case of recklessness, the actor chooses only to create a *risk* of injury. He does not identify with the harm that may eventuate from the risk. He chooses merely the risk.[24]

Obviously some risks are beneficial. We choose to create and expose ourselves and others to risks of driving, flying, using fireplaces, smoking, and, these days, of sexual intercourse. In order to talk about reckless behavior, we need to distinguish the bad risks that render conduct reckless from the good risks we accept as the price of modern living. The conventional approach to this distinction is to insist that a reckless risk be both substantial and unjustifiable.[25] The point of the "substantiality" requirement is simply to set a threshold of seriousness. The issue of "justifiable" risk speaks to the question whether the risk was worth running under the circumstances.

On the charges of recklessly assaulting the four youths, there was not much question at the trial whether the risk was substantial. After all, Goetz shot at them. The burden of analysis on those charges fell on the question whether the risk was "justified" under the circumstances. As self-defense could justify an intentional assault, it could do the same for a reckless assault. Thus the issue of self-defense would control liability for reckless as well as for intentional assault.

As 19th-century penology generated the crime of attempt, 20th-century thinking yielded a crime of recklessness in which no one is hurt. This crime of pure risk-taking first crystallized in American legal thought in the 1950s, when the Model Penal Code proposed its adoption. In 1965 the New York legislature improvised on the theme introduced in the model code by distinguishing misdemeanor and felony versions of reckless endangerment. The former, reckless endangerment in the second degree, requires merely that the actor recklessly create a "substantial risk of serious physical injury to another person."[26] The latter, the first-degree charge, is more demanding in several respects[27] and most significantly in requiring that the defendant's act evince "a depraved indifference to human life."

These two offenses closely track the wording of manslaughter in the second degree and murder in the second degree. Take manslaughter in the second degree, committed by "recklessly causing the death of another person,"[28] then subtract the element of suffering and death. The remainder is the misdemeanor of reckless endangerment.[29] Take murder in the second degree[30] without the consequence of actual harm, and the balance is reckless endangerment in the first degree.[31]

This offense aptly captured the alleged danger that Goetz's shooting generated toward the other passengers on the train. Though the felony of reckless endangerment technically speaks to the risk Goetz created to the four youths as well as the other passengers, the prosecution treated the offense as addressing the potential harm to the noninvolved bystanders. It was a matter of "providence," Gregory Waples argued, that shooting five times in a crowded subway car did not injure one of the other passengers. In contrast, the defense maintained that the bullets were fired either directly into the bodies of the victims or, in the case of the one stray bullet, into the steel side panel of the car. Despite the suggestion of one witness,[32] no bullet ricocheted through the car; no one except the four targets, the defense maintained, was in fact endangered by the shooting.

These argumentative forays never, as lawyers say, "joined issue." With Waples relying on the potential of harm and the defense stressing what actually happened, these arguments passed each other by. Waples relied on an abstract conception of risk-taking, defined generally as shooting in a crowded subway car. Baker and Slotnick relied on a more concrete notion of the relevant risk, defined by this suspect's shooting under these unique circumstances.

There are in fact an infinite number of ways of describing the risk that Goetz created. It would also be correct to say that he fired the gun in a crowded place, without specifying that it was a moving train, or that he fired a weapon, without distinguishing between a machine gun and a pistol. One could get more concrete and fill in details about where the passengers were sitting, the speed of the train, and the force of air currents at the time of the shooting. All these factors are relevant to the likelihood that a bystander would be hit. In the end, the danger of Goetz's shooting posed a problem of physics, not of providence.

Yet as soon as we pin down all the physical variables and predict the path of the bullets, a paradox arises. It turns out that bullets that do not strike innocent bystanders *could not* have struck them, for the path of the bullet is physically determined at the moment of firing. If a bullet did not in fact strike a particular passenger, it was physically impossible that it strike him. According to this logic, if the bullet did not strike a bystander, it did not endanger him. In a physically determined world (that we can know in principle) it is not clear that it makes sense to talk about recklessly endangering but not injuring another.

The only way to avoid this paradox is to retreat from the quest for a total description of the physical variables. We have to think about classes of cases, such as those of firing in the direction of a passenger, or in the vicinity of a passenger or in the same subway car the passenger is sitting in.[33] In these cases, the marksman's accuracy may vary. The physical forces may vary. An element of chance enters into the analysis. And in a world of chance, we can say that perhaps someone could have been hit who was not hit.

As with many other theoretical conundrums raised by the Goetz case, Justice Crane never had to cut through to the core of the problem. He rejected the defense's motion to dismiss on the ground that there was no risk at all to anyone other than the four kids, but he never had to formulate a view on the correct description of the risk. He avoided the issue by instructing the jury in the language of the statute. It was up to the jury to decide precisely what risk Goetz took by firing the gun under those circumstances.

Even those who sympathized with Goetz in his struggle to vindicate himself relative to the four youths thought that he might have a weak case on the charge of reckless endangerment. That he was justified relative to four apparent aggressors does not mean that he was justified in scaring the daylights out of the 15 to 20 other passengers in the car. They, after all, were totally innocent bystanders. How can the provocative behavior of four youths on the train justify depriving innocent people of their peace and security on the subway? The prosecution developed an ingenious argument about why the argument of justification as to bystanders could not be based on the criteria of self-defense.

Waples argued that self-defense should be limited to cases of justification relative to the alleged aggressors. So far as a risk is justified relative to innocent bystanders, the argument should be grounded in the statutory provision on necessity, an innovation in the 1965 Penal Law.[34] The difference between the two provisions, as Waples developed his theory, is that the provision on self-defense generates a full justification any time the defender reasonably believes that he is under attack—whether in fact he is being attacked or not. The provision on necessity seems to require that an "imminent public or private injury" actually be "about to occur."[35] If the four youths were not in fact about to attack Goetz, that fact would not preclude a claim of self-defense, but it would bar—at least under Waples's plausible reading of the statute—a claim of necessity. Thus Waples sensed an important advantage in seeking a ruling that the proper justification in cases of reckless endangerment is not self-defense, but necessity.

Neither the defense nor Justice Crane adequately responded to Waples's argument on this point.[36] The defense never countered the theoretical thrust of the argument and they never had to; for tactical reasons, Waples decided midtrial that he preferred that the question whether the four youths were actually committing a robbery not be treated as a relevant issue in the case.[37]

The defense may have sensed that they had a weak case on the charge of reckless endangerment, for after the impaneling of the jury in the trial, they approached Gregory Waples with an offer to plead guilty to two felony charges, possessing a loaded gun in public and reckless endangerment in the first degree.[38] This plea would have seemed to vindicate Goetz in his confrontation with the four youths[39] and yet satisfy the public interest in condemning and deterring violent conduct on the subway. But the District Attorney refused the deal. It was too important, in his view, to try the case and let a jury of ordinary New Yorkers resolve the issues.

The law remains ambivalent about the relevance of human suffering in defining criminal conduct. Both kinds of charges—those of actual harm and those of potential harm—were levied against Bernhard Goetz. There would be no plea bargain, no plea of guilty. The jury would have to make the ultimate decision about whether Goetz acted in self-defense and, if he did not, how his victims' suffering should be gauged.

The relevance of the victim's suffering in the criminal law poses a serious hurdle to the struggle for reasoned principles in the law. Generations of theorists have sought to explain why we punish actual homicide more severely than attempted homicide, the real spilling of blood more severely than the unrealized intent to do so. Our combined philosophical work has yet to generate a satisfactory account of why the realization of harm aggravates the penalty. Yet the practice persists in every legal system of the Western world. We cannot adequately explain why harm matters, but matter it does.

The law can and should go only so far to implement a rule of reason abstracted from the sensibilities of common people. It is after all common people, speaking in the voice of the jury, who ultimately decide whether an accused offender is guilty under the law. This is not to say that the law should surrender to the irrational passions that thrive in racial antagonism and the lust for vengeance. But neither should the drive for reason in the law make us forget that the law serves human beings. Oliver Wendell Holmes captured this elementary point in the best-known aphorism of American law: "The life of the law has not been logic; it has been experience."[40] The collected wisdom of tradition is expressed in the learned arguments of those who seek to refine the law on the basis of reason, but it also demands continual reinforcement from the jurors who bring to criminal trials their common sense and intuitive sense of justice.

5
People Matter

THE criminal courts building on Centre Street is not far from the Chambers Street stop on the IRT subway. That subway stop was on the minds of a small group of people—Justice Stephen Crane, lawyers for both sides, a court reporter, and an observer or two—who met in the winter of early 1987 around the table in the jury's deliberation room to interview jurors for the trial of Bernhard Goetz. The Chambers Street station is the closest stop to where the shooting occurred; Goetz escaped the subway by running along the tracks to Chambers Street and jumping up to the platform. As though Manhattan were a small town, the processes of justice were unfolding a few blocks from the alleged crime.

If the observers or prospective jurors, all residents of Manhattan, came to court from West Harlem or the Upper West Side, they would get off at Chambers Street and walk several blocks past seedy drugstores, bookstores, and newsstands to the complex of governmental buildings, among them the Centre Street courthouse. As they passed the newsstands, the prospective jurors might well see headlines about the impending trial of Goetz, the folk hero. They would surely be tempted to take a peek at the article on the case; after all, they themselves were at the center of the incessant media attention. Beginning with their selection to the list of over 300 possible jurors, however, they were admonished not to follow the public commentary on the case and not to discuss it with friends and family. They were being absorbed slowly into a nearly sacred function in the system of justice. Eventually, the power of decision would be theirs and theirs alone. Like novitiates preparing for a religious order, they had to cut themselves off, step by step, from the secular world of personal and media influence.

The purpose of screening the jurors is to find first whether they are prepared to serve. Would their employers permit them to miss five or six weeks? Would they suffer a financial, family, or professional hardship? Day laborers find it difficult to serve, for their salaries are not guaranteed. Middle-class professionals routinely seek to be excused because their time is too important to them. Jurors are called to serve only two weeks. A longer trial requires a voluntary commitment.

If they are prepared to serve, the inquiry moves on to whether they lean too heavily for or against the defendant. The interviews take place in these relatively intimate surroundings so that the jurors can speak their minds freely, without embarrassment and without influencing the other candidates waiting their turn in the courtroom. For Justice Crane as well as the lawyers, this is the first chance to engage in probing discussions about the case with a cross section of Manhattanites.

The first prospective juror who presented herself one morning, an attractive young black social worker from Harlem, turned out to be unusually frank. In response to Justice Crane's gentle questioning, she admitted to thinking that all whites harbor fears of young black men moving in groups, and she said, "Sometimes these fears are played out in very ugly ways."[1] There was some connection, she thought, between the Goetz case and the recent racially motivated attack in Howard Beach—at least to the extent that the behavior of the defendants in both cases reflected stereotypical thinking about blacks.

The lawyers had to think fast. The woman had strong opinions and was obviously biased, but did this bias help the defense or the prosecution? Her views about whites' fear of blacks would further the defense insofar as they rendered Goetz's fear of the four youths more understandable and therefore more likely to be seen as reasonable under the circumstances. But if she thought that all whites are bigots, she might lean toward the prosecution, thereby expressing solidarity with the black victims of a white man's attack. The informal rule at this stage of the proceedings is that unless both sides agree to dismiss the candidate, all jurors willing to serve are put into a pool for later, more intensive questioning in court.

The assumed purpose of jury selection is to find impartial and unbiased jurors. The faith that this is possible in any trial, let alone one of the most sensationally publicized cases of recent years, would strike many of us as naive. The prevailing view these days, at least in the universities, is that subjective interest always shapes our efforts to find out what "really happens" in the world. The observer is part of what is observed. Yet the law remains committed to the idea of jurors' determining the facts as though they had no distinctive window on reality.

In practice, however, only judges need subscribe to the official faith in objectivity. Lawyers naturally seek jurors who lean to their side, but not so obviously as to be subject to challenge by opposing counsel for bias or cause. Before the jury is finally sworn, each side can make as many motions as it likes to remove particular jurors for what it claims is good cause and in addition, in this type of case, can remove 15 peremptorily—without having to give any reason at all.

The prosecution and the defense agreed to let the social worker go. It was not likely that she could withstand a later challenge: her open bias was a wild card that could unpredictably strengthen or weaken either side. Sometimes, if the bias shown is relatively weak, the lawyer who stands to benefit continues the questioning in an effort to make the prospective juror appear neutral and more discriminating. This process is quaintly called "rehabilitation."

One solemn and intense-looking middle-aged white man recalled that he was once shot by a black mugger and as a result spent a year in the hospital. He insisted that he could not be a fair and impartial juror: he thought that Goetz did the right thing. It looked as if the defense would have to consent to his being dismissed. Unexpectedly, Goetz himself intervened with a question: "You sympathize with me because you once were a victim of a robbery. If the prosecutor could prove to you that I was not the victim of a robbery and I shot four people without justification, would you lose your sympathy for me?"[2] "Yes, of course," was the immediate reply.

Baker and Slotnick tried, usually without success, to keep their client quiet. Here his intervention worked. By raising a hypothetical question contrary to what he believed to be true (of course, he thought he had a good reason to shoot), Goetz brought a message home to the prospective juror. The man realized that his initial judgment, based on his assumed understanding of the facts, would not preclude his being open to proof of other facts at trial. If it is believable, this degree of open-mindedness, plus fidelity to the judge's instructions on the law, is all that can be expected from a juror. "Rehabilitated" by Goetz's question and his answer, the former crime victim was kept, for the time being at least, in the pool of qualified jurors.

Bias finds a ready outlet in the vision of Goetz's trial as representing a greater political struggle—between black and white, between crime victims and predators. If the jurors should see the case as standing for something more than an inquiry into Goetz's personal guilt, e.g., as a referendum on black dignity or on crime, their investment in the symbolism of their decision would incline them toward reading the facts to support the verdict they preferred. In the trial of Bernhard Goetz, most people were inclined to see the case as standing for something more. If it had been merely a dispute between a young man carrying a gun and four perceived assailants, all five of unspecified color, it would not have received media attention; the defendant would not have become a folk hero.

For some the larger issue was race. Nothing seemed to worry the defense more than the difficulty of perceiving the true dispositions of the numerous blacks and Hispanics interviewed as prospective jurors. A poll taken in March 1985 by the *Daily News* and "Eyewitness News" revealed, albeit on the basis of a limited sample, that far more New York blacks (51 percent) than whites (19 percent) supported the indictment for attempted murder. Yet this is not the message one got from listening to the minorities called for jury service. If they expressed a position at all, it was for, rather than against Goetz. The young black social worker, dismissed by both sides, proved to be an exception. One young black man said he might have thought there was a racial factor in the case—at least until a year ago, when two black men from his neighborhood approached him from behind and broke his arm with a pipe.

Virtually all the prospective jurors knew the racial constellation of the five men. And they were well informed in other respects. Most remembered that one of the victims was seriously injured, paralyzed, and that another was prosecuted and convicted for a rape that occurred after the subway shooting. These were the key facts that profiled the case in the public mind.

The process of prescreening wound down in early March, with a list of 135 potential jurors, more or less able to serve, more or less unbiased. This pool of candidates returned for the second round of selection, the public *voir dire,* on March 23. Again the press assembled en masse; once again Goetz was in the headlines, once again the television screens showed him in a familiar pose, head down, surrounded by his lawyers and court guards, rushing in and out of the courtroom.

As the public phase of jury selection began, Justice Crane explained the rules to the lawyers. Eighteen potential jurors would be selected at random from the pool and would be seated in the jury box. Crane and the lawyers for both sides would pose questions in an effort to elicit bias, and then they would retire to the adjoining courtroom to consider the jurors one by one. Each side could challenge a candidate for cause, and if Crane turned down the challenge, the side that had made it would have to decide whether their objection was sufficiently strong to make use of one of their 15 peremptory challenges. If a juror passed these hurdles, he or she would be included in the 12. Neither side could accept a juror contingently and then, at the end, go back over the list with additional challenges.

As this critical phase of jury selection began, the defense had at its side a consultant, Howard Varinsky, a psychologist from Oakland, California. Varinsky's task was to sharpen the defense's intuitive judgments about the types of people and the particular individuals who were likely, in the final analysis, to view the shooting as a defensive reaction against criminal aggression rather than as an irresponsible and hostile act. His primary standard for selection for the jury was whether particular jurors would be more likely to identify with the victims of crime than with perpetrators. At a deeper level, Varinsky looked for clues whether individuals had basically a passive attitude of resignation toward problems or showed inclinations of initiative and self-reliance. The latter, he surmised, would sympathize with Goetz's striking back against the four youths—particularly if the jury thought of the act as a symbolic defense against crime in the large.

The prosecutor had straightforward criteria for selecting jurors. He obviously preferred people who had not been victims of crime. With an eye to the political dimensions of the case, he would prefer, as he put it, left-leaning "Greenwich village types," people who would appreciate the public danger generated by armed gunmen stalking the subways.

Accordingly, both the defense and the prosecution were receptive to jurors like Mark Lesly and Carolyn Perlmuth. Both were articulate, neither the direct victim of crime. They were about as liberal in their orientation as Waples could find in the pool of available jurors. From the defense's point of view, they stood out by virtue of their experience studying and teaching martial arts. As a Tae Kwon Do expert, Leslie might be contemptuous of someone who had to resort to using a gun. But Varinsky thought otherwise. Leslie's basic attitude toward the necessity and legitimacy of self-defense made him a good bet for the defense. Similarly, Perlmuth's experience with judo made her an easy choice.[3]

A debate that erupted about seating an Episcopal nun illustrates the concerns of the defense. Though the candidate's religious order believes strongly in social action, Varinsky suspected that her contemplative life reflected a passive attitude toward problem solving. Baker had other reasons for challenging her as probably biased. Because she came to court in her nun's habit and apparently regarded wearing the habit as a religious obligation, Baker was afraid that her presence in the jury room would give her too much moral authority in the deliberations. That factor alone, he reasoned, should disqualify her. Justice Crane denied the motion, reasoning that she had a First Amendment right to wear the habit and serve on a jury. There was no difference in principle, he explained, between her habit and the yarmulke that an orthodox Jew would wear in deliberations. In response to the court's ruling, the defense interposed one of its peremptory challenges to disqualify her.[4]

The defense did not want to take the chance that a resolute juror would hold out against a possible majority favoring acquittal. They did not want someone with conviction and moral authority to stand up and halt the momentum for Goetz that they anticipated in the jury room. Thus they argued for the dismissal of other candidates who seemed likely to take an independent stand. They challenged a psychologically trained social worker who had 20 years experience working with veterans who suffered from battle shock as well as other psychiatric problems. The social worker was modest in her views; she claimed that she knew less about the phenomena of fear and anger in battle situations than she thought she knew at the outset of her career. Yet her field of expertise bore directly on the analysis of Goetz's reaction under stress. Slotnick vigorously maintained that "we don't need an expert in there . . . someone who can direct the jurors. . . ."[5] Waples resisted the motion to dismiss, maintaining that life experience should not constitute the kind of bias that would disqualify a juror. "Am I entitled to get every person who has been mugged off the jury?" he complained.[6] Justice Crane was "unsettled" by the challenge. Finally, recognizing that he might be "doing [the social worker] an injustice,"[7] he ruled that her expertise on the psychological issues of the trial should disqualify her.

Waples was indeed concerned about keeping mugging victims off the jury, particularly if they were the victims of repeated or violent attacks. He challenged a Puerto Rican woman who said that she had been mugged five times. Of course, that would not be enough to make her self-evidently biased toward someone who struck out against the mugging class. But she also revealed an inclination to think in terms of "them" against "us":[8]

> I mean if they have records, they have been arrested, because they had done something because a person doesn't get arrested for not doing anything. I have been in this country for 40 years and I have never been arrested.

As she disclosed in the prescreening phase, her son was then serving time in prison, and she had no doubt that he deserved it. Her attitude made her ripe for an argument that Goetz's four victims got what they deserved. Waples challenged her for cause. His motion foundered, however, for Slotnick had induced her to make the right kind of verbal commitment to being fair and impartial. She claimed that she understood the proper use of prior criminal records: they were admissible only to impeach the credibility of witnesses, not to prove that the witnesses were bad people. Waples called her comments a "hollow incantation of no prejudice,"[9] but apparently Crane was impressed by her sincerity. He denied the motion to dismiss for cause, whereupon Waples used a peremptory challenge against her.

As a general matter, however, Justice Crane inclined toward granting motions for cause. Waples challenged another candidate who was unclear whether she would "infer criminality from the complaining witness's prior record." It was a close case, but Crane granted the motion. "If I err on that," he said, "I am simply going to be replacing one fair and impartial juror with another."[10]

The comment reflected Crane's growing confidence that contrary to the pessimistic predictions of many observers, the two sides would soon agree on a jury. Indeed both sides were cooperating. Waples seemed willing to take jurors who were victims of nonviolent crime. And the defense made no concerted effort to keep blacks off the jury. These were the two groups of people who, considered superficially as stereotypes, were likely to be biased for and against Goetz.

There were simply too many crime victims in this cross section of the Manhattan population to find a jury that would have no sympathy for Goetz's predicament. Justice Crane would ask each group of 18 jurors to raise their hands if they had been the victim of a crime, but then noticed that so many raised their hands that he turned the question around: raise your hands if you have not been the victim of a crime. In an effort to clarify possible racial undertones of the prior crimes, he called each crime victim to the bench where they could speak without being overheard by the other candidates and asked about the race of the perpetrators. The point was to probe whether the candidate had forged a link in his or her mind between racial bias and fear of crime.

Aided by these delicate efforts to filter out those who would be unduly sympathetic with the defense, Waples accepted the first candidate interviewed, James Hurley, a young financial analyst, who lost a few dollars in a subway holdup; by the luck of the draw, he would become the foreman of the jury. Catherine Brody, a 59-year-old English teacher and college administrator, was also acceptable, even though she had recently been the victim of an attempted mugging in the subway. She resisted and scared off her assailants. D. Wirth Jackson, a retired civil engineer, and Francisco Figueroa, a 32-year-old computer operator, had both suffered burglaries but no more serious criminal attacks. Diana Serpe, a 33-year-old airline sales agent, had her car stolen. Carolyn Perlmuth's mother was mugged in her presence. But none of these experiences was sufficient, in Waples's judgment, to generate a reflex action of support for someone who "struck back" against the street toughs of the city.

Under New York law as it stood at the time, the defense could have made a systematic effort to keep blacks off the jury. The prosecution may not exercise its peremptory challenges in a discriminatory pattern, but the high courts in Albany and Washington had not yet ruled that the same constitutional limitation applied to the defense. Nonetheless, the defense was very concerned not even to generate an impression that it feared blacks as a group on the jury. They protested any innuendo to the contrary. Yet Slotnick, Baker, and Varinsky did seek black jurors who, like the white jurors they accepted, would be more likely to sympathize with the victims than with the perpetrators of street crime. Thus they had no objection to Erniece Dix, a 23-year-old administrative aide in the police department, or to Robert Leach, a bus driver in his mid-fifties. A young woman and a middle-aged man were not likely to sympathize unduly with black street kids who wreak more criminal harm on other blacks than they do on the white majority.

On the whole, the prosecution and the defense had a good idea of the types of jurors the other side was looking for. But Waples's strong interest in selecting the young, good-humored James Moseley surprised the defense. Coming from Evansville, Indiana, describing New York as a "rough town," Mosely struck Waples—also from the Midwest—as a person of good judgment and common sense who would grasp the justice of the prosecution's case. But as Howard Varinsky analyzed the situation, Moseley's small-town background would make him less fearful than typical New Yorkers of guns and their use. Varinsky thought that in most cases, Mosely would be good as a prosecution juror, but that in this topsy-turvy case, Goetz stood for the values of order and suppressing crime. These psychological hunches are hardly scientific, but they are the kind of intuitive judgments that lawyers must make in picking a jury.

The selection process was obviously going well. By the end of the second batch and an evaluation of only 36 jurors, the prosecution and the defense had agreed on 11 for the jury—seven men and four women, nine whites and two blacks.[11] One more juror and their job would be done.

The opportunity to address the jurors directly, to engage in dialogue with them, provided the lawyers with a unique opportunity. They could establish personal rapport with the people who carried the power of decision. As soon as the trial actually began, the personal interaction would become one-sided: jurors would watch and listen, but they would not be able to ask questions or talk to the lawyers in or out of court. This was an unusual opportunity to talk before a curtain of disengagement descended between the jurors and the lawyers.

Both sides used their access to the jurors to educate them in the moral and legal issues that would dominate the trial. For the prosecution, it was important to test the jury's understanding of the difference between the subjective and objective standards of self-defense. Waples used this hypothetical example to explain the requirement of reasonableness:[12]

> Let's assume, because of the very peculiar way my mind operates, that I believe that everyone who smiles at me is secretly plotting to kill me and that someday when I go back to my hometown in the midwest I am walking down the street and the first man I encounter smiles at me and I kill him because I am in mortal fear of my personal safety.

Like a teacher in a classroom, Waples could ask the jurors whether they got the point that believing that a smiling pedestrian was dangerous was not the same as reasonably believing it. If the juror failed to get the point (or at least pretend to get it), he or she would "fail the course": dismissal for bias would follow.

Waples also prepared the jurors for the special problems of judging self-defense in the count of attempted murder against Darrell Cabey. Explaining the limits of self-defense, he supposed that[13]

> at some point if the attack had stopped and people were walking away, in your own mind you probably would not have gone chasing them and shooting them. . . . If a person had slipped and fallen to the ground . . . you would not have walked up to that person and shot him?

Slotnick pressed the prospective jurors hard on their understanding of the presumption of innocence and the burden of the prosecution to prove guilt beyond a reasonable doubt. Of course, once the trial bell rang, the defense would come out swinging in an effort to knock out the prosecution. But they were not obligated to lift a finger. Cloaked in the presumption of innocence, they could sit by, say nothing, and observe whether the prosecution managed to prove Goetz's guilt beyond a reasonable doubt. Therefore when one of the prospective jurors said that he would want an explanation of why one of the youths was shot in the back, Slotnick was appropriately suspicious about whether he understood the presumption of innocence and its implication that the defense need not explain anything. He successfully challenged the prospective juror for cause.

Everyone involved in this process of educating the jury, Justice Crane as well as all the lawyers, demanded that the jurors display considerable skills in compartmentalizing information. They would have to seal off what they thought they already knew about the case from the evidence that they would see and hear at trial. They would have to keep distinct the use of the victims' criminal records to show that they might be testifying falsely in court and the use of the same prior criminal acts to prove that these kids were likely to have been the aggressors in the conflict with Goetz. But by far the most demanding feat of compartmentalization would be separating in their own minds the legality of possessing the gun from the legitimacy of using the gun in self-defense.

The prospective jurors' tendency to run the two issues of legality together cropped up in the prescreening as well as the public interviewing. A sophisticated young Puerto Rican doorman reported for his interview. He had gained a solid impression of the case from the media, concluding that Goetz had shot four blacks on the subway, that one of the victims was paralyzed for life, that another was subsequently convicted of a serious felony. When pressed about his opinions, he said that he felt that "Goetz was right in a way, wrong in a way."[14] He understood that using the gun might have been necessary, but the very act of carrying the gun bothered him. It was like "Western days." He rode the subway every day, but he did not carry a gun. He was afraid that Goetz's example would mean that "anybody who rides the subway could carry a gun."[15]

Mark Baker pressed him on the relationship between carrying the gun—an act that he took to be illegal—and subsequently using the gun. Could he keep these two acts distinct in his mind? Or would the initial illegality color his judgment of self-defense? He was afraid that he could not keep the issues clearly distinct. In his mind there seemed to be a clear moral connection between creating the possibility of using the weapon and actually using it. The initial illegality tilted his thinking away from finding that Goetz might have acted in self-defense. This "tilt" was sufficient to induce Waples as well as Baker to consent to his dismissal.

This was in fact a widespread sentiment among potential jurors in the Goetz case. Yet the official position of Justice Crane, shared by both sides, was that Goetz's alleged status as a wrongful possessor of guns had no bearing on the legitimacy of his using one of those guns. Any juror who could not grasp that distinction would be dismissed. The problem, however, was explaining to the jurors as well as many people puzzled by the issue exactly why "you can't have it, but you can use it." In more general terms, the question was whether Goetz's prior illegality of arming himself with the gun should curtail his right to use the gun.

The problem cuts across the law of criminal and tort liability, raising deep questions on the relationship between criminal status and individual rights. It has mattered in the law of torts, for example, whether an accident victim engaged in wrongful conduct and thereby brought on his injury. If he has assumed the status of a burglar or a trespasser by entering the premises of another person, the tradition has supported restricting his right to recover for injuries occurring in a place where he had no right to be.[16]

In the field of self-defense, the use of entry-triggered spring guns as protection against burglars has led many people to argue that the spring gun should be treated as a substitute for the owner of the premises. If the owner would have the right to shoot a burglar, then the spring gun's shooting him automatically should have the same legal effect.[17] This way of thinking about the use of spring guns to protect property, which admittedly has wide support in the public at large, recalls Slotnick's punitive theory of self-defense. The burglar deserves to be repelled and even injured by a spring gun. To paraphrase the witness Andrea Reid and Barry Slotnick, "The burglar gets what he deserves."

The implications of this argument of desert based on prior illegal status would be far-reaching for the Goetz case. Perhaps the fact that the four youths jumped the turnstile, that they were trespassers on the subway, should affect their right to complain about being shot while they were riding illegally. If the status theory really took hold in our thinking, it would not matter what Goetz knew and did not know at the time of shooting. The only relevant question would be what the four youths were in fact doing. Their possessing screwdrivers as potential weapons would be relevant, even though Goetz did not know it.

In the course of the Goetz trial, however, no one suggested that their riding illegally was a factor bearing on Goetz's liability. And the law on what Goetz had to know seemed clearly settled; the screwdrivers did not bear on Goetz's claim of self-defense because there was no evidence that he knew of them when he fired. The screwdrivers might lead some people to think that these kids were professional muggers and that therefore "they got what they deserved," but the New York courts have tried to distance themselves from this way of thinking. Whether the jury would be influenced by the victims' supposed status as muggers and Slotnick's punitive theory of self-defense remained to be seen.

The impact of status on liability poses more difficult questions when we turn to the liability of the person causing harm. As the cases have come up in the criminal courts, the harmful event has typically been the victim's death. The offender drives a car or practices medicine without a license and thereafter accidentally causes death to another driver or to a patient. Or in a more egregious case, someone commits a burglary and then accidentally kills the occupant of the home.

The rule took hold in common law textbooks and in 19th-century statutes that if the preliminary wrong was a misdemeanor, thereafter causing death was treated as manslaughter. If the initial crime was a felony, then because the felony cast a darker shadow, the subsequent killing had to be punished more severely, as murder. The way these rules worked, it did not matter whether the killing, considered on its own terms, was purely accidental; the background illegality, depending on whether it was classified as misdemeanor or felony, determined the gravity of the resulting homicide.

These rules resolve the question of liability for manslaughter and murder, respectively, by inquiring merely about the gravity of the background crime committed.[18] The actual behavior of the defendant at the moment of causing death turns out to be irrelevant. The decisive question is the status of the offender at the time the death occurs. If the offender has the status of a misdemeanant (i.e., someone committing a misdemeanor), he is guilty of manslaughter; if he has the status of a felon, he is guilty of murder.

The same mode of reasoning would lead us to conclude that Goetz's committing a felony by arming himself illegally should lead to his forfeiting, or at least to curtailing, his right to use the gun. But the courts have struggled to curtail the impact of this formal, status-based approach to liability. They have rejected the rule most consistently where the initial violation is a regulatory offense that does not by itself cause harm, an offense like driving or practicing medicine without a license or, as in Goetz's case, possessing a weapon without a license. Even if Goetz's shooting as an outgrowth of his illegal possession had resulted in the death of one of the four, it is highly unlikely that any court, even one that generally accepted the relevance of background illegality, would have applied the formal rule and found him guilty of manslaughter. Reason rebels at interweaving a passive felony, like criminal possession of a weapon, with an offense of aggression, like manslaughter or murder.

Yet there are many who protest this separation of the two offenses as artificial. The jurors who ran the two together in their own minds would find considerable support, even among our best legal minds. Their argument is that if the legislature has passed two statutes, one on the possession of guns and the other on self-defense, the two legislative programs should be read together. The law of self-defense should reflect the democratic policy judgment that no New Yorker should possess a handgun without a permit. Suppose that the legislature outlawed the possession of the deadly breed of pit bull dogs. It would seem very questionable to allow someone to use an outlawed pit bull in self-defense. The same should be true, arguably, about the use of an illegally possessed gun.

The response to this argument requires that we recognize two dimensions of criminal law. The traditional law of crime and self-defense derives from moral judgments about wrongful aggression and the rightful use of defensive force. Modern criminal law is designed not to punishing wrongdoing, but to regulate dangerous instruments in the hope of minimizing decisions to act wrongfully. Possessing a gun without a permit is hardly a moral wrong, a wrong in itself; it is only wrong because the legislature has decided to regulate the field. The separation of the issue of use from the issue of possession reflects a strong intuitive sense that traditional criteria of criminality should not get mixed up with modern regulatory offenses. Traditional crimes of aggression must be judged on traditional criteria of right and wrong; the regulatory wrong of possessing a gun without a permit has to be assessed on its own terms.

In explaining this required separation to the jury, neither Justice Crane nor the lawyers could take time for a philosophical lecture on the nature of criminal wrongdoing. They had to appeal to the jurors' intuitive understanding that self-defense was logically and morally prior to modern efforts to regulate the possession of weapons. Waples's explanation was apt:[19]

> Let us assume that I am in my apartment lying on my bed, reading a book, when a burglar comes crashing through the window, and he sets upon me and is trying to kill me or hurt me, and, trying to save my own life, I reach under the nightstand, and I pick up a letter opener, and I stab him with it and injure him or kill that person.
>
> Let's assume that is perfectly proper in self-defense, that's self-defense.
>
> But let's assume, instead, now, that instead of having a letter opener on my nightstand, I had an illegal gun.
>
> Can you accept the proposition that if I reached for the gun, as the person was about to kill me, and used it to defend myself, I might still be guilty of illegally possessing the gun, but that would not diminish my right to use that weapon to protect myself?

This was as good an explanation as one could give the jurors, and if they wanted to be on the jury, they would say they understood, but doubts might return later. If they began their thinking about the problem with an analysis of self-defense and then asked whether a statute regulating guns should compromise a basic right of survival, they would be likely to appreciate the separate and distinct role of the two legal institutions, self-defense and gun regulation. But if they began by focusing on the prohibition of unlicensed guns, they might be inclined to think that if this regulatory program were carried through, it would affect the right to use guns in self-defense.

On most of these issues of educating the jury, the defense and the prosecution cooperated with Justice Crane in a united front defending the received principles and distinctions of the law. But the competing lawyers could not avoid exploiting this unique opportunity of interacting with the jurors to work in some of the ideas they wanted the jurors to accept. Waples began referring to Goetz's mental instability. And Slotnick referred a few times to the four youths as "thugs and hoodlums." Justice Crane admonished the lawyers that this kind of pejorative discourse was inappropriate in selecting the jury. The lawyers would have to wait for the trial itself to bring out their rhetorical guns for full-scale attacks on Goetz and his four adversary victims. Slotnick also tried at one point to sound out the jury's willingness to vote their feelings in the face of strict legal instructions to convict. Justice Crane clamped down hard on any suggestion that the jury had the discretion to "nullify" the law. He made it clear that if they found Goetz guilty on the law as applied to the facts, they must convict.

In interacting with the jurors, asking them questions, hearing their answers, the lawyers tried to sense whether they had sufficient personal rapport with each of them to trust the case in their hands. They accepted eleven on that basis and now came the task of picking the twelfth. The candidate was Ralph Schriempf, a veteran of World War II, a man of considerable personal talent and experience. He had been an actor, singer, dancer; he was a former high school civics teacher, now a statistical word processor. The lawyers tried to address him in personal terms, but he spoke back:[20]

WAPLES: Can you be perfectly fair to me if you're selected in this case?

SCHRIEMPF: How do you mean fair to you?

WAPLES: Fair and impartial to the case I am presenting to the jury?

SCHRIEMPF: I can be fair to the facts of the case, not to you, not to this gentleman [Slotnick], but just to the facts. Whether you present them or whether he presents them.

Schriempf was acceptable to the prosecution, but the defense had doubts. He conformed to the profile of the strong, independent-minded juror that made Baker suspicious. Varinsky too had his doubts; Schriempf seemed like the kind of person who wanted to be onstage, the center of attention. But Slotnick liked him; in totally nonanalytic, nonscientific terms, he felt comfortable with him. He established a rapport with him by alluding in their exchange to a little-known theater in Schriempf's home town (Sandusky, Ohio, also the home town of Slotnick's wife). The "vibes" were good, perhaps because Slotnick is a theatrical personality and he sensed a kinship with Schriempf. Before the defense made their decision whether to accept him, they asked for a two-minute pause so that they could confer in private. They left the courtroom and then came back and said, "Yes." There would be no objection to Ralph Schriempf.

The job was done.[21] The 12 members of the jury were in place. Both the defense and the prosecution had used only about half of their peremptory challenges. Crane breathed easy and expressed his gratitude to the lawyers in a comment that would probably be heard only in a New York City courtroom: "We have a jury. Mazel Tov. Thank you."[22]

6
Trying the Truth

GOETZ's moment of truth finally arrived. The long process of manuevering had come to an end. The jurors had taken their oath and now Goetz and the public would learn whether the prosecution could establish his guilt beyond a reasonable doubt. On April 27, after a two-week break for the holidays, Waples and Slotnick set forth their claims in their opening arguments to the jury.

The thrust of his defense rested almost entirely on the claim that Goetz had shot, reasonably, in self-defense. The prosecution would have to prove to the satisfaction of the jury that his reactions were unreasonable, that even if he believed he was under attack and that shooting the four youths was necessary in response, his fears and beliefs were excessive and subject to censure as unreasonable. If the prosecution could prevail on that central question, the jury's collective voice would resonate at the end of the trial with one finding of "guilty" after another.

The trial turned not on a simple question of fact, but on a question of moral interpretation. The question was not whether Goetz did the deed, but whether his judgment in doing it was good or bad. Everyone agreed that he fired those damaging shots in the subway, and in light of his confession there was little controversy that he intended to kill the four youths. Beyond the agreed-upon factual premises lay an unexplored realm of value. Goetz's shooting required evaluation—was it reasonable in a moral sense?—and that kind of moral judgment does not lend itself to easy proof. Indeed the pivotal issue of reasonableness did not lend itself to any proof at all.

No witness could take the stand and testify, "This act was [or was not] reasonable under the circumstances." Reasonable conduct is defined in the law, without much clarification, as the conduct of a reasonable person under the circumstances. Yet the reasonable person is a purely hypothetical standard. He, she, or it does not exist in reality. No one can testify in court, "I am a reasonable person, so let me tell you what I would have done if four tough kids had approached me on the subway." The law distinguishes for various purposes between the sane and insane, the competent and incompetent, but no one is ever awarded the label "reasonable person." At one point the defense tried to bring in witnesses to testify about the impact of a mugging on the sensibilities and reactions of a reasonable person. Yet Justice Crane saw through the verbal confusion and ruled against the defense. The reasonable person, as he explained, is a hypothetical standard; no one can claim that he is a certified reasonable man and that therefore his reactions are evidence of what a reasonable person would do.

We are accustomed to thinking of trials as turning on questions of fact. The jury determines the facts and then applies the law to the facts to determine guilt or innocence. But though there were factual questions underlying the analysis of Goetz's claim of self-defense, the ultimate question of his guilt had little to do with facts that might have been perceived by people on the train. The general standard of self-defense required an inquiry into two propositions contrary to the facts as they unfolded. The jury had to speculate about what would have happened under other possible scenarios. What would have happened if Goetz had done nothing in response to Canty's overture? Would Canty and his friends immediately have started pummeling Goetz? Would they have left him alone? And what would have happened if Goetz had merely pulled the gun and pointed it? Would that have deterred the potential mugging? Or would one of the youths have taken the gun away and shot Goetz? These speculations are critical to the analysis of the claim of reasonable self-defense. Yet none of them is a question of fact in the ordinary sense.

It is difficult to find a New Yorker, black or white, inclined to believe that Goetz could have avoided a violent confrontation simply by ignoring Canty's request (demand?) for money or deflecting his request with an offhand remark like "I wish I had five dollars." But this is precisely what Gregory Waples believed. After spending hours talking to Canty and Ramseur, in particular, he came to the conclusion that they would not have risked a mugging on a Saturday afternoon in a crowded subway car. These are the kinds of kids, he says, that he prosecutes every day, and he believes himself to be a good judge of their streetwise behavior. Like others who ply their trade, they know the difference between the risks of being apprehended stealing from video games (30 days at Rikers Island) and the consequences of being caught in a robbery (a longer term at Attica or another prison upstate). Waples was sure that he could convince the jury of their limited intentions when they confronted Goetz.

But how could he do that? He could not re-create for the jury the hours of one-to-one conversation that generated his personal conviction. The mode of the trial limits the inquiry to the highly formal process of posing questions to a witness in the dock. And the defense would surely maintain, as Barry Slotnick signaled in his opening statement, that the "gang of four" were "savages" and "predators" on society.

The difficulty of proving the ultimate issue of reasonable self-defense generated a trial in which the primary struggle centered not on questions of fact, but on background assumptions about the kinds of people who confronted each other that Saturday afternoon in the subway. If the prosecution could establish that Goetz was basically an eccentric, irresponsible person, the jury would be more likely to believe that he behaved unreasonably in the shooting. If the defense could establish that the "gang of four" were lawless "predators," the jury would be more inclined to believe that they were about to rob and assault Goetz and that his response, therefore, was reasonable under the circumstances.

The logic of these arguments does not comport well with the law's formal emphasis on what these five people actually did on December 22, 1984, rather than on who they were. Yet by attacking the character respectively of Goetz and the four victims, both the prosecution and the defense encouraged the jury to make an inference from who the players were to a judgment about the moves they actually made. Ultimately, the jury would have to evaluate the events of December 22, 1984, but the path to this evaluation proceeded from premises about the kinds of people involved.

Waples signaled his attack on Goetz as a person in his opening statement:[1]

> These terribly destructive shots that were fired on December 22, 1984 were fired not by a typical New Yorker, not by a reasonable person such as yourselves, responding to provocation in an appro-

priate and limited manner, but by an emotionally troubled individual.

Waples claimed that the evidence would "reveal a very troubled man, a man with a passion but very twisted and self-righteous sense of right and wrong."[2] And further: "Bernhard Goetz was a tormented man, an emotional powder-keg, one spark away from a violent explosion."[3] He stressed peculiarities of Goetz's behavior—such as his not wearing gloves in winter so that he could remain fast on the draw—that made him seem eccentric, if not slightly obsessed by his guns. If the jury would accept this background truth, they would be more likely to infer that Goetz acted unreasonably in drawing and shooting in response to the provocation.

Typically, the defense—and not the prosecution—presses the defendant's mental instability or insanity as a defense against criminal responsibility. It serves the defense's interests to show that the defendant is mad but not bad, sick but not wicked. The defense can invoke the insanity defense and thereby secure a verdict of not guilty by reason of insanity, or it can seek a reduction of some charges by relying on a defense of partial insanity—sick enough at the time of the crime not to be fully responsible. In New York, this defense is called "extreme emotional disturbance."[4] Its impact in the Goetz case would have been to lower the charge of attempted murder to attempted manslaughter. There was no sign, however, that the defense wished to rely on either complete or partial insanity. Though they had earlier criticized Waples for not raising the issue of "extreme emotional disturbance" before the second grand jury, they seemed, at trial, to want to stay as far away from the issue as possible.

For good reason. Goetz wanted to win the case on the issue of right and wrong. Slotnick had declared at the outset of his taking charge of the defense in mid-January 1985 that they would win on the issue of self-defense. Goetz probably fired his first, court-appointed lawyer Frank Brenner because as Brenner hinted on the television show "20/20," he was toying with some version of the insanity defense. Goetz had his reasons for wanting to avoid reducing his moment of truth to the blind reaction of a madman. He saw himself as the courageous everyman, the mild-looking "bait" who turned the tables on his aggressors. He could hardly maintain that image, in the media's eyes or in his own, if he came to court on his knees and sought compassion for his mental condition.

This is precisely why Waples sought to undermine Goetz's normalcy. He had to induce the jury to distance themselves from the man whose actions they had to judge. If Goetz was a hero in their eyes, the jurors would identify with him and they would hear the evidence as favorably as possible. If, however, they came to see him as a "tormented" and sick man, they would be inclined to view him from a greater distance. Paradoxically, therefore, Waples ended up arguing that Goetz was responsible for a crime of self-defense because he was sick. The conventional argument that if you're sick, you are not wicked, became in the topsy-turvy Goetz case the argument that the defendant was wicked precisely because he was sick.

The effort to portray Goetz as sick and tormented led Waples to rely heavily on the two-hour videotaped confession that Goetz delivered to New York law enforcement officials in Concord, New Hampshire, on December 31, nine days after the shooting. The defense also wanted the videotaped confession shown to the jury, but for another reason. Compared with an audiotaped confession to New Hampshire officials made earlier the same day, the videotape more vividly expresses Goetz's fears at the time of the shooting. If the defense had made a timely motion in the early stages of the prosecution, they probably would have been able to have the confession declared inadmissible on grounds that the law enforcement officials conducting the interview did not adequately advise Goetz of his *Miranda* rights, including his rights to remain silent and to have a lawyer present if he chose to speak, and secure a waiver before they proceeded with questions. If the defense had objected, Waples would not have challenged their motion to suppress the videotape.[5] Yet calculating their own interests in having Goetz speak to the jury from the videotape—without having to take the stand and subject himself to cross-examination—the defense decided to waive their constitutional objections. Of course, the defense and the prosecution would stress different portions of the tape in their arguments to the jury.

For the prosecution, the most revealing parts of the tape were those that suggested that Goetz had little patience when confronted with danger or even irritation on the street. Goetz's recollection of a prior incident struck Waples as particularly revealing of the defendant's penchant for unreasonable overreaction:[6]

> A fellow on the street, this was just a crazy kid on drugs. He was coming up behind me . . . he asked me for some money or something and I just kept on walking. He was walking behind me and this was on Sixth Avenue at about 8:00 P.M. and I don't even

know when it was, what date it was. He threatened me. Okay, he said . . . "I hope I catch up with you cause I'm gonna . . ." [or] "I hope I don't catch up with you, because when I do." . . . and I got pissed off and pulled out the gun. And that was stupid because I didn't have to pull out the gun and showing it was enough to make him run away. . . . I could have just as easily run in one of the stores.

Asked why he pulled out the gun, Goetz says, "I was pissed. But I didn't shoot him. He deserved to die. . . ." Waples hoped that the jury would draw an analogy between that incident and the subway shooting. If in one case he got "pissed" and made a judgment that someone who harassed him "deserved to die," a jury might find that this was the kind of person Goetz was and that, therefore, he probably responded to equally irrational sentiments in the subway confrontation.

The defense was always on its guard against Waples's pushing and probing on Goetz's mental condition. They were not going to concede an inch to the claim that Goetz was abnormal, somehow different from the ordinary people in the jury box who sat in judgment of him. When they called a psychologist, Dr. Bernard Yudwitz, to the stand, the defense was concerned that on cross-examination, Waples would elicit damaging psychological comments about Goetz's mental condition. Dr. Yudwitz was supposed to testify that when people start firing their guns in situations like that which Goetz confronted, an adrenalin-induced response in the autonomic nervous system displaces reasoned control of behavior. In popular language, when people start reacting as did Goetz, they go on "automatic pilot." Yudwitz had not examined Goetz and there was no way for him to argue that Goetz himself went on automatic pilot, but the general claim nonetheless provided the defense with an argument that would resonate through the rest of the trial. If the jury thought that Goetz was on automatic pilot, they would tend to see all five firings as beats in one stanza of self-defense. If they would be willing to acquit for the first shot injuring Troy Canty, then they would be inclined to acquit on the final shot that paralyzed Darrell Cabey.

Dr. Yudwitz had at his fingertips persuasive case histories based on his experience with the Boston police department. Slotnick hinted at these supportive examples in his opening statement:[7]

And you will hear that police officers in the same position, seasoned and trained law enforcement men, suffer the same, the absolute same type of reaction. You will hear that when a police officer fires his gun and he's asked thereafter how many times, he won't know.

This testimony would be advantageous for the defense, but the risk in putting a psychologist on the stand might, if Waples elicited comments about Goetz's mental condition, redound to their detriment. Waples too had reason to fear the impact of Yudwitz's testimony, particularly the impact on the jury of his reciting case histories of police officers' emptying their guns without realizing it. Because each side feared what Dr. Yudwitz might say, an unusual bargain emerged that limited the scope of his testimony. Waples and Slotnick agreed to trade one form of silence for another. Dr. Yudwitz would remain silent about the police case histories if Waples would refrain from questioning him, on cross-examination, about Goetz's mental condition. When Dr. Yudwitz took the stand, he encapsulated his comments on "automatic pilot" in a few minutes, omitting reference to the parallel police experiences. Waples kept his cross-examination to a minimum—no questions about whether these general propositions of science held in the case of a man who refused to wear gloves in the winter so that he could have quick access to his guns.

The background truth asserted by the prosecution, that Goetz was abnormally fearful of crime, never became an issue on which the prosecution would introduce evidence. The allegation remained at the level of epithet and innuendo, for Goetz's mental condition was not officially an issue in the case. Waples wanted to establish this background assumption in order to move the jury toward an inference on the ultimate question of unreasonable defensive response.

The defense, too, asserted a background truth that bore on the issues that the jury actually had to decide. From the first moments of his opening statement, it was clear that Barry Slotnick intended to vilify the four victims Troy Canty, Barry Allen, James Ramseur, and Darrell Cabey. He declared his intent to turn the tables on the prosecution and put the "aggressors" on trial. The charges that Slotnick had in mind went beyond any specific crimes prohibited by the Penal Law. He accused the four youths (and implicitly all street toughs like them) of being "vultures" and "savages." He referred to them repeatedly as the "gang of four" and as "predators of society."

Slotnick took his role as prosecutor of Canty, Allen, Ramseur, and Cabey so seriously that when, a few days into the trial, a journalist inquired about his client, he responded, "Don't talk to me about my client. I have no client. The people of the state of New York are my client."[8] Slotnick assumed the mantle of law enforcement. He would set out to prove the background assumption that the four victims were "predators" and that they "got what the law allowed." He launched into an attack on the character of all four, and particularly of James Ramseur, who five months after the shooting allegedly engaged in a gruesome attack on a pregnant woman, Gladys Richardson, in his housing complex. Slotnick spared none of the gory details of rape and sodomy. "And to add insult to injury," he added, "Mr. Ramseur and his friend took her earrings, and her ring and left her bleeding on the rooftop landing."[9] Slotnick came back to Ramseur's participation in the rape of Gladys Richardson so often that at one point Justice Crane admonished him, "Why don't you get off this, Mr. Slotnick?"[10]

The move that permitted Slotnick to dwell on the rape was Waples's announcement that he would call Ramseur as a witness. Technically, all Slotnick was doing was announcing his intention to undermine Ramseur's credibility as a witness by eliciting from him admissions of his prior criminal acts. The assumption behind the practice of impeaching credibility in this way is that convicted criminals are likely to lie. Yet the inference that the jury was likely to draw from Ramseur's felony conviction for rape, sodomy, and robbery was not only that he might commit perjury, but that he had a violent, aggressive disposition. That disposition, of course, is precisely what Slotnick wanted to establish as part of the his background claim about the "gang of four."

Waples's announcement that he intended to call Troy Canty and Barry Allen as witnesses permitted Slotnick to recite their criminal records as well. Canty has a string of convictions for petty theft; Allen was arrested for chain snatching, which led to the revocation of his probation on a previous conviction of disorderly conduct. The jury might well infer a pattern of assaultive, violent behavior from these convictions, even though the brunt of their illegal behavior was petty thievery.

In order to bolster his case that these kids were "savages" and "predators," Slotnick reached beyond the rules of evidence to allude to an alleged criminal act that Darrell Cabey committed shortly before the subway shooting:[11]

> Who are they [this gang of four]? You will find that there was not a touch of pity when by a shotgun Tyrone Grant, Lionel Lee

and Curly Reid were robbed by Darrell Cabey. Not a touch of
pity in his eyes when he robbed them.

Waples had made it clear that Cabey's medical condition precluded his appearing as a witness. Therefore, Slotnick did not have
the formal legal pretext of impeaching credibility as a cover for
referring to Cabey's alleged crimes. Yet there is no way for a lawyer
to stop his opposing counsel from talking except to object, stop
the line of inquiry, and request the judge to make a corrective comment to the jury. As soon as he heard the reference to Cabey and
his three alleged victims, Waples leapt to his feet.

Out of the hearing of the jury, at a "sidebar" conference, Waples
accused Slotnick of committing "a direct breach of the ruling" that
Justice Crane made two weeks before the trial.[12] If Cabey was not
going to testify, then his credibility was not subject to attack. Slotnick
tried to defend himself by suggesting that he would call Cabey as a
witness:[13]

> He will testify that he and his three friends got up to rob Goetz.
> His credibility will come into issue. I have a right to bring out
> his conviction before he does. There's nothing wrong with that,
> Judge.

But Crane ruled that even if the defense intended to call Darrell
Cabey, they could not undermine his character before they heard
him testify. Now Slotnick was expressly prohibited from referring
to the incident between Cabey and his three alleged shotgun robbery
victims. If he did it again, the judge could impose a range of persuasive
sanctions, such as embarrassing him in front of the jury and ultimately
citing him for contempt of court. In this particular case, the harm
had already been done. There was no way to erase the impression
left with the jury that Cabey as well as Ramseur was capable of
violent and aggressive assaults.

The defense tried a more frontal approach to attacking the victims'
characters. If they could bring into evidence all of the victims' prior
criminal acts, both those for which they were convicted and other
alleged criminal acts that could be substantiated by witnesses, the
defense could prove that the four youths were likely to have been
the aggressors in the subway confrontation. Under this approach,
the reference to Darrell Cabey's alleged shotgun robbery would be
proper. Under New York law, however, there were only two ways

that the defense could introduce this evidence to establish the aggressive propensities of the four victims. The basic New York rule is
that prior bad acts of an alleged aggressor are admissible if the
defender knew about those acts and if his knowledge had some
bearing on the reasonableness of his fear and his response at the
time of the confrontation. But Goetz obviously did not know of
these acts at the time, and therefore this exception was unavailable.

In addition, the courts have recognized a basis for admitting
evidence of prior criminality even where the defender in a self-defense
case is unaware of these prior crimes. Called the *Molineux* theory
after the leading case in the field,[14] the doctrine permits prior criminal
acts to be used to demonstrate a specific pattern of aggressive behavior, either with the same intention or with the same mode of executing
the aggressive behavior. For example, if the four youths had allegedly
menaced Goetz with the screwdrivers, prior acts of using screwdrivers
in intimidating others would be admissible to prove their *modus
operandi*—their mode of committing robbery. If they could invoke
the *Molineux* theory, the defense would achieve a major breakthrough
in establishing their background claim that the four youths were
habitual criminals.

The problem for the defense was pinpointing an aspect of the
subway confrontation that appeared to replicate the prior criminal
activity of the four youths. They needed to establish a pattern of
mugging and robbing in a particular way. They ventured the argument
that the four youths tended to commit crimes in groups. If permitted
to do so, they would prove that Darrell Cabey and Barry Allen
menaced a woman named Jane DeWitt in 1982 by approaching
her and asking her for money (she picked out their photo after
Cabey and Allen became well known as a result of the Goetz shooting). They would also show that Darrell Cabey, working with others,
robbed Tyrone Grant, Lionel Lee, and Curly Reid at shotgun point
(the charges were dismissed after Cabey suffered permanently disabling injuries in the confrontation with Goetz). Further, they would
show that Troy Canty plus three to five others followed and menaced
Elizabeth Mays in a subway train and that Barry Allen and another
engaged in a chain snatching that occurred either (they were not
sure) in an elevator or in a movie theater.[15] The only link between
these prior acts and the alleged plan to rob Goetz on the subway,
however, was the practice of acting not alone, but with the assistance
of others. Justice Crane was not going to make it easy for the defense
to establish their background truth that the "gang of four" were

hardened and violent criminals. The mode of acting in groups, he intimated, would not be a sufficient basis to bring in evidence of these alleged crimes in the past.

But the defense had another tack for circumventing the general rule against admitting this form of evidence. Another acknowledged exception under the *Molineux* theory permits the use of prior criminal acts to prove the intention of someone suspected of a criminal act. The problem with this maneuver was that the intentions of the four youths were not immediately relevant to the analysis of self-defense. The criterion for a valid claim of self-defense is not whether Canty, Allen, Ramseur, and Cabey really were going to rob Goetz, but whether he reasonably thought they would. The youths' intentions appeared, therefore, to be even more tangential than the alleged pattern of group criminality; the defense's effort to bring in prior criminal acts to prove this intention seemed destined for failure.

But the lawyers in a criminal prosecution can concur in making an issue relevant even if under a strict interpretation of the law, it is beyond the scope of the trial's inquiry. This is called "opening the door" to a question that would otherwise remain sealed in silence. Early in the trial, Waples initiated the inquiry about the youths' criminal intentions that Saturday afternoon by asking Troy Canty on the stand whether he intended to rob or attack Goetz. Slotnick initially objected and then withdrew the objection, permitting Canty to answer "no": his intentions were innocent. Thus Waples cut an exception in the law and with Slotnick's concurrence invited debate about whether the four youths actually intended to do what Goetz feared they would do.

With the issue of the four youths' intentions under debate, the defense had a solid basis for introducing their prior criminal acts in order to prove under the *Molineux* exception that their intentions on December 22, 1984, were indeed criminal. Waples tried to fend off this result by arguing that the alleged criminal acts were too distantly related, particularly in their mode of execution, to have evidentiary value in a debate about what was really going to happen in the subway encounter. Justice Crane announced his decision to let in the evidence about Canty's and Cabey's prior criminal acts; the defense would be able to prove to the jury that Canty menaced Elizabeth Mays and that Cabey engaged in intimidating Jane Dewitt as well as a shotgun robbery against Lionel Lee.[16] Waples said that he was "flabbergasted" by the impending ruling, but Crane justified his tentative decision by saying that Waples had brought him to this conclusion by "opening the door" to the issue of whether the four youths were actually about to commit an assault or robbery. Waples was in trouble. If the prior criminal actions came to the attention of the jury, the defense would go a long way toward establishing their background assumption that the "gang of four" were the kind of people whom one might reasonably shoot in self-defense. How did he get himself in this position? Why did he invite debate about what the youths intended to do?

Even before the trial began, Waples had crafted the ingenious legal argument that the proper justification on the charge of reckless endangerment was not self-defense, but the claim of necessity under a distinct provision of the Penal Law.[17] The difference that Waples perceived between self-defense and necessity was that the former turned solely on whether Goetz reasonably believed that he was about to be robbed or attacked; the latter required not only belief, but an actual attempted robbery or physical attack that would justify Goetz's endangering the lives of the innocent passengers in the subway car.

Waples sought to generate a fallback position to rescue his prosecution in the event that the jury found that Goetz's behavior was reasonably motivated as to the four youths. As to the other passengers, Waples reasoned, the proper inquiry should be not what Goetz perceived, but what was *really* going to happen. It would be more difficult for the defense to prove* that Goetz was actually under attack than that he believed he was under attack. Thus, Waples thought, the jury might acquit on attempted murder and assault but nonetheless convict Goetz on the charge of reckless endangerment. Waples prepared this argument in a memorandum of law he submitted before trial. But Justice Crane had yet to rule on the issue.

Waples insisted that the only reason he "opened the door" to the question of the youths' intentions was that he anticipated Justice Crane's ruling in his favor on the justification required for reckless endangerment. He also expected to prove that Canty and the others had no malicious intent. Now he found his legal ingenuity backfiring on him. Crane refused to rule on the criteria for justifying reckless endangerment and threatened nonetheless to let the defense bring in the youth's prior criminal acts in order to prove their intentions in the subway confrontation. As the argument proceeded, however,

---

* I sometimes use the term "prove" in speaking about the defense's case. It should be remembered, however, that the defense's "proving" means merely refuting the prosecution's effort to prove their case beyond a reasonable doubt.

Crane hinted that he might change his mind about admitting the prior criminal acts into evidence if Waples "closed the door" on the issue of the youths' intentions. He could do that, Crane suggested, simply by withdrawing his argument that the justification of reckless endangerment required proof of an actual robbery. Waples got the hint and decided to choose the lesser evil. He withdrew his ingeniously crafted argument about the justification for reckless endangerment, whereupon Justice Crane ruled that the prior criminal acts were not admissible to prove that Canty and Cabey were the kind of people who probably intended to pull off another crime of violent intimidation. Waples checked Slotnick's relentless attack on the character of the victims, but only at the price of his claim that for some purposes at least, it mattered what the four youths were actually intending to do.

The effort by both the prosecution and the defense to establish their background assumptions resonated through the trial. Waples was committed to creating an image of Goetz as mentally unbalanced, and the defense countered with their relentless attack on the criminal character of the four victims.

The careful use of language proved to be an effective aid for both sides in generating a negative image, respectively, of Goetz and the four youths. Waples made his mark on the lexicon of the courtroom by arguing persistently that Goetz was not a "reasonable person" like the jurors. Though the quality of reasonableness should attach solely to deeds and not to people, Waples's usage established a pattern that the defense picked up as well.[18]

Barry Slotnick proved to be the master of the carefully chosen word. He carried forward his attack on the criminal character of the four youths by skillfully turning ambiguities to his advantage. On the cross-examination of Troy Canty, he repeatedly asked him whether he made his living from "robbing and stealing." Canty admitted that he and his friends had engaged in the routine pilfering of money from the coin boxes of video games. He insisted, however, that he limited his illegal activities to stealing when there was no element of using force or intimidation against another person—the factor that converts larceny into the more serious felony of robbery. Nonetheless, Slotnick could get him to say that he engaged in *robbing* video games when all Canty meant was that he engaged in *larceny* from the cash boxes of video games. Trading on this ambiguity, Slotnick could argue to the jury that Canty and others engaged in robbery for a living—precisely the form of criminal aggression that Goetz allegedly feared in the subway encounter.

As he played for the advantage of ambiguity in this context, Slotnick sought elsewhere to draw artificial distinctions in the name of verbal precision. He and Baker refused to refer to the four victims as "victims" on the ground that the term communicates too much sympathy. If they were the wrongdoers in the subway confrontation, then they supposedly forfeited their right to be called victims. In the defense's lexicon, the four youths were the "perpetrators" or, worse, the "predators." Yet the conventional way of describing people who are injured is to call them "victims." Even people injured in legitimate self-defense are ordinarily called "victims." Nonetheless, the defense prevailed upon Crane and Waples to follow their preferred usage. When one of the People's witnesses, Detective Michael Clark, referred to "the four victims on the train," Slotnick objected and the following exchange ensued in front of the jury:[19]

MR. SLOTNICK: Your Honor, I would object to the characterization of the word "victim." That's a decision the jury will have to make.

THE COURT: Can you use another word, Detective? Or was that Mr. Goetz' word when he related this to you?

MR. WAPLES: Why don't we just use "young men."

Waples conceded these linguistic points to Slotnick when he could have easily objected. He participated in banning the perfectly appropriate word "victim" from the debate before the jury.

As Slotnick seemed to realize more than Waples, language is the lawyer's paint for casting images for his side of the case. The word "victim" casts an image far different from "young men," and getting Canty to concede that he was engaged in "robbing" sends a message more incriminating than does the more accurate description "stealing."

On other points as well, Waples ceded linguistic terrain when he could have fought back. Slotnick and Baker balked at calling Goetz's four-hour taped admission of guilt a "confession." For them, the confession was merely a "statement"—a neutral term noncommittal about the "statement's" accuracy. What Goetz delivered in New Hampshire was clearly a confession, and it would have been appropriate to call it that in the course of the trial. By adopting the defense's term "statement," Waples unwittingly advanced the defense's thesis of skepticism about whether the confession was 100 percent accurate.

Similarly, Slotnick repeatedly invoked the epithet "license to lie" to describe the impact of the prosecution's granting immunity to

Canty and Ramseur. The implication was that the two victims could lie under oath, that is, commit perjury, and get away with it. Nothing could have been further from the truth. The immunity they enjoyed by virtue of testifying before the second grand jury did not extend to committing perjury, either before the grand jury or in court. Despite the distorting effect of the defense's impugning their veracity by suggesting they had a "license to lie," Waples did not object to Slotnick's use of the phrase. Trials may not be won and lost by conflicts over the language of discourse, but the side that controls the image-making lexicon of the trial unquestionably argues in a more persuasive idiom.

That Waples and Slotnick engaged in a struggle to establish their background truths—Goetz as abnormal and unreasonable, the victims as a "gang of four"—did not mean that they would not fight equally hard on the detailed factual issues that would inform the jury's finding whether Goetz acted reasonably in face of a feared attack. Much of the day-to-day discourse of the trial focused on such details as how many youths approached Goetz, where were they standing, where did the bullets hit the victims, what was their posture at the time of impact—these are details on which the witnesses from the train were called to testify. The details as well as the larger background truths would invariably influence the jury's overall assessment of Goetz's response.

In his opening statement, Waples stressed specific factual allegations, such as the claim that Goetz shot Barry Allen in the back and Darrell Cabey as he was sitting down. Slotnick maneuvered hard to create the impression that the prosecution's burden of proof attached to these specific factual claims. He insisted, for example, that[20]

> Mr. Waples knows [that he] must prove to you that Barry Allen was shot squarely in the center of the back as he tried to flee. Not only does he have to prove that to you, but he's got to prove that to you beyond a reasonable doubt.

Waples objected to Slotnick's effort to treat this specific factual claim as an ultimate legal issue in the case. Justice Crane sustained the objection and explained to the jury that only the legal elements of offense need be proved beyond a reasonable doubt, even though he would not explain these "elements" to the jury until the very end of the trial.

A subtle logical point lies behind the distinction between the factual claims about how the shooting occurred and the legal elements of the offense. The legal elements are the ultimate issues in the case, such as whether Goetz intended to kill Barry Allen and whether he had a reasonable belief about whether Allen, specifically, was about to rob him or attack him with deadly force. Whether Allen "was shot squarely in the center of the back as he was trying to flee" is relevant to the inquiries about both intent and the claim of self-defense. But the particular factual claim about the way Allen was shot is far from a necessary condition for the prosection to prevail on the issues it must prove. Even if Goetz had not shot Allen in the back while he was running away, Goetz might well have intended to kill without an adequate ground to fear for his safety. Waples's claim was one way to establish his case, but it was not the only factual basis on which the jury might find Goetz guilty.

From the outset of the trial, therefore, Waples faced a contradictory situation. In order to make his version of what happened on the subway plausible, he had to commit himself to a story of what happened. Yet he had to avoid overcommitting himself. He had to avoid the impression that if he failed to prove his particular story, he thereby failed to prove that Goetz was guilty of assaulting and attempting murder without justification.

The debate between the prosecution and the defense took place, therefore, on numerous levels at the same time. There was the ongoing effort by both sides to establish their background truths about the kind of people thrown together in an epic subway shooting. There were the less visible negotiations about the language that would be used to talk about the victims (youths), about their crimes (robbery or stealing), and about Goetz's confession (statement). As the trial proceeded, however, the argument over the details, such as whether Cabey was shot sitting down, would dominate the day-to-day hearing of witnesses. The ultimate moral question, whether Goetz acted reasonably in self-defense, receded into the background as the parade of witnesses attempted to reconstruct exactly what happened in those few seconds of explosive violence on the downtown IRT express.

7

What the Jury Saw and Heard

LAWYERS at trial are directors as well as performers in presenting their client's vision of the truth. They make theatrical decisions about the order in which to present their witnesses, they coach them like directors in rehearsal, and they lead their witnesses gently through their parts.[1] Their presentation of the truth reflects art and rhetoric as well as rational argument.

The prosecution had extraordinary material for a dramatic unveiling of the historical truth about the subway shooting. Waples had two hours of Goetz speaking on audiotape, two hours on videotape. He had Troy Canty and James Ramseur, who, given immunity from prosecution for their part in the events of December 22, had testified before the second grand jury and would presumably testify again that they had no intention to mug Goetz on the train. He had a surprisingly large number of witnesses who had been in that subway car and seen or heard some aspect of the shooting. He had medical and ballistics experts who would testify about possible inferences from the impact of the bullets on the victims' flesh. Most of this evidence had been kept under wraps until the trial. No one except the lawyers and court officials had seen the tapes. Not even the defense knew until shortly before the trial who all the subway witnesses would be.

Waples decided to set the stage with the tape-recorded confession and to present Goetz's physical likeness on the videotape as the climax of his case. The story on the two tapes is essentially the same, but the dramatic impact of an agitated and angry Goetz quarreling on the screen with prosecutor Susan Braver made the videotape the ideal climax of the prosecution's efforts to cast Goetz as eccentric and unreasonable. Waples's decision to begin with the audiotape provided the framework, therefore, for the rest of the trial. The story as told on this tape by a relatively relaxed Goetz, speaking with New Hampshire detectives whom he liked and trusted, became the standard for the jury's judging the witnesses' testimony and the other evidence that would come in. Everything that came after the confession would be seen as either confirming or disconfirming Goetz's own story.

As the tape played, the mood of the courtroom shifted from excited observation to the meditative silence of parishioners absorbing an awesome moment. Goetz's voice from the police station in Concord, New Hampshire, made the events of December 22, 1984, eerily present in the cavernous courtroom. Goetz enters the car at 14th Street through the door closest to the north end of the car and sits down opposite Canty, who is leaning or lying on the long bench next to the door. Goetz is alone at that end of the car with the four youths. Canty turns to him and says, "How are you?"[2] Goetz responds, "Fine," and looks down to avoid eye contact.[3] Then Canty and Allen, who was sitting on Goetz's right, get up, "saunter over," and position themselves on Goetz's left, between him and the other passengers sitting in the center and the far end of the car. Canty, who is closer than Allen, says, "Give me five dollars." Almost simultaneously, Goetz notices one of the other two, presumably Ramseur, putting his hand in his coat pocket and sees that the pocket is "bulging out." Goetz notices that Canty is smiling at him and his eyes are shining. Then Goetz asks Canty, "What did you say?" and Canty responds, "Give me your money."[4] At that point, Goetz stands up,[5] draws his gun from his belt holster worn inside the front of his trousers, under his jacket, and begins shooting from left to right, first Canty and Allen, then Ramseur and Cabey, both now standing on his right. Then Goetz "runs back" to check out the first two, finds them out of commission, then "spins" around and notices that Cabey is now sitting. Unsure whether he had hit him, he says, "You seem to be [doing] all right; here's another."[6] Cabey jerks his right arm and Goetz shoots at him a second time.

This is the most detailed account that the jury would hear. Yet a number of critical details go undiscussed. The listener does not learn from either this or the second, videotaped confession how close Canty was standing to Goetz, whether Canty was leaning over him, whether he had his face next to Goetz's. Nor do we get a precise statement from Goetz about how close he was standing to Cabey when he shot the second time. The popular interpretation is that Goetz was standing right next to Cabey, but this assumption is uncorroborated by Goetz's words. There is considerable ambiguity about whether Goetz ever moved from the spot where he started shooting. He does say on the audiotape that he "ran back to the first two" and then "raced back to the other two," but he hints that he did all this with a concentrated gaze: "your eyes just race across them, that's all you need." And in response to his interviewer's following up on this ambiguity, he says, "looking and acting are the same thing, virtually." Goetz seems to be saying that he "raced" over to Cabey by looking at him intensely. The key question of fact whether Goetz actually ran over to Cabey would have to be resolved by the witnesses from the subway car, who, one would expect, glimpsed whether Goetz moved at the time of the firing or not.

The audiotape not only rehearsed the shooting details, but gave the jury extraordinary insight into Goetz's personality. The two hours of rambling free association reveal the frustrations and anger that brought him to the point of pulling the trigger. If Goetz had testified in person, the constraints of courtroom ritual would have inhibited the personal exposure of self that spills forth on the tape. He repeatedly comes back to his mugging in 1981, his unsuccessful efforts thereafter to obtain a permit to carry a gun, his understanding of the mugging culture and how it operates, and his fear of being "played with" and "beaten to a pulp." He reveals a personality disturbed about what happened and anxious whether anyone in the legal system will understand him and the terror that he experienced before he aimed and shot at Troy Canty and then pulled the trigger four more times.

Significantly, the tape bears the marks of a reliable account of the shooting as Goetz understood it nine days later. He makes concessions that he need not have made and that he might not have made if he had accepted the constitutionally required offer to have a lawyer present at his interrogation. He says, almost boastingly, that he did not regard it a "threat" for Canty to approach him and ask for five dollars. Nor was it a "threat," he says, for Ramseur to create the appearance that he had a weapon in his pocket. His confession of an "intention . . . to murder them, to hurt them, to make them suffer as much as possible"[7] incriminated him far more than his deed standing alone. The prosecution could cite and the press could quote this out of context and easily generate the impression that Goetz was a vigilante out to revenge himself against the criminal underclass of the city.

The jury heard two hours of unstructured information about the shooting and about Goetz as a person. How would they absorb this data and relate it to their task of judging the reasonableness of Goetz's shooting? Each statement requires clarification in the context of the surrounding statements. It was the task of the lawyers to interpret the two hours of free association, but after the confession was played, the trial continued with a parade of witnesses. The lawyers would not have a chance to speak, in their own argumentative voices, until their closing statements at the end of the trial.

The jury was left alone to ponder what Goetz meant by admitting, for example, that "his intention was to murder them, to hurt them, to make them suffer as much as possible."[8] When taken out of context, this statement incriminates Goetz as an intentional killer, as someone who fits the profile of the vigilante stalking victims and firing upon them as a cold-blooded avenger. Yet neither Goetz nor any other suspect is in a position to render an authoritative description of a legal issue like the intention required for attempted murder or assault in the first degree. If he was acting in reasonable self-defense, there would be nothing wrong with his intending to kill as a means to ward off the attack. And even if in the fear of the moment his defensive act included an aggressive and hostile component, he would still be acting within his rights. The guilt that he felt about the hatred in his heart could incriminate him, but it also lent itself to lawyerly interpretation in his favor. He arguably felt guilty about the malice that exploded within him at the moment of his defensive action. As Slotnick might argue at the end of the trial, that self-assessment only showed him to be a man basically opposed to violence.

The jury would also have to ponder Goetz's repeated statements in his confession that he was afraid only of physical violence, not of robbery. The demand for money, he said, was "bullshit. The robbery has nothing to do with it."[9] This is a significant concession, for paradoxically, under the New York law of self-defense, defending against a robbery carries broader rights than defending against physical violence.* Goetz might have been more concerned about his

* For clarification of these issues, see Chapter Two, page 22.

physical safety, but he might also have expected that his assailants would take his money after they had "beat the shit out of him."[10] His statements about his fears have to be understood in the context of his prior mugging, which left him with a permanently damaged knee. He might not have cared about the money, but it does not follow that he should be treated as having forfeited his personal autonomy, his right to be free of aggressive intrusions, including attempts to rob him.

The confession hints at a value supporting this individualist, autonomy-based theory of self-defense, namely that the defender should not have to bear the risk of uncertainty about the outcome of the attack. What Goetz feared was "not knowing what's going to happen from moment to moment." He could tolerate being killed instantly, but not being played with as a "cat plays with a mouse."[11]

Significantly, the confession provides little fuel for the defense's punitive theory of self-defense, for the view that the four youths got what they deserved. Goetz admits saying to a bleeding Canty lying on the floor of the train something to the effect that "you better learn a lesson from all this."[12] Yet there is no hint of pride or satisfaction in his tortured recollection of the deed. He never refers to any of his four adversaries or the class they represent as "thugs" or "toughs" or by any other epithet. Indeed he never volunteers that both they and Fred Clark, who mugged him in 1981, are black. The New Hampshire detective inquired matter-of-factly about race and Goetz answered, but so far as one can tell from his anguished and uncontrolled rambling, it did not matter to Goetz that his adversaries were the type that New Yorkers describe as "tough black street kids."

The confession itself provided the defense with all the arguments that it needed in order to build a fortress against the prosecution's onslaught of witnesses who observed some aspect of the shooting. Slotnick would add his punitive theory, and the defense witness Bernard Yudwitz would add some technical jargon about the "autonomic nervous system" to support Goetz's self-interpretation that his rational mind had shut off and that he, in effect, was on "automatic pilot." Goetz incriminated himself with his self-deprecating description of his intentions, but he also made the best case he could for himself.

There was one critical part of his case that he could not make, and that was the suggestion that he might have been somehow mistaken about some of the more damaging statements in the confession—particularly his widely reported pausing before the fifth shot, approaching Cabey, and remarking, "You seem to be [doing] all right; here's another." But the confession contained hints that perhaps Goetz did all of this by running with his eyes rather than with his feet, and as the witnesses began to come forward, the defense stitched together evidence for a radical undermining of the confession.

As the confession was neutral ground, subject to interpretation and argument either for or against the defense, so it was with the witnesses from the train who came forward to testify. Waples called every available witness of the shooting and its aftermath, whether or not their testimony was likely to be strongly supportive of the prosecution. As soon as Waples concluded his direct examination of the witness, Slotnick could begin probing the witness for material useful to the defense. The striking result of this phase of the trial was Slotnick's eliciting a theory of the defense from the admissions of the witnesses.

The first witness who testified from among those on the train, Sally Smithern, heard the shots from the next car. Waples gained virtually nothing from her testimony that strengthened the prosecution's case. On cross-examination, however, Slotnick began to collect significant concessions. Amidst a long examination in which Slotnick called into doubt whether Ms. Smithern was really on the train, he inserted this series of questions:[13]

Q: Now, you heard how many shots?
A: I heard four shots.
Q: And that's all?
A: That's all.
Q: In rapid succession?
A: In rapid succession, yes.

The admission that she heard only four shots could make one wonder whether Ms. Smithern was there after all. But Slotnick had a different point in mind in this exchange. The tactic became clear on the cross-examination of the next witness who heard or saw the shooting, Victor Flores, who claimed actually to have seen Goetz fire at two of the youths as they were running toward him and away from Goetz. He heard four or five shots "one after another."

On cross-examination, Slotnick took advantage of his legal option to restate Flores's testimony in his own language and ask Flores to answer "yes" or "no" whether that was his view of what happened.[14]

Thus he reformulated Flores's first statement about the pattern and rapidity of the shots by asking, "And the three shots or the four shots . . . that you heard in rapid succession after the first shot, were all going in your area, is that correct?"[15] Having gained Flores's assent to the phrase "rapid succession," Slotnick began using the label over and over again in cross-examination. The jury heard Flores say "yes" to this description so often—five more times—that the words came to seem like his own.

The case that Slotnick was eliciting on cross-examination became clear in a question that he put solely for the jury's benefit:[16]

> So it is fair to say that as far as your witnessing what occurred, the fact that he might have walked over to a rear seat and shot somebody and said something to them, like "you don't look bad, here's another," something like that, that really never happened?

Waples's objection to the question was sustained. Flores never answered the question. Nor could he have testified plausibly about what might not have happened. Yet the argument was on the table—something for the jury to think about as they heard the witness assent repeatedly to the description of the shots in "rapid succession" without the pause necessary for Goetz's own description of the events to be accurate.

Flores's testimony signaled an emergent pattern in the testimony. Slotnick would ask the witnesses whether they heard the shots in "rapid succession," and they would say "yes." This is the way Armando Soler heard the shots from the next car (he actually volunteered the phrase "rapid succession"). Loren Michals and Garth Reid—the husband of Andrea Reid—were in the car, each witnessing a portion of the action, and they too heard only four or five shots firing so rapidly that they accepted Slotnick's label "rapid succession" as apt for their recollection. Garth Reid, who is a Jamaican and speaks in a crisp accent, offered the quaint phrase "snap of time"[17] to express how rapidly he heard the shots fire in close proximity.

Mary Gant was one of the two women who remained in the car, crouching on the floor, after the shooting. Goetz approached her and asked her whether she was all right. She did not get a good view of the shooting because after becoming concerned about the four kids carrying on at the north end of the car, she hid her head in the book she was reading. She did hear the shots, however, and on cross-examination she accepted the description "rapid succession" for the four shots that she heard.

Josephine Holt also missed the action because she kept reading her newspaper after she took note of the youths "talking loud and saying dirty words."[18] She too heard only four shots, and she concurred in Slotnick's description that "it was all very fast and very rapid."[19]

The same line was confirmed by Solitaire McFoy and Andrea Reid. None of these witnesses objected to Slotnick's systematic effort to generate a picture of the events that would have made it temporally impossible for Goetz to pause, walk, and talk to Cabey before he fired the fifth shot. As the roster of witnesses from the train took the stand, testified, and stepped down, it became clear that only one—Christopher Boucher—provided significant corroboration for the popular belief, based on the confession, that the shooting of Darrell Cabey was different from all the others.

Christopher Boucher, an articulate 33-year-old window display artist from San Francisco, had come to New York to visit his friend Loren Michals. They were riding together on the fated train. Boucher noticed the four youths "talking loud and joking"[20] as soon as he entered the train at 96th Street. After the train left 14th Street, his attention was arrested by Andrea Reid's getting up with her child and falling over Loren sitting next to him. He heard gunshots but his view was blocked. After Andrea Reid got up, his could see the north end of the train and his "eyes went directly to the action."[21] He saw Goetz standing with a gun and more:[22]

Q: And what did you notice about [Goetz] when you looked at him, what was he doing?

A: He was standing, looking down at the man in the seat.

Q: Where was this man in the seat?

A: On my side of the car in the rear, by the conductor's cab, the bench for two that's at the end.

Q: What was that individual doing at that moment?

A: Sitting back.

Q: Can you show the jury exactly what he was doing?

A: Sitting back with his hands like grasping the bench and a frightened look on his face.

Q: How far was the defendant from him?

A: Two to three feet. . . .

Q: Were you looking when that shot was fired?

A: Yes.

Q: Was the individual still sitting down?

A: Yes.

Q: Did you see the gun at any point?

A: Yes. . . .

Q: And what did the person who was sitting down, do at the moment the shot was fired?

A: Well, he was sitting, grasping the bench, and he just tightened.

Now there was someone who actually saw Goetz act out what he says he did on both the audiotaped and the videotaped confession. The defense would have to labor hard to undermine this corroboration of the shooting of Darrell Cabey. Slotnick tried virtually everything on cross-examination. He tried to imply that Boucher was influenced by media accounts of the shooting, but Boucher denied watching television and paying attention to the media accounts. He tried to get Boucher to concede that he was "shaken and traumatized" by the violence, but Boucher responded calmly, "Actually no [he was not disturbed at the time]. That's the funny thing."[23] But he was shaken up afterward.

Slotnick switched his attack to minor inconsistencies between Boucher's testimony and the police report prepared by the officer who interviewed him several hours after the shooting. The report has Boucher saying that when Goetz shot Cabey, two young black men were sitting in the seat next to the cab, but Boucher denied saying that to the officer. Then there was the prolonged, detailed probing of Boucher's initial report that Cabey was sitting in a one-seater by the cab and Boucher's learning when he testified before the March grand jury that it was a two-seater. None of this seemed to impeach his testimony.

The major omission in Slotnick's cross-examination was an attack on Boucher's motive for coming forth with testimony so damaging to the defense. Questioning the witness's motives served Slotnick well in confronting other witnesses for the prosecution. He implied, for example, that Canty and Ramseur had a financial interest in lying; they are both suing Goetz for millions of dollars in damages, and their prospects for recovery would be greatly enhanced by a conviction on one of the charges of violence against them. He drew Andrea Reid through a swamp of self-interest, suggesting that she was testifying in order to further her career as a police officer. Yet he could find no motive that might have moved Boucher to improvise testimony against Goetz.

It seemed as if Boucher had emerged from cross-examination with his testimony unchallenged. But in fact, Slotnick had elicited one minor suggestion of impropriety and one glaring set of inconsistencies that would haunt the rest of the trial. The minor peccadillo was Boucher's insistence that he and his fellow witness Loren Michals had not discussed the details of the latter's testimony several days before, even though they are close friends and Boucher was staying with Michals at the time. When Slotnick asked Boucher how far he was away from Goetz at the time he shot Cabey, Boucher unhesitatingly answered, "About 40 feet."[24] Michals had given the same estimate, but only after overcoming doubts and confusion about the distance.[25] That Boucher came up with the same number seemed like more than a coincidence. Slotnick immediately picked up the hint of collaboration and reminded the jury, in his follow-up question, that Michals had said the same thing.

The single most blatant inconsistency emerged when Slotnick asked Boucher to step down from the stand and demonstrate for him how Goetz had shot Cabey. Boucher sat down in a chair in front of the jury box and acted out his perception that Cabey sat motionless, with his hands holding the front lip of the bench. He moved Slotnick into the position where he saw Goetz standing and shooting downward at the sitting Cabey. The position that Slotnick assumed, in line with Boucher's instructions, is not recorded in the trial transcript. But everyone who was there knows that according to Boucher's demonstration, Goetz was supposedly standing directly in front of Cabey when he shot. Boucher testified further that Cabey did not jerk his arm or motion in any other way before the gun went off. He obviously did not know that according to the undisputed medical evidence, Cabey was shot on the left side with the gun pointing laterally across his body. He could not possibly have been shot from the front unless he had jerked at the last second, twisted his body, and exposed his left side to the barrel of the gun.

Immediately after Boucher's testimony, Waples played the videotape to the jury. The two events together generated powerful support for the People's claim that Goetz did in fact stand over a defenseless Cabey and fire a fifth shot downward, severing his spinal cord. Yet the People's witnesses had generated doubts on significant fronts. The testimony of numerous witnesses that they heard no pause before the fifth shot must have troubled the jury. And Boucher's testimony would stand or fall on whether the inconsistency with the medical evidence about the angle of the shot would strike the jury as a flaw that undermined his credibility or as a normal discrepancy in observing an event from 40 feet under tense circumstances.

As the initiative in presenting evidence passed from the prosecution to the defense, the analysis of the Cabey shooting shifted to new ground. The defense changed the focus of evidence from eye (and ear) witnesses to experts on analyzing bullet wounds and re-creating crime scenes. Slotnick's expert, former New York City Medical Examiner Dominick Dimaio, asserted that according to the angle of the shot's entry and the path of the bullet straight across the back, Cabey could not have been hit while sitting down. Therefore, and this was asserted as scientific truth, if Cabey was sitting at the time of the fifth shot, it must have been the case that he was shot by the fourth bullet while he was standing up. An intriguing remark in Boucher's testimony tended to support this theory. Boucher said that at the time of the fifth shot, Cabey was sitting motionless and looked like he was already paralyzed. Slotnick could have used that remark to his advantage, but he was understandably reluctant to vouch for Boucher as a credible witness.

The question whether Cabey was shot on the fourth or fifth shot, standing or sitting, became almost a preoccupation of both sides as the trial nearing its end raised the level of anxiety. Legally speaking, however, it did not matter all that much whether Goetz hit Cabey with the fourth or fifth shot. True, Goetz had a better chance to prevail on his claim of self-defense as applied to the fourth shot rather than to the problematic fifth shot after an alleged pause and approach toward Cabey. But if he had intended to kill on the fifth shot, the attempted murder charge would stick, regardless of whether he hit Cabey with that shot or not.[26] Apart from these legal subtleties, it would obviously matter whether Goetz brought about the permanent injury to Cabey with a shot like all the others—while Cabey was standing—or by a categorically different assault against someone sitting down.

Dr. Dimaio's testimony seemed to catch Waples off guard. Unable to shake the doctor's unwavering insistence that as a matter of medical fact, Cabey could not have been hit while sitting down, he cut his cross-examination short. With only a few days notice, he put together a team of doctors to rebut Dimaio's argument; the most important voice for the prosecution on rebuttal was Suffolk County Medical Examiner Dr. Charles Hirsch. His purpose being to refute Dr. Dimaio's claim of medical certainty, he testified that Cabey could have been shot while sitting down if he had turned in his seat and exposed his left side to the shot. Waples unintentionally provided some comic relief by demonstrating the various possibilities of bullet entry and body angle using a dressmaking manikin made of soft material, an amply busted female figure. He twisted the manikin at various angles, and with Dr. Hirsch providing explanatory commentary, he illustrated the way the bullet could have entered at various angles by sticking long sticks through the manikin. The point of this demonstration was that the physical evidence could not resolve the dispute about whether Cabey was sitting or standing when he was shot. With Hirsch's skepticism seemingly canceling out Dimaio's dogmatism, the jury was thrown back on the uncertainties of Goetz's confession and Boucher's testimony.

Of course, neither Dr. Hirsch nor prosecutor Waples had any scientific proof that Cabey was shot sitting down. Or at least it seemed that way. Later, when it came time for Waples to make his summation to the jury, he would surprise everyone with a strikingly original interpretation of the scientific data to argue just the opposite of Dr. Dimaio—that Cabey must have been sitting when he took the damaging blow.

The basic strategy of the defense was to show that the fourth and fifth shots were not different from any of the first three. If Goetz had a good claim of self-defense against Canty, Allen, and Ramseur, he should get the full benefit of that defense in his assault against Cabey. Goetz's confession provided the raw materials for a solid defense based on his fear of being robbed and more acutely of being beaten to a pulp, of being maimed. Yet there remained the problem of assessing that fear as reasonable under the circumstances. This was the legacy of the long appellate argument that established the objective standard of reasonableness as a limit on the right of self-defense; having lost that skirmish, the defense confronted the elusive task of proving that a reasonable person would have been afraid in that confrontation and would have reacted as Goetz did.

From the defense's point of view, the raw material of reasonableness was fear—and particularly, fear of young black kids approaching on the subway and asking for money. In his opening statement, Slotnick broached the theme of fear by displaying blown-up pictures of the four youths as they looked in December 1984. These were, of course, not poses in cap and gown or the kind of snapshots shown off in a family album. Nor were they colorless police mug shots. They were poses that showed the four kids in their street garb looking self-confident and ready for action. Slotnick repeatedly showed these photographs to the jury in an effort to re-create in their minds what Goetz might have seen on the subway in those few minutes before he pulled his gun.

As he was presenting the defense case, Slotnick sought various

ways to dramatize Goetz's predicament in the subway car. He wanted
the jury to visit the car itself, and he wanted each juror to sit in
Goetz's seat and experience somehow the scene that led Goetz to
"feel trapped like a rat."[27] After some argument and resistance from
Waples, he got permission for what Baker called the "class trip"
to the subway. Yet as Justice Crane ruled, the visit would be carried
out under a cloak of silence. The press would have a chance to
photograph the jurors outside the courtroom, but Slotnick would
not be able to impress upon them the terror of the confrontation.

The morning after Justice Crane ruled against theatrics in the
subway, on Thursday, May 28, Slotnick surprised everyone in the
courtroom. As the public was waiting for the trial to begin at the
scheduled 9:30 A.M., he and his investigator Frank King took an
hour to prepare a full-scale, taped outline of a subway car on the
floor of the courtroom. When the trial reconvened, the jury sat at
one end of the floor plan of the car. The tables for the prosecution
and defense were adjusted so that the floor plan would be in full
view; both sides accepted the taped lines on the floor as a replica
of a standard New York subway car, and Justice Crane ordered
that the lines be retained until the end of the trial.

Slotnick called as his witness a ballistics expert, Joseph Quirk,
a former police officer, and elicited sufficient credentials for him to
be recognized as an expert on the re-creation of crime scenes. His
purpose was to try to re-create the confrontation on the subway
floor directly in front of the jury. As an aid to Quirk's testimony,
Slotnick proposed bringing into court four "props"—four young
men whose bodies would serve as the basis for illustrating the witness's claims about the likely position and physical attitude of the
four youths. Waples protested the plan to bring in outsiders; it would
do just fine, he maintained, to use the uniformed court guards as
props. Slotnick importuned that his people were properly prepared
and that this would save the court time. Justice Crane concurred.

Slotnick then requested in open court that his four props be
allowed to sit in the front row, adjacent to the jury box, until needed.
He directed everyone's attention to the back of the court, where
four black young men dressed in dungarees and T-shirts were standing. Next to them stood another black youth wearing a Guardian
Angels jacket. Having supported Goetz's brand of grass-roots justice,
the four volunteers from the Angels had now come to his side.

Slotnick's effort to have the four T-shirted black kids sit next
to the jurors turned down, he called his live "props" one after another
("number 1," etc.) with the aim of positioning them around his

white investigator Frank King, who was playing Goetz in the defense's version of the shooting. The expert Quirk provided a running commentary, based on information given to him by Slotnick, about where the youths must have been standing in order to receive their wounds. Canty was shot as he was facing Goetz, but Allen, Quirk reasoned, was not running away when hit; he was supposedly leaning over toward Goetz, and the bullet struck him in the upper back. This is a significant claim about Allen. But Slotnick obviously had another purpose in staging this demonstration.

As the four black youths, dressed like street toughs, began to group themselves around "Goetz" in a version blatantly favorable to the defense, the scene began to reek with danger. The jury had a full view of the black youths standing in for Canty and Allen. Then, as Slotnick called "number 3" to play Ramseur, Waples grasped that this demonstration had an intended message more far-reaching than illustrating possible inferences from the paths of the bullets. He had to find a way of frustrating Slotnick's effort to have four T-shirted black kids standing around a white prop in the narrow space circumscribed by the taped lines on the courtroom floor.

Fortunately for Waples, he was sitting on the opposite side of the putative subway car, and the stand-ins for Canty and Allen blocked his view of the position that "Ramseur" took on the other side of "Goetz." He asked that "Canty" and "Allen" sit down so that he could see the rest. There followed an amusing interaction in which Slotnick tried to get Waples to move his seat so that the demonstration could go forward and all four could stand in that narrow space around "Goetz." "Perhaps Mr. Waples could sit over here."[28] Sensibly, Waples refused to budge, and his "arguing with his seat" was rewarded. Crane ordered "Canty" and "Allen" to sit down at the far end of the courtroom and the demonstration proceeded.

There is no doubt that the dramatic power of this re-creation of the crime was enhanced by having four street-clad black kids standing in for the four alleged aggressors. If one were re-creating the incident on the stage, there is no doubt that one would want to cast young blacks in the roles of Canty, Allen, Ramseur, and Cabey. Authenticity demands no less. But the purpose of the demonstration was solely to clarify Quirk's claims about possible inferences from the established paths of the bullets. There was, therefore, no legal warrant for Slotnick's calling black youths—and he had specifically requested that the Guardian Angels send him four blacks[29]— in order to illustrate points about bullets' passing through human bodies. The witness was not authorized to speak about the rational inference of danger from being surrounded by four young black toughs. But Slotnick designed the dramatic scene so that the implicit message of menace and fear would be so strong that testimony would not be needed.

Justice Crane quickly recognized that he had made a mistake in allowing the four blacks to serve as stand-ins for the four victims. When court reconvened after the weekend break, he ordered that thereafter the court officers would serve as props for the remaining hour or so of this demonstration and implicitly for all future demonstrations.

Art is sometimes more powerful than rational argument, and on a deep emotional issue such as the fear a normal person would feel in Goetz's situation, there is probably no better means of communication than the jury's actually seeing and feeling the danger. The behavior of James Ramseur in the courtroom probably brought the jury closer to Goetz's moment of decision than any other event in the trial. Waples warned the defense that even though Ramseur had received immunity before the second grand jury, he might not testify at the trial.[30] He might be, as one says, contumacious; he might violate the duty incumbent on all witnesses to testify under oath. The Fifth Amendment privilege against self-incrimination provides an exception to this duty,[31] but immunity is granted precisely to overcome the privilege and induce a valuable witness to testify.

Ramseur had no good reason for not wanting to testify at the trial as he had at the grand jury hearing. He was simply angry at the system. He felt, apparently, that he was "set up"—prosecuted in order to eliminate him as a witness—in his conviction for rape and sodomy that, as the jury in his trial found, occurred five months after he was shot in the subway. Shortly after he was released from the hospital, he submitted a false report of his own kidnapping. It is not clear why he did this, but he has hinted that he was so fearful that Goetz's friends would be after him that he wanted to test the degree of his police protection.

By May 5, when James Ramseur was scheduled to testify, a well-dressed, mild-mannered Troy Canty had already put in several days on the stand. It was a shock for everyone to see a surly, sullen Ramseur ushered into court in his prison clothes—dirty dungarees and windbreaker. It was as though we were all transported back to the subway encounter of December 1984.

No one knew what Ramseur would do. He was led, almost forced forward, to the witness stand, and there he balked. Then his rebellion: "I'm not taking the stand. I refuse to,"[32] he uttered under his breath. Just in case the jury did not hear this act of defiance committed within a few feet of the jury box, Slotnick interjected immediately, "Sorry, Your Honor, I can't hear the witness."[33] Ramseur repeated, "I refuse to take the stand."[34]

There followed a tense sidebar conference—a huddle of the lawyers and judge outside the hearing of the jurors. Waples indicated that he would extend Ramseur's immunity to cover possible perjury, not usually covered. Slotnick claimed that he needed Ramseur's testimony. His mere presence helped the defense so much that he wanted him around as long as possible. When the lawyers broke from their huddle and returned to the field, Slotnick blurted out, so that the jury got the point of Ramseur's risk-free situation, "Your Honor, is the witness aware of the fact that he will receive immunity?"[35] Crane chided him: "Please no speeches at this time."[36] Slotnick wanted the dispute to continue. But Waples eventually decided to cut his losses and protest further proceedings in the matter of James Ramseur. With the measure of James Ramseur now taken by the jury, Crane held him in contempt and had him taken from the courtroom. Slotnick and Baker had fought hard, in legal skirmishes behind the scenes, to have precisely this scene acted out in front of the jury. The defense had gained much from the jurors' direct experience of James Ramseur.

Everyone assumed that was the end of James Ramseur, but then, after Crane offered him another opportunity to testify and purge his contempt, he returned to court on May 19, this time dressed in a coat and tie and prepared to testify for the prosecution. His direct testimony, denying that Canty had a malicious purpose in approaching Goetz, surprised no one. Tension began to mount when Slotnick began his cross-examination. Ramseur was the first witness prepared to joust from the stand with the combative Slotnick. He fought back on subtle points. When Slotnick asked him whether he had "stolen and robbed" with the other three in the past, he picked up on the linguistic point that Waples had let pass:[37]

RAMSEUR: We never stole and robbed nobody. We broke into machines. Why you put "robbing" in? We never robbed anyone together.

SLOTNICK: When you break a machine?

RAMSEUR: Don't try to convince the jurors that I'm a robber.

More provocatively, Ramseur traded insults with Slotnick. As Slotnick taunted Ramseur about his criminal past, Ramseur gratuitously accused him of being a mob lawyer.[38]

SLOTNICK: When was the last time . . . that you . . . committed a crime against a human being?
RAMSEUR: When was the last time you got a drug dealer off?

Slotnick loved every insult. When Ramseur accused him of fixing his conviction for raping Gladys Richardson and paying the jurors then watching the scene, Slotnick gave him another opening:[39]

SLOTNICK: Mr. Ramseur, have we ever met?
RAMSEUR: No, we never ever met, but I heard about you.
SLOTNICK: I hope it was nothing unpleasant.
RAMSEUR: It was unpleasant. I know about you, baby.

The more Slotnick could provoke the witness, the more likely he might lose his cool and show himself once again to be, in the favored expression of the *New York Post*, "Raging Ramseur."[40]

Tensions were high when at one point Ramseur took off one shoe and scratched his foot. The three or four guards standing near the witness stand moved in immediately. Ramseur never raised the shoe. Nor did he make any motion suggesting that he might throw the shoe. Yet Slotnick was prepared to interpret the incident as a life-threatening assault. The *Post* and the *Daily News* treated the event as newsworthy, though ambiguous. At his regular press conference after the day's events, the "five o'clock follies" as the press dubbed the defense's efforts to try the case in the media, Slotnick said, "If he had a gun he would have shot me."[41] The next morning he began with a florid, mellifluous tribute—mercifully out of the presence of the jury—to the courtroom guards who came to the rescue against the vicious witness. Waples could not avoid smirking.[42]

The *Times* ignored the incident except for this wry comment in Kirk Johnson's "Reporter's Notebook" on May 24:[43]

> Mr. Slotnick . . . even began saying several days later that a court officer had jumped in front of the witness box to block the shoe in the event that it might be thrown. Other witnesses to that aspect of the exchange are still being sought.

At a certain point, after a day of cross-examination and hostile interaction, Ramseur apparently had had enough. Slotnick began a line of questioning that seemed inoffensive. He asked Ramseur what he did the day before the shooting; Ramseur answered that he was with his girlfriend. What about the day before that? Same answer. This line of questioning continued, one day at a time. Reaching the 19th of December, Ramseur refused to go on. He simply stopped. There was nothing particularly provocative about the pending question, but he refused to answer. By chance, it seems, Slotnick hit on the question he was looking for. He pushed Ramseur over the edge and managed to show the jury—live—an irrational and furious man who could commit the crime of contempt rather than answer a question about his whereabouts three days before the shooting. Crane was at his best in patiently coaxing, almost pleading with Ramseur to continue his testimony. Yet all Ramseur could reply was "Take me out of here."[44] Justice Crane complied after citing him for contempt five times for refusing to answer five routine questions about his whereabouts and his acquaintances.

At the sentencing hearing on May 22, Crane rebuked Ramseur for irrationally helping the man he hated. The judge opined that his conduct before the jury[45]

> had conveyed viciousness and selfishness more effectively than words could. . . . Your conduct has played right into the hands of Mr. Goetz's lawyer. He owes you a vote of thanks. . . . The jurors saw your contemptuous conduct. That can never be erased from their minds.

Ramseur's lawyer, Ronald Kliegerman, argued that these probing questions about his private life should not have been allowed. This argument had little impact. Crane found that the questions were relevant and permissible and therefore concluded that Ramseur was guilty of contempt. He sentenced him to a fine of $1,500 and an additional term of six months in jail—the maximum permissible without a jury trial. The fallout from the incident that bothered Justice Crane the most was that he would have to accord the defense the option of striking all of Ramseur's testimony. Because Slotnick had not finished his cross-examination, requiring the testimony to stand would deprive Goetz of his constitutional right to confront one of the witnesses (nominally) against him. The situation was painful for Justice Crane. Not only had they devoted several days of trial time to the testimony and the haggling about how they should cope with Ramseur's threatened contumacy, but striking his testimony would leave Troy Canty as the only witness who had testified about the victims' perceptions of what happened in the subway car.[46]

A single message to the jury emerged from Slotnick's bringing Ramseur's rage into the open and his staging of the crime with four young black Guardian Angels playing the four would-be assailants. The implicit message was simple: In a subway encounter with these four black toughs, any normal, reasonable person would have feared the worst. You, ladies and gentlemen of the jury, you would have been afraid.

The examination and cross-examination of Andrea Reid intensified the message of fear. She was nervous as soon as she took the stand. Slotnick exacerbated her anxiety by telling her at the outset that he had had his investigator surreptitiously tape-record his interview with her at her home in the Bronx less than a week before she took the stand. Every time she committed herself to a version of the facts, Slotnick intimidated her with the suggestion that she gave the investigator a different version of her recollections of the subway shooting. Sometimes Slotnick had the tape to back up his intimidating cross-examination. Sometimes he did not. He repeatedly pressed her, for example, on whether she told the investigator that she saw one of the youths approach Goetz and stand "in his face." She repeatedly denied ever saying that, and it turned out when Slotnick revealed the content of the secretly made tape that it was his investigator who used those words and who tried, unsuccessfully, to get her to accede to them.

At first Andrea Reid denied ever telling anyone that she told her husband immediately after the shooting, "Those punks got what they deserved." When she heard herself saying that to the investigator on the tape, she admitted it. Slotnick's questionable maneuver of taping a private conversation with a witness had paid off. He secured a critical statement that he deployed relentlessly in developing what he declared at the outset of the trial would be his prosecution of the four youths. Goetz should be acquitted not only because he was afraid, but because he turned the tables on his assailants. He gave back to those "predators of society" what they deserved, just "what the law allowed."

Slotnick continued to interweave his message of "just deserts" with an appeal to the jury's compassion for those who act out of fear. Andrea Reid admitted she was afraid of getting involved in the case because she had met Darrell Cabey's mother at a neighborhood "crystal party" and one of her sons was with her at the time. Just as she was fearful of the Cabeys, Goetz arguably had every reason to be afraid of Cabey and his friends. In his closing statement to the jury, Slotnick returned often to Andrea Reid's fear and her supposedly misrepresenting a few points in her testimony. He had introduced portions of the tape in order to document her inconsistencies. But fear, as Slotnick was to argue in his summation, fathers unusual reactions—in the case of Andrea Reid as well as Bernhard Goetz.

At the close of all the evidence the major issues seemed to be clearly framed. There was virtually no conflict in the evidence about the gun charges. Myra Friedman had testified that Goetz gave her two guns in a cardboard box on December 30 when he was hiding from the police and that she turned them over to her lawyer and the police on January 2. Gun dealers in Connecticut and Florida testified that they sold these particular guns, identified by their serial numbers, in 1970 and 1984. There seemed to be little doubt about whether Goetz was guilty of the misdemeanor charge of possessing unlicensed guns at home. Similarly, there was little doubt that he had carried a loaded gun in public, making him guilty of a felony carrying a maximum jail term of seven years. Whether he was also guilty of the more serious charge of possessing a loaded gun with the intent to use it unlawfully lurked in the background of the proceedings, but no evidence was produced that went specifically to the question of Goetz's intent when he left his apartment on December 22 and started walking toward the subway.

From the viewpoint of what the jury heard and saw, the key question was obviously the claim of self-defense against the four young men whom Goetz feared. Behind the large question whether Goetz reasonably believed both that he was about to be robbed or attacked with deadly force and that shooting was necessary lay all the detailed factual disputes about the initial interaction between Canty and Goetz, whether Barry Allen was shot in the back when he was running away, and, most critically, whether Goetz actually paused after the fourth shot, approached Cabey, said, "You seem to be [doing] all right; here's another," and then let loose the bullet that severed his spinal column and left him crippled for life.

The jury had to proceed on the basis of what they heard and saw at the trial. They were not entitled to rely in their deliberations on what they heard or read before the trial began, and during the trial they were prohibited from following the media accounts of the events swirling around them. There was a lot of material they did not know or should not have known. They were not acting as free-ranging historians gathering all the information and evaluating it as responsible researchers. They were presented with information filtered through a sieve of legal rules on relevance and appropriateness. They were not told the race of Goetz's assailants in the prior mugging incident, and they were not told that Goetz had allegedly made a racist comment at a block meeting several years before the shooting about ridding the neighborhood of "spics and niggers." Most significantly, they had no idea of what was kept from them and why.

8
What the Jury
Did Not Know

TRIAL by jury is at once the highest form of democracy and the crudest form of censorship. The jury expresses the voice of the community in adjudging Bernhard Goetz guilty or not, but it is constantly exposed to the trial equivalent of a censor's stamp blotting out provocative material with the message "Not for your eyes or ears." Sometimes the censorship takes place in front of the jurors. The lawyers approach the side of the bench and argue privately with Justice Crane. Whenever the argument is likely to be complicated and last more than a few minutes, the jurors leave the courtroom and take up their familiar places around the discussion table in the deliberation room; they wait until called back in, but they are never told what was decided in their absence.

The debates that occur in their absence are the legal heart of the trial. Typically, the debate centers on whether a witness should be allowed to testify about a particular matter. In deciding whether testimony should come into evidence, the contents of the testimony are disclosed to the judge but not to the jury. If the jury were not kept in the dark, there would be no point in deciding thereafter to keep the particular item of testimony from them.

These debates about what the jury should know capture the spirit of our adversary system of justice. European trials, which never turn over the ultimate power of decision to exclusively lay juries, remain more casual about the evidence that is heard at trial. In our adversary system, the lawyers have more to do. Not only do they have to present the material to laymen and persuade them of their position, but they must engage in highly contentious debates about the scope of evidence admissible on their side of the case. The highly technical nature of these debates challenges their lawyerly skills. The debates also generate hundreds of legal decisions that a judge must make in the course of a trial like the Goetz prosecution. Indeed the primary way in which a trial judge in the American system expresses his authority is in rendering these decisions controlling the scope of evidence at trial.

The most significant area of debate in the Goetz case was the admissibility of the various statements made by the four victims shortly after the shooting. Some were made to witnesses in the subway car, others to medical personnel. Some of these statements reflect total bewilderment that Goetz would have shot them; others concede that at least some of the four were planning a robbery. These alleged statements by the victims are obviously relevant. Yet the only way that they could come to the attention of the jury was if one of the youths conceded on the stand that he made the statement or a witness to the statement testified in court that he heard Canty, Allen, Ramseur, or Cabey utter the words.

The problem is that this form of testimony runs squarely into one of the formal rules that characterize the adversary system of justice: the prohibition against *hearsay* evidence. In general terms, the rule prohibits witnesses from testifying about what they heard other people say. But if the rule is a wall, it also is riddled with holes and there are tunnels and paths around it. Sometimes witnesses can testify about statements that they heard out of court without running afoul of the rule. This is where lawyerly skill comes into play.

The prohibition against hearsay expresses many of the values underlying the Sixth Amendment right of a criminal defendant to confront the witnesses against him. Suppose that someone in Goetz's car on the subway (let's call her Ms. Rider) said she had heard another person who could not be located (call him Mr. Gone) say, "That was terrible. He shot him in the back." Ms. Rider is called as a witness and the question is whether she should be allowed to testify to the jury about she says she heard Mr. Gone say about the shooting. If she is allowed to reveal the highly incriminating statement, Goetz will in effect have another accuser to contend with, namely Mr. Gone. Yet he is not in court; there is no way that the defense can confront him, cross-examine him, and probe the accuracy of his claim that Goetz shot someone in the back. Cross-examining

Ms. Rider would not do, for Ms. Rider can only testify to the fact that she actually heard the statement made. She has no idea whether Gone really saw Goetz shoot someone in the back and whether he remembers the event correctly. For this reason, there is an important principle of fair procedure at stake in letting Rider tell the jury what Gone said. In principle, the defendant should be able to confront and cross-examine every witness against him. In this situation, Gone would in effect be the witness against him. If his testimony were admitted, by way of Rider's speaking in court, Goetz would have no way of defending himself against the damaging testimony.

This way of thinking expresses the sporting spirit of justice. However relevant the statement by Gone might be, it should not come into evidence if the defendant would be thereby deprived of a sporting chance to defend himself against the statement's evidentiary sting. The competitive dimension of adversary trials comes through as well in the complex maze of holes and tunnels for maneuvering through and around the wall against hearsay evidence. The starting point for these paths around the rule is the formal definition of hearsay. The same statement made out of court might sometimes be classified as hearsay, sometimes not. Whether it falls under the prohibition depends on the evidentiary purpose of the lawyer who seeks to bring the statement into evidence. If the purpose of having Rider testify about what Gone said is to prove the truth of what Gone said (that Goetz shot someone in the back), the statement would be hearsay; it would be introduced to "prove the truth of the matter asserted." But if there was some purpose other than proving the truth of what Gone said, the statement would glide past the rule into the discourse of the trial. But what alternative purpose might there be? How can a statement be useful in a trial if it is not used to prove the truth of its contents?

As to statements made before the trial by one of the witnesses at the trial, an inconsistent statement tends to show that he is mistaken and perhaps even lying at one time or another. If the witness gave a different story in the past, he was wrong either then or now. The prior inconsistent statement is admissible, therefore, for a purpose other than proving the truth of the statement. The point is not that the prior statement is true, but rather that the inconsistency in itself undermines the witness's credibility.

Troy Canty made two incriminating statements that the defense could bring in through this tunnel under the rule. Detective Charles Penelton testified that when he talked to Canty in the hospital, the latter said, "We surrounded the white guy." Penelton sought to clarify the point: "All of you?" Canty replied, "All of us."[1] Detective Peter Smith testified that while Canty was still lying on the floor of the subway car, Canty said, "We were going to rob him but the white guy shot us first."[2] These statements could not be used—officially—to prove that the four youths surrounded Goetz and that they intended to rob him. But they could be used to prove that Canty told different stories to different people, a tale of innocent intentions in his testimony at trial and an admission of an intended robbery to Peter Smith. Though these two uses of the same statement are technically distinct, it would take a sophisticated juror to appreciate the distinction.

The scope of this exception to the hearsay rule covered only the statements made by Canty, for he was the only one of the four whose testimony officially counted as evidence (Ramseur's testimony was stricken after he committed contempt). The defense had access, however, to several highly relevant statements that Darrell Cabey made to various people. He told John Filangeri, the paramedic who treated him on the way to the hospital, "The guys I was with were hassling this guy, asking him for money. The guy threatened us and then he shot us."[3] He made essentially the same statement to the columnist Jimmy Breslin in late November 1985.[4] In view of the prosecution's decision not to call Cabey as a witness, however, the defense could not introduce or refer to these statements on the theory that the statements served merely to undermine Cabey's credibility. This way of circumventing the hearsay rule was barred to the defense.

The defense desperately wanted to bring that statement by Darrell Cabey into evidence. The charges based on the Cabey shooting were the most difficult to defend against; it might help if Cabey were portrayed as a participant in harassing Goetz. Bringing in Cabey's reference to "hassling this guy" might induce the jury to think of him more as an aggressor than as a paralyzed victim of the shooting.

While the jurors sought ways to amuse themselves in the sealed privacy of the deliberation room, the lawyers engaged in a prolonged debate about whether Filangeri could testify to what he heard Cabey say. The defense explored all the possible loopholes and tunnels for getting past the hearsay barrier. The arguments that the defense invoked read like a course in popular psychology. The exceptions to the hearsay rule rest on seat-of-the-pants psychological judgments about when people are likely to be telling the truth. The principle is that if in the particular situation, someone is highly likely to be telling the truth, his statements should come in—even without a chance to cross-examine him.

First came the argument that the statement should be admissible to prove that the youths were "harassing" Goetz because this was a statement against Cabey's "penal interest," i.e., it would tend to incriminate Cabey in a crime. The psychological assumption is that people are not likely to lie about matters contrary to their interests. This makes good enough sense, but numerous legal hedges on the exception stood in the way of admitting the statement on this theory. Significantly, Cabey does not directly incriminate himself in the statement; he says, "The guys I was with were hassling . . ." and thereby tries to push the blame off on the other three. That self-serving maneuver is hardly as reliable as a contrite expression of guilt. Also, unless the word "hassling" has a special meaning in the vocabulary of street kids,[5] this concession falls below the threshold of a self-incriminating confession of a crime.[6]

With little hope of succeeding on this theory, the defense shifted its argument to another psychological theory for supposing that Cabey must have been telling the truth. The statement might come in on a theory of "excited utterance": subject to the trauma of being shot, Cabey's normal capacity for reflection and fabrication would be in abeyance and therefore he would not have the capacity to fabricate in his self-interest. If "Rider" had heard Cabey scream, "I've been shot" after the fourth shot, she could unquestionably have testified that she heard the statement. Cabey's excitement would be good reason to believe that the statement was reliable. The problem in this case was that the statement was made about an hour after the shooting. Cabey might have well have recovered from the shock of the event and regained his ability to tell a self-serving story.

Justice Crane ruled against the admissibility of the statement on these first two grounds as well as on technical theories ventured by the defense.[7] At that point Slotnick and Baker engaged in the ingenious maneuver of arguing that Cabey's statement should come in as evidence not to show that the youths were hassling Goetz, but simply to prove that the sounds were uttered. They would try to circumvent the hearsay rule by arguing that their purpose was to prove not that the statements were true, but merely that they were made. The idea is that Filangeri would testify, if allowed to do so, not about Cabey's statement as a truthful communication, but simply as an event like any other that the witness might observe.

If Filangeri had heard Cabey scream in pain, he unquestionably could have testified to having heard the scream. By like token, he could testify to verbal statements that would be significant only because they would reflect a certain state of mind, such as pain or fear. The distinction between relying on the content of Cabey's statement and testifying simply about the fact that it was made may be philosophically subtle, but the delicate distinction has a point. In principle, Cabey's statements should not be used either for or against the defense if Cabey cannot be cross-examined. But if someone hears sounds coming from Cabey, that person should be able to testify simply that he has heard the sounds—the content being irrelevant.

Trial lawyers often seek to counter hearsay problems by arguing, in effect, that they want the witness on the stand simply to testify that he heard the sounds. The problem with this tactical move is typically, Why should anyone care about whether the person simply uttered those sounds? If the point is not to prove the aggressive inclinations of Canty, Allen, and Ramseur, why should it be relevant that Cabey uttered words about his three partners hassling Goetz? That Cabey simply uttered words could be used to prove that Cabey was conscious at the time, but that was not a proposition relevant to the inquiry about Goetz's guilt or innocence.

At this point in the argument, Slotnick and Baker devised a rationale for why the fact of Cabey's making the statement was important, regardless of whether the others were in fact hassling Goetz. If Cabey's subjective feeling was that hassling was occurring, then there was a basis for concluding, by analogy, that Goetz felt the same way. And if someone else as closely involved as Cabey felt the situation bespoke aggression, then there was also a basis for concluding that Goetz's belief that he was about to be robbed was reasonable (overlooking the logical leap from "hassling" to "robbery").

The argument was ingenious, but Justice Crane was inclined to think that this was all a maneuver to prove indirectly that the three were hassling Goetz. Cabey's statement struggled for admission into evidence, but the restraints of the hearsay rule proved to be too powerful. Lawyerly ingenuity has its limits, and in this instance, it could find no way through or around the letter of the law.

Though the defense lost this round,[8] the argument exercised many of the legal strokes and counterstrokes that would be critical in the rest of the trial. Slotnick and Baker were better prepared the next time the same issues came up. The prosecution tried to bring before the jury certain exculpatory statements that the injured youths allegedly made to a fellow black passenger, Arnetha Gilbert. Out of the presence of the jury, Ms. Gilbert testified that she was riding in the sixth car of the train, heard the shots, and went directly to the seventh car, where the gunshots seemed to be coming from. There she found three youths lying on the floor. She approached one and felt his pulse, and then another lying next to him—it would have been Troy Canty—said, "He shot me for nothing, I didn't do anything, I only asked for five dollars."[9] Then she went over to another youth at the end of the car, by the conductor's cab, who was presumably Cabey, who said to her, "I didn't do anything, he shot me for nothing."[10]

If these statements came into evidence, they would lend considerable weight to the prosecution's position that in fact the four youths intended no more than to shake Goetz down for a few dollars. They had no money, and their plan, as Canty testified, was to go down to an arcade and engage in their routine activity of jimmying open video machines and stealing quarters from the cash boxes. That was the purpose of the screwdrivers, and according to Canty, they needed a few dollars to play the first video game while they pried open the cash box.

Coming from the lips of Arnetha Gilbert, however, these self-serving statements by Canty and Cabey are clearly hearsay. They could come into evidence only if they qualified under an exception to the hearsay prohibition, and the only exception that seemed available was the doctrine of "excited utterance" under which the defense failed to secure Filangeri's statement into evidence. The critical legal test for determining whether the statements qualified under this exception was whether at the time they were made, the "reflective capacities" of Canty and Cabey had been sufficiently suspended to make the statements so reliable that the jury should be allowed to hear them without Canty's and Cabey's facing cross-examination about what they supposedly said.

The best way for Slotnick to succeed in keeping the statements out was to get the witness Arnetha Gilbert to make concessions about the youths' condition that would lead Justice Crane to rule that the youths retained their capacities to reflect on what they were saying and fabricate self-serving statements. Slotnick managed to secure these concessions in a textbook display of skillful cross-examination. To understand his interaction with the witness, think about a spectrum of reflective capacity ranging from a groggy semiconscious state where the wounded youth does not know what he is saying, at one extreme, to normal capacity to reflect and lie, at the opposite. The debate under the legal standard centers almost exclusively not on the "groggy" end, but on the "normal" end of the spectrum. Yet there was no way the witness was likely to know this. Slotnick pressed the witness on the "groggy" end:[11]

> And you think he was coherent and he knew what he was saying, and he understood you?
>
> Isn't it a fact he [Canty] was really semi-conscious, his eyelids were drooped?
>
> He was mumbling, isn't that a matter of fact?

These questions, coupled with Slotnick's admonition to Ms. Gilbert not to commit perjury, hinted that the issue standing in the way of admissibility was whether Canty was incoherent. Slotnick pressed the same line of questions about Cabey, suggesting that he was in a state of shock, that he was "slurring his words," and that he "didn't know what he was saying." These questions prompted Ms. Gilbert to describe the statements as "clear and concise" and eventually to agree with Slotnick's characterization that "the people you spoke to were coherent and of sound mind and were out of the state of incident and were able to talk to you."[12]

In the legal argument based on this testimony, Slotnick relied heavily on Ms. Gilbert's concessions. If she had wanted her testimony to come to the attention of the jury, Ms. Gilbert would have been more likely to succeed by answering the opposite: that Canty and Cabey were groggy and appeared to be in a state of shock. But Slotnick had coaxed her into avoiding that extreme of the spectrum and stressing the clarity of their speech and their making their statements in a conversational exchange with her. These factors suggested a large measure of control over the statements, enough control so that they would not appear to be spontaneous and beyond their reflective capacities.

The clincher in the argument was that Filangeri had described Darrell Cabey as being in a state of severe shock when they arrived at the hospital and Crane nonetheless ruled that his statement to Filangeri in the ambulance did not qualify as an excited utterance. Consistency seemed to require that he rule the same way on the statements made to Ms. Gilbert. Although the statements in the train were temporally much closer to the incident, Waples could not persuade Justice Crane to distinguish between these inculpatory statements he had already excluded and the exculpatory statements at issue.[13]

If the defense recouped part of their losses in the Filangeri debate by urging that the decision be consistently applied to the statements made to Gilbert, they scored again in a critical skirmish leading to the admission of a witness's hearsay statement that the four youths were "punks." At stake were two statements made by Andrea Reid, a passenger on the train along with her husband Garth Reid and her baby. The defense knew from the police report that before the shooting she called her husband's attention to the four youths with the remark "Look at those punks bothering that white man." And during the trial she told one of Slotnick's investigators, "Those punks got what they deserved."[14] The defense needed these statements in evidence in order to ground its punitive theory of self-defense in the sentiments of ordinary people like the jurors.* Nothing would better support the theory that Goetz justly struck back at the predators of the city than a witness who described these youths as "punks." The problem for the defense was that these epithets were not relevant to any of the formal legal issues debated in the trial.

Andrea Reid, young, black, and attractive, would prove to be an effective source of evidence for the defense. Her hostilely describing the youths as "punks" seemed to reflect the sentiments of an upwardly mobile black woman toward the street toughs who helped perpetuate prejudice against blacks. She wanted to be a police officer, and one of the jurors, Erniece Dix, was also a young black woman working for the police department, and she would obviously identify with Andrea Reid. The problem for Slotnick was how to bring Andrea Reid's inflammatory sentiments to the attention of the jury.

The prosecution called her husband Garth Reid as their witness, but in his testimony he made a few comments that made the youths seem unruly and boisterous in the interactions leading up to the shooting. He said, "People were swinging on the handle in the subway."[15] This observation gave Slotnick an opening for eliciting Andrea Reid's hostility toward the four black youths. He probed the reasons for Garth Reid's first taking note of the kids' horsing around. "Isn't it true," he asked, "that the reason you took notice of these four individuals is because someone said, 'Look at those four punks bothering that man.'?"[16] Waples leapt to his feet, and

---

* See the discussion of the punitive theory of self-defense on pages 27–29.

Justice Crane was sympathetic to his objection. A sidebar conference erupted in hostility:[17]

THE COURT: Gentlemen, I thought we had an understanding that this would not happen again, Mr. Slotnick. . . . That you would not spread upon the record, in front of the jury, in open court, something that's not in evidence on your cross examination.[18]

SLOTNICK: Judge, you can speak a little louder and the jury can hear you.

THE COURT: I'm upset with your conduct.

SLOTNICK: I'm upset with your conduct.

THE COURT: You know where you can go with that.

With this beginning, you would think that Slotnick had little chance to persuade Justice Crane of the soundness of his position. But Slotnick and Baker had an extraordinary capacity to press their arguments even in the face of likely defeat. They came forth with the argument first heard in the Filangeri debate. The claim now was that the statement was important just to prove how and why Garth Reid was alerted to the presence of the four youths. It was as though he heard a scream—not a statement that would tend to show that the four youths were "punks." To Waples's dismay, after long argument, this claim appeared to be succeeding. Crane said that he believed Slotnick was "not offering it for the truth of the communication. . . ." Slotnick was so confident of his maneuver that he indulged in the following:[19]

SLOTNICK: I would ask your Honor not only to give a curative instruction, but to indicate to the jury that sometimes Judges make mistakes when they yell at lawyers.

THE COURT: I did, but I adhere to it. When you spring something like that. . . .

SLOTNICK: . . . I didn't think that I was springing something. To me that's Hornbook law.

When Waples grasped that the tide of the argument was shifting, he asked plaintively, "This objection is being overruled?"[20] Crane said, "Yes." Waples protested vigorously that the statement's coming to the attention of the jury would have a prejudicial impact and it would not clarify any issue at stake in the trial. Even if Garth Reid's testimony was interpreted as showing merely that his wife made the statement, why should that fact—that she made that particular statement—be relevant to the trial? Why should anyone care whether Garth Reid heard certain sounds—if the meaning of those sounds was deemed irrelevant?

At this juncture in the argument, Slotnick harvested the seeds sown in an earlier series of implicit negotiations between the prosecution and the defense about whether they would inquire whether the passengers on the train were afraid of the four youths "horsing around" at the north end of the car. When Waples put this question to two prior witnesses, Victor Flores and Loren Michals, Slotnick initially objected and then withdrew his opposition. He would take his chances on their both probing into the passengers' subjective fears. It was clear, however, that Justice Crane had reservations about letting in evidence on the passengers' state of mind. He thought that effective cross-examination about these private feelings would be impossible; no one could challenge what the witnesses said. He feared also that the entire inquiry would only confuse the jury. Yet Waples and Slotnick had in effect overruled him. They opened the door themselves, and the course of the trial would determine who would win and who would lose from the expanded range of inquiry.

In the debate about whether Andrea Reid's reference to the "punks' " bothering Goetz should be admitted, it became clear that Waples would be the loser. His having opened the door with his pressing prior questioning of Michals now revealed a trap:[21]

THE COURT: I agreed with you this morning but you propounded questions to the passengers about their state of mind.

WAPLES: Judge, there is no question about whether this person looked over. What compelled him to look over is totally inconsequential. He did look over in response to some communication. That's not in dispute. Why is it necessary then to establish what it was? That is prejudicial, without any probative value.

THE COURT: He's entitled to establish that Mr. Reid has a state of mind bordering on alarm. He's entitled to show it circumstantially, as well as to get out from the statement of the witness. I didn't call for the subject being opened in the first place. I rather urged you both to consider not doing it and you both chided me for trying your cases for you. Now it's open and he's going into it.

Thus the jury learned that Andrea Reid regarded the four black kids as "punks." Crane resolved the borderline issue of whether

Garth Reid could testify to what his wife said to him by holding Waples accountable for having initiated the entire line of inquiry about subjective fears and anxieties on the train.

Trials take on a logic of their own. Judges seek to maintain consistency in their rulings, primarily for the sake of their own integrity. Thus if the debate on the "excited utterance" exception to the hearsay rule is resolved one way when Filangeri is a witness, it will likely be resolved the same way when Gilbert is prepared to testify. Yet there is another kind of reasoning that invariably emerges when the judge, as arbiter between conflicting positions, senses that fairness requires a fair distribution of advantage in the course of the trial. This means that if he decides a close question one way in one context, he may well err on the other side of the debate the next time the matter comes up. Sometimes the imperative of logical consistency coincides with this strategy of splitting the difference. In the Filangeri and Gilbert debates, Justice Crane could rule on the basis of consistency and at the same time award one victory to the prosecution (excluding the incriminating statements in the Filangeri debate) and one to the defense (excluding the exculpatory statements in the Gilbert debate). In other situations, consistency may suffer in the interests of sharing the advantage resulting from close questions between the prosecution and the defense. A good example is the extended series of decisions triggered by Ramseur's indication that he was unwilling to testify.

After a long debate, the defense prevailed upon Justice Crane to require the prosecution to bring Ramseur before the jury even though there was considerable uncertainty about whether he would commit contempt rather than cooperate with the court. The defense obviously had much to gain from having Ramseur show the jury precisely how unruly and mean-spirited he could be. The leading case in New York, *People v. Berg*,[22] recognizes that the trial judge should decide as a matter of his sound discretion whether to test a witness's willingness to testify in the presence of the jury.

Yet in that case itself, the Court of Appeals affirmed the defendant's conviction even though the prosecution in the case secured a witness's refusal to testify in front of the jury. The victim of the assault indicated that he might not testify because he did not remember anything. The prosecution called him even though his refusal to testify might suggest to the jury that he feared the defendant. As it turned out, the witness refused to answer questions about his whereabouts at the time of the assault, and he was found in contempt. The implicit message to the jury was that the witness was afraid.

Implications from silence are not subject to rational examination, and that is precisely the reason the Court of Appeals advises trial judges in the state to test the witness's willingness to testify outside the presence of the jury. Nonetheless, in the *Berg* case itself the court was not convinced that the prosecution had engaged in misconduct by insisting on the witness's appearing before the jury; the prosecutor justified his decision on the ground that the formal presence of the courtroom and the judge's admonitions might induce him to testify.

The principle underlying the *Berg* case should arguably have convinced Justice Crane not to risk Ramseur's refusing to testify and thereby displaying his rebellious spirit in front of the jury. The defense sought precisely the kind of unarticulated and unanalyzable communication to the jury that the Court of Appeals identified as unsuitable for a criminal trial. If the prosecutor in *Berg* acted with a proper motive in trying to induce the witness to testify (testimony about the assault would help his case), the suspect motives of the Goetz defense were transparent (they had nothing obvious to gain from Ramseur's confirming Canty's story of innocent intentions).

The defense found a "trump" that won over these apparently sensible considerations. They argued that the purpose of the *Berg* principle was exclusively to protect the defense. The principles of due process protect the defense from prejudicial prosecutorial behavior, but not the prosecution from the same type of conduct by the defense. The prosecutor could not act with improper motives, but they arguably could. Justice Crane found this point sufficiently persuasive to bring Ramseur into court in the hope that he might testify.

It is true that our system of criminal justice is skewed toward the defense. The accepted maxim is, Better that ten guilty go free than that one innocent be convicted. The prosecution cannot appeal a jury verdict of not guilty, but the defense can appeal a verdict of guilty. The prosecution may not use its peremptory challenges to keep specific ethnic and racial groups off the jury, but under New York law as of the Goetz prosecution, the defense could.[23] We act as if only the defense has a due process right to a fair trial. Ignoring the rights of the prosecution is particularly insidious when, as in the Goetz case, the prosecution stands closely identified with the demands of a racial minority for equal justice.

Nonetheless, if the teaching of the *Berg* case is that only the prosecution is prevented from profiting from a witness's refusing to testify before the jury, this teaching should have controlled the subsequent ruling by the court when the prosecution planned to call Barry Allen and indicated that he would probably invoke his Fifth Amendment privilege against self-incrimination and refuse to testify. It was difficult to distinguish the case of Allen from the case of Ramseur. True, Allen had not testified before the second grand jury and therefore, unlike Ramseur, had not received immunity from prosecution for the acts that he would disclose in his testimony. Protected by immunity, Ramseur had no apparent motive of self-interest in refusing to testify and committing contempt; his meanness was all the more manifest. Yet Allen, risking possible prosecution for conspiracy to rob Goetz, had a good reason for invoking the Fifth Amendment. If anything, this should have made the decision in Allen's instance easier than in Ramseur's. The innuendo of the witness's bad character would be less compelling.

Yet after the defense had harvested its undebatable implication of Ramseur's bad character, the equities of the decision seemed different. Deciding directly and swiftly,[24] Justice Crane ruled that he would not allow Allen to appear before the jury until it was clear that he would testify. He did not allow Slotnick and Baker their usual maneuver of arguing after the decision in an effort to change his mind. As it turned out, Allen came into court, took the oath, and then invoked the Fifth Amendment on virtually every question Waples put to him. The jury had no idea he was in the courthouse.[25]

Consistency required that the two witnesses be treated the same way. But this was a close call, a decision at the borderline. Perhaps a distinction between the two cases could be eked out of the difference between committing contempt and taking the Fifth Amendment. But a factor of equity entered into the balance. Rather than give the defense the benefit of both decisions, Justice Crane decided to allocate the advantages and disadvantages of witnesses' refusing before the jury to both sides. The defense got one and the prosecution got one.

Splitting the difference, however, is a precarious way of judging. It might be fair to give both sides an equal share of the advantages of his legal decisions, but doing so only encourages both sides to overstate their demands so that their half of the decisions will be larger. In the aftermath of the Allen decision the defense began to argue as though some compensating advantage were now due to them. They were unwilling to accept the implicit fairness of "Ramseur for them, Allen for the prosecution." As far as they were concerned, the process of allocating trial advantages did not end, but rather began with the decision to keep Allen away from the jury.

They quickly put Waples on the defensive by insisting that he grant immunity to Allen so that the latter could no longer invoke his privilege against self-incrimination. Waples refused, undoubtedly with support from his superior, District Attorney Morgenthau. The defense then mounted a campaign to induce Justice Crane to order Waples to grant immunity. They had no legal support for this demand. The only precedent they could cite on their behalf, *People v. Shapiro*,[26] was obviously inapposite. In that case, the Court of Appeals held that it was improper for the prosecution not to grant immunity to a *defense* witness (Allen was a prosecution witness), but only after the prosecutor had engaged in a campaign to intimidate the witness with threats of perjury prosecutions. The defense in *Shapiro* had demanded immunity from perjury as a way of warding off the browbeating tact by the prosecution. Waples was obviously not intimidating Allen, and therefore there was hardly a foothold for an analogical argument.

The defense buttressed its claims for immunity by invoking the defendant's Sixth Amendment right to confront the witnesses against him. The problem, of course, was just the opposite: Allen was not a witness, and would not be a witness against Goetz. Nothing he said was being used against the defense. Yet by arguing this unfounded constitutional interpretation with insistence and passion, Baker and Slotnick remarkably made the claim seem almost plausible. A respectable journalist even reported that the entire controversy about Allen raised an issue under the Sixth Amendment confrontation clause.[27]

Justice Crane eventually decided against what he charitably called the defense's "novel" theory.[28] Yet the defense won even as it was losing. For the debate about immunity had created the impression that Waples was responsible for Allen's not testifying. His refusal to grant immunity came to appear equivalent to a decision not to call the witness at all. Yet he was obligated to call all witnesses who might give evidence favorable to the prosecution. Ignoring Waples's effort to call Allen and the latter's invoking his constitutional right not to testify, Crane decided to instruct the jury at the end of the case that Allen was in effect a "missing witness."[29] He would instruct the jury the prosecution had failed "adequately to explain" the absence of Barry Allen and that the jury could infer that Allen would have testified in a manner contrary to the prosecution's case.

Thus the bargaining and negotiations for trial advantage finally came to an end. The defense got Ramseur before the jury. The prosecution kept Allen from the jury. The prosecution refused immunity for Allen, and the defense got a highly favorable instruction to the jury. These were decisions driven largely by an impulse to give each side a fair share of tactical advantage: a decision for one side triggered the need to compensate with an offsetting decision for the other side. What was missing in this approach was a strong sense of principle and consistency. If Crane had had good reasons for requiring Allen to take the Fifth Amendment outside the presence of the jury, if the dictates of fair procedure required it, he would have treated Allen's unavailability not as a consequence of Waples's trial strategy, but as an implication of the court's own interpretation of the Fifth Amendment.

These, then, are some of the arguments and the evidence that the jury did not hear. The jurors might have been able to use the hearsay statements by Cabey and Canty in evaluating the intentions of the four youths in the subway confrontation. It is unlikely, however, that knowledge of these statements would have affected their intuitive sense whether Goetz faced serious danger on the train. The one statement that could have an inflammatory effect—Andrea Reid's comment about the "punks"—did come to their attention. It would have been better had they not seen Ramseur commit contempt the first time, but in light of his doing it again at the end of his testimony, their view of Ramseur would not have been more favorable had they been ignorant of the first incident. It would have been damaging to the prosecution's case if they had seen Barry Allen as well as James Ramseur refuse to testify. And there is something questionable, though not strictly illegal, about allowing a jury to think ill of someone—Barry Allen—just because he invokes his constitutional right not to incriminate himself. The law of evidence pointed Justice Crane to the right decision on some of these matters, but it would be difficult to say that the enormous investment of time on these issues of admissibility produced a fairer, less biased trial.

There were other matters on which the jury surely must have been curious. They undoubtedly wanted to hear Goetz testify from the stand. But there never was any likelihood that Goetz would waive his Fifth Amendment rights, swear an oath to tell the truth, and then expose himself to a searching cross-examination about past incidents in which he pulled his gun as well as about shooting on the train. He had little to gain from repeating the four hours of his voice and image already projected to the jury. And if he should change his mind on what happened, he had much to lose from exposing inconsistencies.

The jury quickly got the message that unlike other researchers into the truth, they had a purely passive function as judges of the facts. There would be no agenda for research into the events of December 22, 1984. They would have to wait to see what the lawyers brought them and what the rules of evidence allowed them to hear as evidence. Their being constantly ushered in and out of the room, their sense that major issues were decided in their absence, must have given them a strong sense of being subject to the discipline and control of the lawyers and Justice Crane. Little did they realize how much power they actually had. Theirs was the power of final decision, and unbeknownst to them, the judge and lawyers who exercised control over them were deeply concerned about how they would use their power.

9
Perfecting the Law

AT least since the 17th century, juries have enjoyed a well-established power to vote their conscience, even in the face of judicial instructions to the contrary.[1] In the 1670 prosecution of William Penn and William Mead for allegedly speaking at an unlawful assembly at a London church, the jury initially voted not guilty and the trial judge tried to intimidate the jurors into changing their votes. He ordered the jurors imprisoned without food and water until they would come around. The jurors endured these deprivations rather than change their votes. They were freed finally on a writ of habeas corpus.[2] Their courage etched a fundamental principle into English legal consciousness: judges cannot impose sanctions on jurors for voting according to their own vision of right and wrong.[3]

Decisions by juries that vote their conscience are conventionally described as "jury nullification." The label is unfortunate and misleading, because it suggests that when the jury votes its conscience, it is always engaged in an act of disrespect toward the law. The acquittal, supposedly, nullifies the law. In place of the law, it is said, the jury interposes its own moral judgment or political preferences. There are some who defend this residual power in juries as the highest expression of democracy and community control over the machinery of the state, and others who decry the same power as an invitation to anarchy.

Jury nullification seems to stand in conflict with the rule of law, but careful historical reflection underscores the power of the jury not to defeat the law, but to perfect the law, to realize the law's inherent values. Prior to the middle of the 19th century, the critical cases of jury nullification raised claims of justification that went beyond the incompletely stated body of formal legal rules. Today we assume, for example, that in all criminal and civil actions for defamation—that is, for writing or saying something that exposes someone to ridicule or derision—the defendant can appeal to the truth of his claims as a complete justification for compromising the reputation of those he has attacked. In the 18th century and earlier, however, in cases of published attacks on governmental officials, the law did not recognize truth as a defense. The crime of seditious libel consisted simply in the act of publishing attacks that exposed officials to unwanted criticism.

In a case that became a landmark of jury independence, the colonial authorities in New York prosecuted the newspaper publisher John Peter Zenger in 1735 for seditious libel. His lawyer, Andrew Hamilton, made a ringing peroration to the jury that they were the ultimate judges of the law as well as the facts. The specific principle of law he asked them to recognize was the one that we now take for granted as part of the written law: the jury should not convict Zenger for publishing truthful attacks on corrupt public officials. In acquitting the publisher of *The New York Weekly Journal,* the jury took a stand squarely on the side of truth as a defense to seditious libel.

By the end of the 18th century, the conception of the jury as judge of the law as well as the facts took root and became a standard feature in the law of seditious libel. The Federal Sedition Law of 1798 provided that "the jury who shall try the cause shall have the right to determine the law and the fact . . . as in other cases."[4] More than a dozen states, including New York, anchored this principle, as applied to criminal libel cases, in their constitutions.[5] A few states extrapolated the jury's right "to determine the law" to all criminal cases. For example, the constitution of Maryland provides that "the Jury shall be the Judges of the Law and of Fact."[6] These provisions acknowledge the function of the jury as the ultimate authority on the law not to "nullify" the instructions of the judge, but to complete the law, when necessary, by recognizing principles of justification that go beyond the written law. It would be better if we abandoned the phrase "jury nullification" and spoke instead of the jury's function in these cases of completing and perfecting the positive law recognized by the courts and the legislature.

Unfortunately, in contemporary discussions of the jury's independence, writers fail to distinguish between the rightful authority of the jury to realize the law's inherent values and a distortion of this power that enables jurors to defy the judge's instructions. If the jurors are not to be subject to sanctions however they vote, they have the power in all cases to acquit a defendant guilty under the law or to convict an innocent but unpopular defendant. Nothing prevents them from making these decisions on the basis of their passions rather than a reasoned effort to refine the law. This possibility of perverting the law runs for and against criminal defendants, but the dangers to an innocent defendant are less pronounced than the potential benefits to one who is guilty. If the jury renders an impassioned verdict of guilty, the defendant can appeal on the ground that the evidence is insufficient to support the verdict. But if the jury acquits for the wrong reasons, its finding on the evidence is final. The prosecution cannot appeal an irrational or biased verdict of not guilty.

The term "jury nullification" infelicitously encompasses both dimensions of the jury's power, their power to negate as well as to refine the law, to vent their passions as well as give voice to their reason.[7] The defense in the Goetz case thought they would be able to appeal to the jury's innate power and convince the jury to acquit even if the evidence under the applicable law clearly required conviction. They proceeded as though popular support for Goetz would translate into an issue of conscience that would move the jury to acquit. But fear of crime and racial antagonism are hardly motives of political conscience. There is no hint of universal principle in the claim that Goetz had to carry a gun because if attacked, he would have to "give those punks what they deserved." But this argument with its variations was the foundation of the Goetz defense.

This is not to say that the defense could not have postured the case so that it would appear to raise a basic issue of political conscience. Goetz himself believed and presumably still believes strongly in the right to bear arms as an aspect of the fundamental human right of self-protection. After his success before the first grand jury, he began to urge, publicly, the distribution of an additional 25,000 firearms to well-trained citizens. The nearly forgotten Second Amendment in the Bill of Rights protects this right; even though the prevailing interpretation is that the amendment merely guarantees a right to the states to maintain a militia, convincing evidence indicates that the framers had an individual right in mind.[8] In the years of the American republic's founding, the overwhelming fear was that the central government would become a force of tyranny. An armed and disciplined citizenry was the best possible defense against a government that might seek to enslave us. Goetz's lawyers could have attempted to ground their defense in this plausible interpretation of the Second Amendment. This strategy would have required educating the media, as the defense was adept at doing, to develop an image of the case in the public's mind as testing a fundamental issue of human freedom.

This way of posturing the case would have elevated the defense to a plane of universal principle above and beyond the partisan issue of securing protection against a class of "predators" and "vultures." Building on the spirit of a universal right to protect oneself by bearing arms if necessary, they might have had a chance of persuading Justice Crane that the official law of New York was truncated and insensitive to the larger moral issues at stake. They might then have persuaded Justice Crane that they should be able to address the jury on "higher law" bearing on Goetz's guilt, precisely as John Peter Zenger's lawyers had appealed to the jury to vote their conscience and refine the imperfect law of seditious libel. They might have succeeded, as defense counsel secured permission to speak directly to the jury in the trial of the Camden 28, a prosecution for destroying draft records. In that case, which indirectly raised the legitimacy of the Vietnam war, counsel urged the jury:[9]

> [you are] supposed to decide if the law, as the judge explains it to you, should be applied or if it should not. Nothing the judge would say to you is inconsistent with this power.

Not all judges would agree that the jury should have been encouraged to pass judgment even indirectly on a question of American military policy or on civil disobedience as a technique of protest.[10] But in the Goetz case the defense had failed to articulate an argument, either in the media or in the courtroom, that there was an issue of universal human freedom that went beyond the law of New York on self-defense and the permissible possession of defensive weapons.

The defense may well have thought that an appeal to the right to bear arms would collide with fearful sensibilities and might even be counterproductive. Every survey of public reactions to Goetz indicates that although support for his defensive act cuts across class and racial line, very few people support his political convictions on the right and importance of the citizenry's responsibly arming itself. A nationwide Gallup poll conducted in March 1985 revealed that a substantial majority of 57 percent of the population supported

Goetz, but an overwhelming countermajority of 78 percent stood opposed to there being more guns on the street. After the verdict, in June 1987, another Gallup poll revealed the same intersecting majorities. Substantially more than half supported the verdict of not guilty on the shooting charges, but only 1 percent would have favored an acquittal on the gun possession charges.

When one of the prospective jurors showed up for his interview with a copy of the Constitution and argued that the charges against Goetz violated the Second Amendment, both sides as well as the judge concluded quickly that the man was far too eccentric and biased for serious consideration as a juror. The right to bear arms may be dear to some segments of the population, but this right did not present itself to anyone in the Goetz proceedings—except perhaps to Goetz himself—as a serious issue in the case.

The defense was caught, therefore, in an embarrassed position. They wanted to appeal in some way to the jury's power to vote their sympathy for Goetz, but they could not raise the factor of sympathy to the level of moral principle. They could not make a plausible claim that they needed to appeal to the jury to refine and perfect the law as it stood on the books.

The standard jury instructions used in the New York courts gave the defense hope that they might in any event, moral argument or not, invoke the jury's power to vote its sympathy for Goetz, the folk hero. The conventional practice in New York as in other states is to instruct the jury that if they find beyond a reasonable doubt that all the elements of the crime are satisfied, they *may* convict the defendant. The use of the permissive *may* seems curious, for the standard instructions also say that if the jury makes an affirmative finding[11] on a defensive issue like duress, necessity, or self-defense, they *must* render a verdict of not guilty. Why should the standard instructions require an acquittal if the jury makes a finding for the defense, but only *permit* a conviction if they make an analogous finding for the People? The answer might be that the legal system is ambivalent about whether the law captures all of the factors that make a criminal defendant morally culpable and deserving of conviction and punishment. Even if the defendant has violated the law and he has no defense, the special circumstances of his crime may undermine his moral culpability. Leaving this residual power of moral judgment in the hands of the jury, even if it is expressed only as the subtle difference between *may* and *must,* hints at the power of the jury to decide the case on its own convictions of right and wrong.

Justice Crane was fully aware that in a case in which popular sentiment favored the defendant, jury nullification of the law lurked as a risk in the background. But he decided early in the Goetz proceedings that he would not give the jury even a slight hint of its power to circumvent his instructions. If the legal system is ambivalent about whether the law fully captures the grounds for a just conviction, he was not. He had faith that the law of attempted murder, assault, reckless endangerment, gun possession, and self-defense was just and complete. There was no great issue of moral principle—like the legitimacy of the war in Vietnam—that the conventional rules of law did not express. The defense had not raised a principle of self-protection that went beyond the law as it was written. There was no need, therefore, to open a window to the jury's capacity to act lawlessly. Justice Crane decided boldly that he would change the standard jury instructions and make it clear the jury's function consisted exclusively in applying the law as stated in the court's instructions to the facts as they found them. Therefore, when Barry Slotnick tried to probe the prospective jurors about whether they felt obligated to convict even if they found Goetz guilty beyond a reasonable doubt, Justice Crane intervened. The jurors could not answer that question. They *were* obligated—and that is all there was to it.

At one point Justice Crane was inclined to instruct the jurors at the end of trial that if they found Goetz liable on the facts, they had a "duty" to convict him. But Mark Baker prevailed upon him to make the less noticeable change of converting the permissive use of *may* to a mandatory *must*. Therefore, he would instruct them, in effect, If you find beyond a reasonable doubt that all the elements of the crime are satisfied and that there is no recognized defense, you *must* convict Bernhard Goetz.

The jury never knew about the fretting and the negotiations beyond the scenes about their intrinsic power to vote their feelings and nullify the law. That, of course, was the point. The less they knew about their power to override the law, the more likely they were going to be to defer conscientiously to the law as the judge explained it to them.

Appealing to jury nullification is not the only way to bring to bear efforts to refine and perfect the law. The argument need not be ventured outside and beyond the law; the law itself admits of ongoing moral refinement and political argument. In the political cases of this century, the legal issue that has best captured political aspirations has been the defense of necessity. The defense provides a justification for infringing minor and sometime serious prohibitions of the criminal law when the attainment of some meritorious objective requires the action. If the political motives of the defendant rise to the level of moral conscience, they can support the characterization of the act as the lesser evil under the circumstances. In any sit-in carried out for a political purpose, the protesters can and do urge that conveying their political message necessitated the trespassory act. Sometimes the defense prevails, as in the recent acquittal of Abbie Hoffman and Amy Carter in Massachusetts.[12] In other situations, such as the efforts by an antiwar group called the Silo Pruning Hooks to dismantle missile silos with sledgehammers, the claim of necessity provides a medium in which the lawyers can express the defendants' motives of civil disobedience.[13] They may not secure an instruction to the jury on the issue, but bringing the question of necessity to the forefront profiles the case as raising issues of "higher law" that go beyond the conventional formulation of legal rules.

The claim of necessity can come to the aid of the defense even in prosecutions for more serious crimes. In the case of *United States v. Tiede,* tried in the summer of 1979 in West Berlin before a special court, the United States government prosecuted an East German defendant for having hijacked a Polish airplane in an effort to escape from East Germany.[14] Tiede had intimidated the crew by using a toy pistol he sneaked onto the plane. He hurt no one, though he roughly laid hands on one of the stewardesses. The plane landed at Tempelhof airport in the American zone in West Berlin, still technically occupied by the three Allied powers. The West Germans would not prosecute, and therefore the United States government took the legally unique move of establishing a court in Berlin that, applying American procedure and West German law, would sit in judgment of Tiede's hijacking.

The primary defense was necessity: Tiede had hijacked the airplane as the only way to avoid a pending prosecution in East Germany for his earlier efforts, illegal under East German law, to escape to the West. Though he was convicted on a minor charge, his argument of necessity prevailed and he walked out of the courtroom. The jury of West Berliners was convinced that what was at stake was not simply a criminal hijacking, but an act of risking danger to others as the only available means of securing the freedom that the jury undoubtedly thought was Tiede's inalienable right.[15]

Necessity was the only defense that might rescue Goetz from the charge of criminal possession of a weapon in the third degree. An innovation in the 1965 New York Penal Law,[16] taken directly from the Model Penal Code,[17] necessity has as its underlying principle the balancing of evils. The evil of violating the law is weighed against the evil that would occur if the offender did not nominally breach a statutory prohibition. In other words, the violation of the law is justified if it is the lesser evil under the circumstances. New York law requires further that the need for action arise without the fault of the actor claiming justification.

The necessity defense expresses the same commitment to the welfare of the public that supports the very crime of possessing weapons without a license. In the case of the prohibition, the public interest or welfare is expressed in a benefit to public safety that exceeds the cost to individual liberty resulting from the suppression of guns. Cost-benefit judgments of this sort pervade modern regulatory schemes. They always require a judgment not simply that conduct like possessing a gun is right or wrong in itself (because it is not right or wrong in itself), but that the expected benefits of the regulation exceed the expected costs.

Policy analysts, who rely on this method, do not shy away from assigning quantitative estimates to the expected benefits of a regulatory scheme. Let us suppose, therefore, that the expected increase in safety resulting from a ban on handguns is valued at 60 units, and the psychic costs to those, like Goetz, who want handguns but may not legally carry them is valued at 50 units of welfare. Economic analysts of law would come to this conclusion by determining how much the competing groups—those wanting to suppress and those wanting to possess handguns—would be willing to pay to determine the outcome of the dispute. If those wanting to suppress handguns would be willing to pay a total of 60 units of wealth (a unit would be, say, a million dollars) and those wanting to carry guns would be willing to pay a total of 50 units, then it serves the public interest to decide the dispute in favor of those willing to pay more. According to these hypothetical figures, the public benefit of gun control exceeds the cost and therefore it represents a sound public policy.

But a blanket prohibition against possessing guns would cover many instances and categories in which the benefit of carrying a gun clearly exceeded the cost. Banning handguns is not like banning the private possession of nuclear weapons or even the contemplated ban against possessing deadly pit bull dogs. There are many situations in which a sound analysis of the expected costs and benefits of possession would lead us to recognize exceptions to the general pro-hibition. That is why the statute prohibiting the possession of a loaded gun in public contains a catalog of possible exceptions in which a license to possess guns should be issued by a special office in the New York police department.

No one is entitled automatically to a license, but the statute mentions the following categories, among others, where a strong presumption favors granting a license to carry a loaded gun in public: messengers employed by banking institutions, justices and judges in the New York City courts, employees of prisons and other custodial institutions. A general catchall category provides, in addition, that a license should be granted "when proper cause exists for the issuance thereof."[18] Individuals who claim they are under special danger, perhaps because of their prominence in society, rely on the latter clause. The legislative judgment behind the licensing scheme is that in some special cases, the social benefit of carrying a gun exceeds the danger to society represented by one additional weapon on the streets. Critics of the scheme do not hesitate to point out that the rich and powerful, the Trumps and the Rockefellers, have no trouble showing that "proper cause" exists for awarding them a license.[19] But many other individuals have them as well. By the time of the Goetz trial, over 18,000* private persons, not connected to law en-forcement agencies, had permits to carry concealed weapons, and more than 7,000 had limited permits permitting them to keep hand-guns at home.[20]

As an individualized judgment of the public good justifies granting these permits to particular individuals, the defense of necessity invokes a general appeal to the public good to justify a limited exemption from the statutory prohibition. As the benefits of carrying a concealed gun prevail over the cost in 18,000 particular cases, the same calculus of interests should justify a limited class of individuals carrying con-cealed weapons where time and other circumstances do not permit the issuance of a license. The aim of the regulatory scheme, after all, is not to suppress all handguns, but only to keep guns from the hands of those whose probable use of them would violate the public interest.

The general defense of necessity builds on the premise that the criminal law should serve the public good; actions should be pun-ished only when they represent the type of conduct that the law

---

* This figure represents 0.2 percent of the city's 7,200,000 residents.

should deter. In particular subclasses of cases covered by sweeping regulatory schemes like the prohibition against possessing handguns, whenever the benefits of carrying a gun outweigh the costs, the public interest is served not by condemning and punishing, but by justifying and exempting these cases from the scope of the statute.

Necessity is a problematic defense, largely because in many cases in which it might apply—like hijacking an airplane to escape East Germany—the conduct imposes costs on totally innocent bystanders. The aggressor in a case of self-defense brings the harm on himself: with his aggressive act, he induces the defender to respond with force. But the passengers on the plane that Tiede hijacked did nothing to expose themselves to the risks entailed by his commandeering an airplane. That a totally innocent person suffers for the good of others made jurists prior to the last half century reluctant to recognize a general defense of necessity. It still has not been recognized in England.

The specific areas where the defense has made inroads, almost everywhere in the Western world, are abortion (when necessary to protect the life and health of the mother) and the destruction of property (when necessary to protect more valuable interests). In the face of an innocent victim, the doctrine of necessity has great difficulty accommodating homicide, attempted homicide, assault, and other crimes of aggression to persons. Respect for the autonomy of innocent persons makes us balk at justifying killing or injuring them for the sake of someone else's good. Significantly, these crimes of aggression invite application, under appropriate circumstances, of self-defense as a justification. It matters, obviously, whether the person who suffers the justified force is an innocent person or a wrongful aggressor.

Two distinct philosophical foundations have emerged for the necessity defense. According to one theory, the defense refines and furthers the legislative purpose expressed in the enactment of the basic prohibition—in the Goetz case, the prohibition against carrying a loaded gun in public. The legislature delegates, as it were, authority to the courts to carve out exceptions from the blanket prohibition. It might be difficult to maintain this argument as to the gun control laws of New York, however, for the legislature seems to have delegated the relevant authority to recognize exceptions to the licensing division of the police department.

The alternative foundation for the necessity defense is that regardless of the legislative purpose, conduct that is socially beneficial is by its nature not criminal and therefore ought not to be punished. The defense is grounded in a "higher law" of right and wrong that determines what ought to be criminal. This view of necessity gives the defense its moral force and makes it effective as the means for bringing the drive to perfect the law within the criteria of the law itself. When this version of the necessity defense prevails, the arguments for jury nullification become domesticated within the law as arguments about the higher law of necessity. That is why we have witnessed so many political cases in this century in which the necessity defense plays the role once fulfilled by appeals to the jury to vote their conscience regardless of the law.[21]

The New York necessity provision avoids grounding the defense in any particular rationale. Although the Model Penal Code provides that necessity be a defense only when "a legislative purpose to exclude the justification claimed does not otherwise plainly appear,"[22] the New York legislature modified the Model Penal Code formulation of the defense to omit reference to the legislative purpose. In New York, therefore, little weight should be accorded to the argument that the legislature meant to delegate exclusive authority to the police department to work out the exceptions to the blanket prohibition in the Penal Law.

There is no reason, in principle, why the New York necessity defense should not encompass the injury entailed by violating the prohibition against carrying a loaded gun in public. The statute recognizes the defense in principle anytime the action is "necessary as an emergency measure to avoid an imminent public or private injury" and the

> desirability and urgency of avoiding such injury clearly outweighs the injury sought to be prevented by the statute defining the offense in issue.[23]

In Goetz's case, however, it is difficult to determine what that injury is. He was charged with carrying a loaded weapon in public on December 22, 1984. The crime lasted, presumably, for no more than half an hour. The injury would consist in the risk that he would cause the gun to discharge accidentally or that he would use it to harm another unjustifiably. In his particular case, in view of his knowing how to handle guns, the risk of accidental discharge was minimal. There might have been a risk of an unjustified intentional shooting, but there was no evidence, apart from the subway shooting, that Goetz would actually use the gun, and whether he used the gun improperly in the subway shooting was precisely what the trial was about. For these reasons, it is difficult, in Goetz's case, to get a handle on "the injury sought to be prevented by the statute defining the offense in issue."

The benefit to be gained by Goetz's violating the gun possession law was protection against attack. In order to develop a case for this benefit, the defense would have had to paint the darkest possible picture of the dangers lurking in the New York subways. Crime statistics would be relevant, as would expert testimony on the protection afforded when properly trained persons carry weapons. If the defense developed this argument, they could bring to public attention Goetz's political views about the desirability of widespread distribution of guns in the public at large. This is, after all, his primary political commitment. The trial would become an arena for him to justify himself—not only under the law of self-defense, but under the principles of morality and public safety that in fact, he claimed, guided his life.

Building on the spirit of a universal right to protect oneself by bearing arms if necessary, the defense could well have constructed a limited defense of necessity and thereby countered the rejoinder that recognizing the defense of necessity would defeat the legislative program of suppressing handguns. There were significant, limiting facts in Goetz's situation including, first, that he was well trained in handling weapons; second, that he had been once victimized and was fearful of walking the streets; and third, that though he had drawn his gun too quickly on one occasion,[24] he had not shown any tendencies to use his guns in crimes initiated against totally innocent victims. If Justice Crane had recognized a claim of necessity limited by these factors, there would have been no need to worry that acquittals in this narrow class of cases would nullify the legislative prohibition.

The major legal hurdle to recognizing the defense would have been the New York requirement of "imminent public or private injury." The vague possibility of harm in the future cannot justify the present violation of the interest of others, however slight, in the immediate benefits of gun control. The defense should come into play only when there is no time to appeal to alternative means of preventing the injury. The imminence requirement frustrates many efforts to invoke the necessity defense in cases of political protest and civil disobedience. The standard reply by the government in prosecutions against peace advocates who have damaged governmental property is that the risk of war is not sufficiently imminent to justify nondemocratic means of protest.

The statute requires the imminence of a "public or private injury." The most serious harm Goetz feared was a repetition of the 1981 mugging on the subway. He could not walk the streets or ride the subway without fearing an attack. But how imminent was this harm? He carried the weapon for three years before he felt the need to use it. A more immediate harm would have been the anxiety he would have suffered walking the streets and riding the subways without a weapon. If the court would have recognized that anxiety as a private injury, he would have had a plausible basis for invoking the balancing scheme required for the necessity defense.

It is important to remember that all Goetz needed to do in order to bring the issue of necessity to the attention of the jury was make out a plausible claim under the statutory definition of the defense. The court would then have permitted defense counsel to address the jury on the issue, and the jury would have had to resolve the questions of value raised by the defense. A jury sympathetic to Goetz could well be expected to balance the conflicting injuries at stake (the harm to the public in carrying a gun as opposed to the harm to him in not carrying it) in his favor.

A basic question that could have determined whether Goetz could secure a jury instruction on necessity would have been whether the balancing of the competing interests should be carried out purely objectively or whether Goetz's fearful perceptions should have been allowed to tip the scales in his favor. If Justice Crane had engaged in objective balancing, he might well have decided the public harm of violating the law outweighed the cost to Goetz of complying with the prohibition. But, on this particular point, the New York cases might have given Goetz some legal support. Three recent precedents in New York, including a decision by the Court of Appeals, reverse the trial court for failing to grant the defendant instructions on necessity. All of these decisions stress the relevance of the defendant's subjective perceptions and imply that very little evidence of necessity should be sufficient to generate jury instructions on the issue.

All these decisions turn on the common theme of committing nominal crimes in an effort to avoid or escape from an attack. For example, in *People v. Padgett*, decided by the Court of Appeals in

1983,[25] the defendant had asserted necessity as a defense to a charge of malicious mischief for having crashed through a glass door in an effort to retreat from an assault. The trial court disregarded the defense, and the defendant was convicted. The Court of Appeals reversed on the ground that the judge should have given the instruction on necessity "if on any reasonable view of the evidence the fact finder [the jury or a judge exercising the jury's function] might have decided that the defendant's actions were justified."

In *People v. Green*,[26] decided by the Appellate Division, also in 1983, the circumstances were closer to the problem posed in the Goetz case. The defendant, a prisoner, was charged with "possessing dangerous contraband" in prison for picking up a knife dropped by his assailant in a fight and refusing to give it up immediately to prison guards. He could not invoke self-defense to justify his refusal to surrender the knife (the guards who demanded the knife were not attacking him). Yet he claimed "that he feared for his life and took possession of the knife to prevent his attacker from acquiring it and continuing the attack." In view of this subjective perception of danger, the court held that it was error for the trial court not to instruct that necessity would justify the illegal possession.

The third case, decided by the Appellate Division in 1973,[27] posed a complicated situation in which the claim of necessity, grounded in the defendant's fears of a gunman chasing him, allegedly justified erratic and dangerous driving in an effort to escape. The charges in the case were reckless endangerment and reckless assault against a police officer, who sought to arrest the defendant for his wild driving. If his driving violations were justified as a matter of necessity, then supposedly the police did not have legal grounds for the arrest. And if the arrest was not valid, his subsequent assault against the officer might not have been illegal. The reasoning of this case leaves something to be desired,[28] but the decision is helpful to Goetz in one important respect. The court stresses the subjectivity of the defense. If the defendant feared that "he was approached by a stranger carrying a gun," that was sufficient to warrant an instruction to the jury on the issue of necessity. If Goetz feared for his life if he did not carry a gun in nominal violation of the licensing law, he had a good basis, therefore, for asking for an instruction on the issue of necessity.

Admittedly, there is some authority in New York that would support turning down a request for these instructions on a charge of criminal possession in the third degree (a loaded gun in public).

One case in the Appellate Division[29] rejects the defense in a case of illegal gun possession even where the defendant faced actual threats to his life. More significantly, in *People v. Almodovar*,[30] the most recent relevant decision by the Court of Appeals, the court discusses the problem posed by taking a gun away from an assailant in the course of a fight and concludes that in this and similar cases of short-term possession, the defendant should rely not on a claim of justification, but on the judicially developed doctrine of "temporary and lawful possession."[31] The court continues:[32]

> A person either possesses a weapon lawfully or he does not and he may not avoid the criminal charge by claiming that he possessed the weapon for his protection. Justification may excuse[33] otherwise unlawful use of the weapon but it is difficult to imagine circumstances where it could excuse unlawful possession of it (cf. *People v. Padgett*).

The court goes on to suggest that the claim of justification it had in mind was self-defense rather than necessity.[34] And it is well established that self-defense is not available as a defense to charges of possession.[35] What is true about self-defense, however, need not apply to the distinct justification of necessity.

Significantly, the court approvingly cites the *Padgett* case, where the Court of Appeals reversed a conviction for failure to instruct on the defense of necessity. The most telling point is that there is no plausible rationale for the doctrine of "temporary and lawful possession" except the necessity of temporarily taking hold of the weapon. And if necessity can justify short-term possession, it is hard to see why, in principle, it should not be relevant to longer-term possession.

There is no way of knowing how the court would have reacted to a well-briefed and well-argued effort to introduce necessity as a defense to the charge of carrying a loaded gun in public without a license. There is good evidence that Justice Crane would have been unsympathetic to the argument.[36] But if the argument had been properly raised at trial, the defense would have had a solid basis for appealing the seemingly inevitable conviction on this charge.

A serious effort to secure instructions on necessity is the only path the defense could have followed in order to convert the case into a political challenge to the regulatory scheme that most frustrated and disturbed Bernhard Goetz. It would have been the way to make crime statistics on the subway relevant to the case. It would have been a way to address the root stimulus that governed Goetz's conduct over a period of years. Most significantly, the necessity defense would have provided the defense an opportunity to articulate the political forces that drove Goetz and fueled the outpouring of public sympathy on his behalf.

As it was, the defense preferred a low profile on the factors that made Goetz into a folk hero. They hoped that popular sympathy for their client would trigger defiance of the judge's instructions and an outright acquittal as a protest against crime. But they preferred to avoid systematic argument on the ultimate issues at stake. As they approached their final argument to the jury, they concentrated their energies on the shooting charges and the defense of self-defense. They had hopes of an acquittal on the charge of criminal possession of a weapon in the third degree, but they had not translated either their hopes or Goetz's popularity into an argument on which the jury could render a verdict of not guilty.

10
Arguing Toward
a Verdict

IF we take a step back from the outpouring of details in the Goetz trial, an elementary question presents itself. Why should anyone disbelieve Goetz's confession? The four hours of taped confession was the best guide we have to what happened on the IRT Saturday, December 22, 1984. The confession is so incriminating that one could hardly believe that Goetz was holding back damaging information. No one has ever suggested that the police induced him to tell a particular tale or that he was an innocent person making it all up.

Relying on the confession, the jurors would have a hard time concluding that Goetz acted reasonably toward Darrell Cabey. Even if they concluded that he was not guilty of assault and attempted murder toward his first three victims, the fourth and especially the fifth shots were different. If Goetz really did pause after the fourth shot, physically approach Darrell Cabey, and say, "You seem to [doing] all right; here's another," it would be almost impossible to construe this shot as a reasonable act of self-defense. There was no imminent attack, no need to defend against a passive young man sitting in a subway seat.

If guilt or innocence were to be decided on the basis of the confession alone, an open-minded jury, following the law, would be forced to vote for conviction. This particular jury, it is fair to say, would have voted guilty on the Cabey charges. But unfortunately for the prosecution, there was other evidence in the case, and not all of it squared with the story Goetz tells on the audio- and video-tapes.

Goetz says that he walked over to Cabey. But if he did that, there should have been a pause between the fourth and fifth shots. The witnesses in the car should have heard that pause. But eight witnesses testified that they did not hear a pause. They all testified that they heard the shots, in Slotnick's words, in "rapid succession." The testimony of the witnesses and the confession did not jibe. If Goetz actually walked over to Cabey, looked at him, and uttered a sentence, someone should have heard it.

Christopher Boucher, the star witness for the prosecution, testified not only that he heard the pause, but that he saw Goetz stand over Cabey and fire downward into the seat. Boucher said confidently that Goetz shot Cabey directly in the front of the chest. This was flatly inconsistent with the unrefuted medical evidence that the bullet entered Cabey's body in the lower back on the left side. Boucher also denied that Cabey jerked or twisted at the last second, which Goetz himself asserts on tape and which would have been the only way to reconcile Boucher's claimed perception of the event with the scientific evidence.

There were obviously anomalies in the evidence. When these minor inconsistencies present themselves in any scientific or historical investigation, the most tempting response is to explain them away as probably errors of perception or as problems on the fringes to be dealt with another time. Anomalies exist only by reference to a particular hypothesis. And the hypothesis that made the "rapid succession" of the shots ring inconsistent was the presumed accuracy of the confession. To hold onto the confession as the starting point for judging Goetz, the jurors had to dismiss the anomalies as problems at the fringe of the case.

When people are inclined to ignore or dismiss anomalies, they surely are able to do so. After all, in no field of inquiry does the evidence line up like the data in double-entry bookkeeping. In real life, some inconsistency of perception is normal. If Boucher had testified precisely as Goetz confessed, one would properly suspect foul play, perhaps that the prosecution had let him see the tape before his testimony. Talmudic lawyers were so sensitive to this danger that if two witnesses before the Sanhedrin agreed on every detail, the judges dismissed them as unreliable. In real life no two people see and experience the same event in the same way.

The jurors had direct experience with this phenomenon in court. In trying to re-create her recollection of hearing the shots, one of the witnesses, Sally Smithern, repeated "bam, bam" a number of times. Controversy followed among the lawyers and Justice Crane about the rhythm and spacing of the shots.[1] The press corps was also uncertain about how many shots she simulated. If those in the courtroom could not be certain about what they heard, how could the jurors expect the passengers on the train precisely to recall how many shots they heard and in what pattern?

The same uncertainty surrounded the observers' perception of Ramseur's intentions when he took his left shoe off. Did he intend to throw the shoe or merely to scratch his foot? Slotnick and some observers adamantly insisted that he intended a hostile act. Others, including the court officer standing next to Ramseur, said that he was just massaging his foot.[2] Perceiving an aggressive intent is often a matter of projecting our assumptions about the type of person the alleged aggressor appears to be. It is no surprise, then, that reasonable people might disagree about Canty's intentions when he asked for or demanded five dollars from Goetz.

When people are inclined to dismiss anomalies, there is no shortage of arguments for downplaying the significance of inconsistent data. But the defense had a different approach to these anomalies in mind. They wanted the anomalies to grow in number and significance to the point that they could not be ignored. When the inconsistencies generated by accepting the confession gained the upper hand, the jurors would no longer be able to assume that the confession, particularly the sequence about approaching and shooting Cabey, was accurate. If the defense was successful, the anomalies would overwhelm and then displace the hypothesis that generated them.

When the accumulated weight of anomalies overturns a reigning view of the world, one paradigm, or worldview, replaces another. The terminology of paradigmatic shift has its origins in the history of science, where contrary to popular belief, researchers do tolerate anomalies—so long as they do not stand out too prominently. For example, the Ptolemaic conception of the universe, the hypothesis that the earth was at the center of the universe, provided a perfectly good account of most of the observable data. The conception of orbits around the earth could explain everything that could be seen in the heavens, except that it had some difficulty accounting for the movement of the planets' moons, in particular Jupiter's moons. These moons sometimes appeared on one side of the planet and sometimes on the other side. These were anomalies, but to a point they were tolerable.

When the weight of these anomalies grew to the point that they could not be ignored and explained away as "epicycles," the Ptolemaic hypothesis simply caved in; a paradigmatic shift occurred in our understanding of the earth and its place in the universe.[3] The Copernican heliocentric system could explain the orbits on the planets' moons more simply and elegantly, and therefore it became the reigning conception of the solar system. Like every other hypothesis that simplifies the world, the Copernican system generated a few anomalies,[4] which, for the time being, were not disturbing.

The revolution from Ptolemaic to Copernican conceptions of the universe was a paradigmatic shift on a grand scale; the Goetz defense sought to bring off a shift that, in the total world of the Goetz trial, seemed of equally grand proportions. By hammering hard on the anomalies reflected in the thesis of "rapid succession" and the inconsistencies in Boucher's testimony, the defense sought to overturn the confession as the starting point for thinking about what happened in the subway shooting. They urged a paradigmatic shift: from confession as hypothesis to the alternative thesis that Goetz fired five shots in one continuous defensive response. If they could bring off this shift in thinking, the jury would judge all the shooting charges together. They would not distinguish victims and differentiate between self-defense against Canty and self-defense against Cabey.

To support their alternative hypothesis, the defense relied heavily on the testimony of their expert, former New York City Medical Examiner Dr. Dominick Dimaio, who claimed that according to the angle of the shot's entry and passage directly across the back, Cabey could not—a matter of physics—have been shot while sitting down. He was medically certain that a standing gunman could not have shot a sitting man at that angle. It followed, according to his logic, that Goetz must have shot Cabey with the fourth shot while both were standing up; the fifth shot missed and hit the cab wall. If Dimaio was right, then the defense had generated the biggest anomaly of all. The confession could not be accurate on Goetz's interaction with Cabey, for Goetz said that he shot him while he was sitting down. Either Goetz was wrong or Dimaio was wrong.

Dimaio was so certain of his position that Waples could do little on cross-examination to buttress his case against this scientific juggernaut. When it was his turn for rebuttal, Waples produced his own expert, Dr. Charles Hirsch, who testified that of course it was possible for Goetz to shoot Cabey while he was sitting down. Perhaps Waples had sealed up the hole that Dimaio had driven through the confession, but other troubling anomalies remained.

Slotnick and Waples devoted their closing arguments to the jury to attacking and defending the confession. Slotnick grounded his attack in two catchy slogans: "rapid succession" and "automatic pilot." The first summarized testimony of eight witnesses who failed to hear a pause after the fourth shot; and the second captured the testimony of Dr. Yudwitz, who provided an account of why Goetz might have emptied his gun without a pause.[5] Together these theses constituted the alternate hypothesis of the defense. If the jury felt the weight of the anomalies generated by the confession, their minds would rebel at the inconsistencies and they would accept Slotnick's alternative version of what happened. To back up his case, Slotnick tried as well to confirm his background truth that the four youths were the "gang of four," "predators" on society "who got what the law allowed."

When Waples began his response, he faced an uphill fight in vindicating the confession as the best explanation of what happened. Without Goetz's self-incriminating description of the deed and particularly of the Cabey shot, the prosecution hardly had a case. In contrast to his opening statement when he "was shaking like a leaf,"[6] Waples confidently approached the jury box and began his prepared statement with strong rhetoric designed to counteract Slotnick's assertion that the four "predators" got what they deserved:[7]

> Almost a century ago the highest Court in New York wrote, "The worst man has the same right to live as the best and no one may attack another because his general reputation is bad. The law protects everyone from unlawful violence, regardless of his character." This case, I submit, presents a monumental challenge to this most precious tenet of a free and democratic society.

Slotnick, Waples continued, was not committed to the principle of equal justice for all. The defense sought to establish that some "persons are above the law's sanctions and worse, that some people are below the law's protection."[8] This is as close as anyone came in the trial to addressing the unspoken racial dimension of the case.

Waples turned immediately to the major problem of his case: the fifth shot's crippling Darrell Cabey and, particularly, the confession as the centerpiece of his theory of the case. He sought to buttress the general reliability of the confession with a point-by-point breakdown of the factual components of Goetz's description of the train confrontation and a demonstration that each of his 17 listed components was corroborated by the testimony of others who were there.

The 17 points encompassed details ranging from whether Goetz stood up before he began shooting to the manner in which he escaped from the scene of the shooting.[9] The point of the exercise was to demonstrate that if the confession was reliable on so many points, there was no reason to doubt its validity on the critical question whether he approached Cabey and said, "You seem to be [doing] all right; here's another."

Despite the analytic finesse of his effort to bolster the confession, Waples made a significant concession in his argument that may have undermined his efforts. Trying to counter Slotnick's claim that if the jury should believe the witnesses' report that there was no pause and therefore no time for this interaction to occur, Waples conceded,[10]

> In all probability, the defendant uttered these words only to himself and probably not even mouthing the words, but just saying them in his own mind as he squeezed the trigger that fifth time.

Waples might have thought that he bolstered his credibility by acknowledging a weak point in his case. By backing off from the confession this far, however, he encouraged the jury to think that perhaps the confession was not as reliable as he, in other portions of his summation, claimed that it was.[11]

In order to fend off a paradigmatic shift to the twin theses of "rapid succession" and "automatic pilot," Waples had to counter the damaging testimony of Dr. Dimaio. If the jury believed Dimaio's claim that it was physically impossible for a standing Goetz to shoot a sitting Cabey, the confession would be overthrown. In an effort to turn Dr. Dimaio's testimony on its head, Waples built an entire theory around the undeniable fact that Cabey's jacket had two bullet holes in it.

On the second day of the trial the prosecution's ballistics expert, Detective Charles Haase, testified that there were two entrance points on one side of the jacket and two exit points on the other side.[12] One point had blood around it. Haase said this on the second day of the trial and no one sought thereafter to explain the obvious anomaly. Cabey had only one gunshot wound! There were two holes in the jacket, but only one hole in the body.

Waples seized on this fact and made it into an issue that cast its shadow on the rest of the trial and the jury deliberations. He introduced the novel theory that the fourth shot passed through the jacket without hitting Cabey and the fifth shot hit him, sitting down, precisely as the People had been arguing all along. Moving quickly, like an inexperienced actor anxious to get through his lines, he started to demonstrate his claim that both bullets passed through the jacket. He took a chair, positioned it in front of the jury box, took Cabey's jacket, and though this was a seemingly tainted object that everyone had handled gingerly, he suddenly put it on. He stood as Cabey was allegedly standing when the fourth bullet went through his jacket and crashed directly into the cab wall, then he sat down and re-created Cabey's helpless posture when the fifth bullet arguably entered his left back and severed his spinal column.

But Waples did not leave the matter at a simple claim that two bullet holes implied two bullets. He developed an argument to attack Dimaio's position that Cabey could not have been shot while sitting down. Waples's essential claim was that if the bullet that hit the cab wall also went through the jacket, that bullet had to have been fired while Cabey was standing up. The angle of impact precluded its having been fired downward while Cabey was sitting down.[13] From this sensible but by no means compelling premise, Waples made a gigantic logical leap: "And the shot that Dominick Dimaio, this expert, said could not have been fired while Darrell Cabey was sitting down, was fired when Darrell Cabey was sitting down."[14] The point of the demonstration was not only to refute Dimaio's scientific argument, but to show that the confession had to be right: Cabey was shot while sitting down.[15]

Slotnick listened to the argument without protesting. As soon as the summation was over, however, he acted as though Waples had committed an unpardonable prosecutorial sin. Never in the course of the trial had Slotnick fumed indignation as he did at Waples's demonstration. He had already given his summation and would not have another chance to address the jury. He demanded a mistrial, and if not that, at least an opportunity to call an expert to rebut the two-bullet thesis, and if not that, at least a chance to address the jury on the issue.

The fight about the two-bullet thesis raged through the last days of the trial, almost as though Goetz's guilt or innocence hung in the balance. It was never clear whether Slotnick was genuinely outraged or whether he simply tried to use this issue as a way of securing the right to address the jury once again. At first neither the defense nor Justice Crane seemed to understand Waples's arguments. Backed up by his investigator Frank King, Slotnick argued both that Waples

had impermissibly introduced new evidence in his summation—
Waples insisted his theory was a permissible inference from the evidence—and that Waples had told the jury something that was physically impossible. The defense's view, which they never presented to
the jury, was that one bullet made both holes. Yet if anything, this
was the impossible theory, for there is no way that a single bullet
can make two and only two holes in a jacket, unless the material
is folded and the bullet enters the inside of the jacket, exits, and
then reenters from the outside. Detective Haase had testified, however,
that both holes on the outside of the jacket were entrance holes
and thus there was no way to reconcile the single-bullet hypothesis
with the evidence received in the trial and binding on the theories
the lawyers could present to the jury.[16]

The demonstration had a powerful dramatic impact. The message
was not so much in the solution of the logical puzzle, one bullet or
two, but in Waples's medium—his putting on the jacket, his becoming
Darrell Cabey, if only for an instant, in the eyes of the jury. The
jacket was ragged and filthy; it bore the bloodstains of a man paralyzed for life. Waples's putting it on made Cabey, never seen at the
trial, seem that much more real. His sitting in the chair disturbed
Slotnick not because of Waples's logical legerdemain, but because
the jury could see, perhaps for the first time, This was someone
like us who was wearing that jacket and shot while he was sitting
down. As Slotnick conceded in the course of his protesting Waples's
action over and over again:[17]

> I could certainly think of a million things I could have said in
> summation that would have a dramatic impact. . . . I think the
> most telling thing that Waples did was put on that jacket, sit down,
> and talk about two bullets.

Whatever Slotnick's reasons for his apparent outrage, he would
not stop arguing the issue. Justice Crane denied his motions to reopen
his case and to address the jury on the issue of one or two bullets.
But his vehemence left its mark. Justice Crane too was confused by
the argument. Crane apparently thought that Waples had claimed
that both bullets had passed through the jacket while Cabey was
sitting down, which he deemed to be inconsistent with the physical
evidence on the angle of impact against the cab wall. Crane thought
the demonstration might lead the jury to think that there were six
bullets—an additional one to account for the second hole. He communicated his concern to the jury early in the charge:[18]

I am not telling you what evidence does not establish, nor is this example an approval or disapproval of any argument in summation by respective counsel. . . . But, for example, you heard from Detective Haase that there were two bullet holes in . . . Darrell Cabey's jacket. The People, in summation, *postulate* that one of these holes under the arm was made by the first bullet while Cabey was standing and that the second hole lines up with the bullet that entered his body. You heard testimony that the bullet that did not enter his body hit the conductor's cab wall more or less flatly. You are not to speculate that there was yet another bullet unaccounted for. . . .

The use of the word "postulate" instead of "infer" or "conclude" reflected Crane's identification with the defense's complaint that Waples's argument went beyond the evidence. Referring to the possibility of another bullet to make sense of the argument confirmed his message to the jury that there was something suspect about the prosecution's maneuver. Yet Slotnick was not satisfied even with this concession. As the jury retired to begin its deliberations, the defense continued to press its offensive for some last-minute advantages that Slotnick might derive from Waples's supposed sin in making a novel argument from the evidence.[19] Waples had made a grand effort to save and bolster the confession as the reigning hypothesis of the trial, but the surprise and the dramatic impact of his demonstration generated a counterreaction by the defense and the court. He triggered a debate that took on a life of its own. The outcome was an instruction to the jury that subtly undermined his credibility as an advocate.

Paradigmatic shifts do not occur, either in science or in law, on the basis of reason alone. Relying solely on the data and the construction of a reasoned hypothesis, scientists could still use the Ptolemaic system to explain the movements of the planets. The Copernican system is simpler and more elegant, and for that reason it triumphed in the history of science. But neither this nor other scientific revolutions are fueled simply by the "truth" of the competing hypothesis. There are always personal and psychological factors that induce a younger generation of scientists to shift their loyalties to a new hypothesis that more simply accounts for the anomalies generated by the old system.

Similarly, the shift from the confession as the reigning explanation of the Cabey shooting to the defense's theory—"rapid succession" and "automatic pilot"—would hardly occur just on the basis of reasoned argument. Of course, reason plays the role of demonstrating inconsistencies. But the problem always is, How many inconsistencies can we tolerate before we shift our loyalties to a new hypothesis? Our tolerance level is inescapably affected by personal influences.

In a trial, with the jurors constantly focused on what the combative lawyers are doing and saying, a minor slip, a personal offense, can make the jurors more receptive to a competing hypothesis on the evidence. Waples made one such slip. It is difficult to know whether the slip actually drove some people over to the defense's theory on the evidence. But offend them he did.

Waples suggested that perhaps Goetz brought the problem on himself. At one point in his closing argument, he said:[20]

> one really has to wonder why the defendant deliberately seated himself in an area of the car that is not only in the middle of this group of rambunctious young teens, but . . . is in a location where he is at least psychologically isolated from all the other passengers on the train.

The implication was that Goetz should have ceded the subway car to the "rambunctious young teens." But for most concerned New Yorkers who followed the Goetz case, the issue was precisely the right of decent citizens to hold their ground against the terrorizing effect of the mugging subculture. Waples compounded the error:[21]

> If this defendant, simply because he's been mugged by a group of young teens in the past is now so anxious about his own safety, that he's going to perceive every unpleasant encounter such an ominous threat that it must be answered by gunfire and possibly death then I suggest a solution is not for the defendant to pull out his gun at the mere indication of approaching danger. I suggest a solution for the defendant [is] to pack his bags and go somewhere else where his fragile sensibilities will not be so easily assaulted.

Of course, Waples had a point, but it was the right psychological insight at the wrong time. The jurors were under strict orders from the judge not to discuss the case prior to their formal deliberations, but one of the jurors, Michael Axelrod, responded to Waples's pushing some of the blame for the confrontation onto Goetz by muttering, "This guy is insulting my intelligence." Carolyn Perlmuth, who regarded Waples's summation as impressive, did not regard the remark as "excessive," but another juror, Mark Lesly, thought the suggestion that you had to be tough to live in New York "alienated everyone."[22]

Waples had entered treacherous territory. He crossed the line between psychological analysis and arguments about personal rights. The jury was presumably more concerned about whether Goetz had a right to defend himself than with his propensity for suffering avoidable problems. But only the deliberations would reveal whether this slip took its toll in moving the jury to reject the confession and adopt the defense's paradigm of what happened in the shooting of Darrell Cabey.

After two days of closing argument and then nearly a day of Justice Crane's explaining the elements of liability and of self-defense, the jury finally retired on Friday, June 12, to their windowless room behind the courtroom. They knew the place well—the mismatched chairs, no two alike, the seminar table dominating the room with its lacquered-on wood sides splitting off, the two tiny bathrooms at the far end of the room. They had already spent hours there every day while the lawyers and Justice Crane fought out the contours of the evidence they would be allowed to hear.

During the six weeks of rigorous discipline, they could not read newspapers or watch the media coverage of the case. They could not speak to each other or to their friends or family about the matter that was most on their minds—the barrage of evidence and innuendos that they were exposed to every day. By and large, according to two jurors interviewed in depth,[23] the group held to this discipline. They busied themselves in the jury room during the trial by playing cards and shooting baskets with paper balls into a hoop rigged up at one end of the room. Now as they entered the room on June 12, the discipline was relaxed. Newspapers were still off limits, but they could talk freely. They could finally share their feelings and thoughts about whether Goetz committed a crime or acted in self-defense.

How were they to begin? The only rule they had to guide them was that their verdict, guilty or not guilty, had to be unanimous. They were given a charge sheet, which called for a verdict of guilty or not guilty on the 13 original charges[24] plus five lesser charges that would come into play if they found Goetz not guilty of the most serious felonies.[25] They did not have any of the exhibits used in the course of the trial, and they did not have a copy of Justice Crane's prolix charge explaining the law. They had to rely on their memories, but they knew that if their memories failed or if they disagreed about the evidence, they could have specific exhibits sent into the jury room or they could return to the courtroom and have specific passages of the transcript read to them.

As the first juror whose name was picked out of the hat, James Hurley, a 29-year-old white financial analyst, was their foreman. He would speak for the jury when they returned to the courtroom to request information or to deliver their verdict. The jurors agreed that he would chair the discussion. It was clear at the outset that the jurors brought to their deliberations a strong sense of orderly procedure. They agreed they would raise their hands and speak when recognized. And they immediately tackled a problem they could easily have deferred. Should they vote by secret ballot or by voice vote?

The issue was charged. One of the jurors, Catherine Brody, a 59-year-old English professor in a New York technical college, sensed immediately that she might be in a minority favoring conviction. In the face of social pressure, she could hold to her position more readily if the voting was anonymous. She urged her fellow jurors to proceed by secret ballot, and they agreed. But at that moment, Carolyn Perlmuth, a 31-year-old editor from the Upper West Side, was in the bathroom at the end of the jury room. When she returned to the deliberations, she was informed of the decision. "What do you mean, secret ballot?" she protested. "That is what we decided," replied Brody. At Perlmuth's insistence, the question was reopened, and she argued strongly that they should know who might be holding out and why. That would be the only way, she maintained, to address the objections of the minority. One of the jurors related an experience of deliberating in another case with secret ballots; they never knew who the holdout was until in desperation the majority forced a voice vote. The Goetz jury finally agreed, over some objections, that they would proceed by openly declaring their votes.

The charges given to the jury were listed in the following order: the counts from the first indictment and then from the second indictment, both listed in order of decreasing gravity. The most serious charge returned by the January grand jury was criminal possession of a weapon in the third degree. There was little room to question the allegation that Goetz knowingly possessed a loaded gun away from his home or his office. That he fired the gun on the subway made discussion almost superfluous. The defense claimed neither that he had a permit nor that he carried the gun out of self-protective necessity. There was no issue, factual or legal, on which jurors sympathetic to Goetz could gain a foothold and develop even a speculative case for acquittal. It took the jury about 15 minutes to convict on the first charge.

The charges of criminal possession in the fourth degree, based on the possession of two guns in Myra Friedman's apartment on December 30, 1984, would seem to have been equally straightforward. Carolyn Perlmuth says that she was convinced at the outset that the prosecution's case on this charge was "open and shut"; accordingly, she voted guilty on the first couple of ballots. Myra Friedman testified that Goetz came to her apartment on December 30 with the guns in a cardboard hatbox and that she kept the box until she took it to her lawyer's office three days later and Detective Michael Clark opened the box and found the guns. Two gun dealers testified that Goetz had bought from them precisely these two firearms, identified by their serial numbers—a Smith & Wesson model 60 .38 special revolver (similar to the gun used in the shooting) bought from a Connecticut dealer in 1970, and a 9-mm semiautomatic pistol bought in Florida a few months before the shooting in 1984. Thus the jury had a full explanation of how Goetz acquired the guns and how they ended up in the hands of the police. It did indeed appear to be an "open and shut" case.

Yet, in contrast to the first charge, where the law fit the facts like a glove on a fat fist, the law on this charge left room for speculation. If the jury did not believe Myra Friedman's testimony about Goetz's giving her the guns, the prosecution's tight case might begin to come apart. Justice Crane himself had thrown a legal conundrum at the jury that could readily instill doubts about Friedman's testimony. If the jury should find that Myra—as everyone called her—was an accomplice, then they could not accept her testimony unless it was corroborated by independent evidence "tending to connect the defendant with the commission of the crime."[26] An accomplice is someone who participates in committing the crime and whose testimony might therefore be questionable, if only because he or she might be trying to shift responsibility onto the other party.

The jury's willingness to disbelieve Myra required only the slightest encouragement. Early in the deliberations, juror Robert Leach, a black bus driver from Harlem in his mid-fifties, declared that he did not believe Myra. How could he not believe her? She indisputably turned the guns over to her lawyer and the police: were they lying too? No, the problem, as the jury began to pick away at the prosecution's case, was whether Goetz gave her the guns on the date alleged. Perhaps he sold them to her at some earlier date. At that point, Carolyn Perlmuth reports:

People were coming up with the wildest scenarios as reasons for doubt. There were people who doubted Detective Clark's testimony that they opened . . . the box with the guns . . . at the lawyer's office. There were people who thought Clark was lying about everything he said. That . . . I couldn't figure out at all. . . .

The majority was still for conviction, but doubts were growing. Before the day was out, the jury had passed a note to Justice Crane requesting clarification of the legal concepts that bore on the charge of criminal possession in the fourth degree. They needed to know more about who is an accomplice and what was corroboration. Also, they were so puzzled by the arcane legal language used to define "constructive" possession,[27] which is used in turn to define the range of the possession prohibited by the statute, that they could barely identify the problem.[28]

Instructing a jury is an exercise in teaching. But the teaching is restricted to lecturing without feedback and questions. The judge as teacher cannot try one explanation and then ask, "Do you get it now?" If the jury as students do not understand, they cannot raise their hands and ask questions. All they can do is formulate a question in a note for transmission to the judge; the question gives the judge an opportunity to clarify his original instructions. The jury must then return to their deliberation room, ponder the response, and, if they are still puzzled, write another note. The formality of communication seeks to secure the jury's privacy and insulation from the impromptu opinions of the judge, lawyers, and others in the course of their deliberations.[29]

Justice Crane sought to ease the jury's confusion by reading the vague statutory definitions of an accomplice as someone who participated in the crime and then adding the dictionary definition of "participation" as someone "sharing in" the commission of the crime. It certainly seemed as if Myra shared in the possession of the guns; what Justice Crane did not tell the jury is that if she possessed them only temporarily with the intent to surrender them to the police at the first convenient moment, then she was not an accomplice. The court's clarification of corroboration was more helpful, for Justice Crane told the jury what was at stake:[30]

> such other [corroborating] evidence standing alone must satisfy the jury that it tends to connect the defendant with the commission of the crime in such a way as may reasonably satisfy you that the accomplice is telling the truth.

He supplemented this instruction by suggesting that either the testimony of the two gun dealers or the recovery of the two guns by the police might be sufficient to validate Myra's testimony. But the seeds of doubt were already sown and sprouting in the jury's deliberations. Mark Lesly, one of the younger members of the jury, emerged quickly as a strong voice in the discussions. He zeroed in on Myra's motives:

> Now, with Myra, she is a writer. We had established in Goetz's statement [i.e., confession] that Goetz sold guns for cost to his friends. Let us suppose, hypothetically, that Myra bought these guns from him two years ago. Then she finds out that he is the subway vigilante. You know, if I make a story out of this,[31] I can get a front page article in New York Magazine and make several thousand dollars with it. I am not saying that happened. But it is a reasonable motivation for her lying.

This is not an absurd scenario. Myra Friedman did in fact tape Goetz's telephone conversation with her shortly before he turned himself in, and, as the jurors were told, she used that conversation as a basis for an article in *New York* magazine.[32] It is not clear, however, if the guns were hers, how surrendering them to the police and saying that her friend Bernie gave them to her would add to the marketability of her story. And why should one believe speculative theories about Myra's motives rather than her unrefuted testimony? But then again, if Goetz took pains to burn his clothes and disassemble and discard one Smith & Wesson .38 revolver in the Vermont woods (the one he used in the shooting), why would he deliver the other one in a hatbox to his neighbor?

Amidst this controversy about whether Myra was lying, the jury came back to court with a request to hear her testimony reread and to hear anything that Goetz might have said about giving her the guns on December 30. If Goetz had said something on this point, that would probably have settled the matter in the jury's mind. But he had not. And that left Myra—the woman who had already exploited her friendship with Goetz—as the backbone of the prosecution's case. Saturday at noon, on the second day of deliberations, a third note came out of the jury room, again requesting all references to Myra in the four hours of taped confession. There were none. Doubts were growing. In the end, the backbone of the case buckled under the weight of imaginative brainstorming about why an uncontradicted witness might be lying. The 12 jurors eventually came around to the position of the skeptics and, to the surprise of the trial observers, voted unanimously that Goetz was not guilty of criminal possession in the fourth degree.

Though this charge had the minor status of a misdemeanor (which the jury did not know), the method of deliberation must have given the jury a sense of confidence in their ability to reason together and to reject, if they so desired, the testimony of a witness they did not believe. The deliberations on the next set of charges, attempted murder against each of the four youths, confirmed their ability to reason through a problem together. Everyone assumed that the problem with both the attempted murder and assault charges would be self-defense. Before they could get to the issue of self-defense on the attempted murder charges, however, the jurors had to be convinced that Goetz's shooting satisfied the basic elements of the offense, including the requirement of an intent to cause the death of each victim by shooting him.

The defense made only an indirect approach to the question of Goetz's intent to cause the death of Canty, Allen, Ramseur, and Cabey. Mark Baker argued to the court (not to the jury) that Waples's emphasizing Goetz's mental instability was tantamount to alleging his insanity at the time of the act and, therefore, that Waples could not simultaneously argue that Goetz was insane and that he intended to kill the four youths. Baker was appealing to a more complex conception of intention, one that presupposed a responsible choice to engage in the action. Because an insane actor is not responsible for his choices, he or she cannot harbor this complex version of criminal intent. Though there are some cases and legal materials to support Baker's view, lawyers generally think of intent in narrow terms, defined independently of responsibility. Accordingly, Justice Crane defined intent to mean nothing more than "having the conscious aim or objective" of bringing about a particular result. Even if insanity had been an issue in the case, the jury would have been expected to find first that Goetz intended to kill in this limited sense and then subsequently to assess his responsibility or sanity at the time of the deed.

Apart from this indirect legal attack, the defense never seriously challenged whether, as a matter of fact, Goetz intended to cause death by shooting the four youths. The jury never heard an argument that perhaps Goetz did not "have the conscious aim or objective" to kill. Indeed the defense seemed willing to let Goetz's confession stand on this point. They made no effort to interpret his own repeated admission that his intention "was to [do] anything [he] could to hurt them. . . . to murder them, to hurt them, to make them suffer as much as possible." Goetz had not doubted that he was a murderer in his heart. The defense seemed willing to fold on the issue of intention and place its bets entirely on the justification of self-defense.

The objective facts and Goetz's own declarations bespeak a clear objective to kill his perceived aggressors, if only to ward off the attack. As lawyers look at the problem, denying Goetz's intent to kill would seem to require the hypothesis that he intended merely to injure the youths. This might have been the case if he had fired at their legs, but he purposely and systematically fired directly at their midsection. They were all hit in the chest or back. With the exception of Baker's claim that the insane do not intend their actions, intent seemed to be an issue beyond dispute.

Yet the jurors had another way of thinking about the intent to kill. Apparently D. Wirth Jackson, a 74-year-old retired engineer, posed the question "Where have they proved the intent to murder?"[33] The jurors began thinking seriously, in ways that the lawyers had not even contemplated, that perhaps Goetz did not really have the required intent. As Mark Lesly recounts his experience, he initially argued to his fellow jurors that "anytime you point a handgun at somebody, with hollow point bullets no less, that's attempting to murder somebody." He changed his mind, however, and became convinced that unless there was a clear motive to murder, there was no intent to kill: "We needed a motive for murder. The only motive that Waples presented us was this revenge. And we didn't buy it."

Mixing the issues of motive and intent moved the jury closer to a moral conception of intent. The cold factual judgment that an actor sought to bring about a particular result was not enough to find an intent to murder or to kill. In the jury's lay understanding of the term, the required intention has to be an impulse that makes you morally blameworthy for the act. If the motive for the killing is not heinous, there is no intent worthy of moral censure.

Carolyn Perlmuth concurred in this line of thought:

> It was obvious that if you shoot someone, you run the risk of killing someone. [Goetz] was aware of that possibility but I don't think he identified that one thing as what he wanted by shooting them.

Ms. Perlmuth interpreted the definition of intent as "conscious aim or objective" to require not that the intent be in the service of a bad motive, but that the desired end of the action be death and only death. That Goetz admitted his intent to kill was not persuasive, for she once had a similar experience of murderous rage after a mugging:

> I did have this one incident where my mother was mugged . . . we were together and my mother was mugged. I just felt fear at the time, but afterwards I really felt that I wanted to kill the guy. I wouldn't have dreamed about being serious, I really want to kill. . . . this did influence me [in the deliberations].

Another juror, Diana Serpe, a 33-year-old airline employee, reasoned in much the same way that Goetz's recollections of his intention might well have reflected rage that set in after the event. A majority eventually came over to this position and found Goetz not guilty on all four counts of attempted murder. They never even reached what everyone thought would be the critical issue: self-defense. Their moralist conception of the intention required for attempted murder led them to think that if he could not have intended to kill.

Indirectly and implicitly, they incorporated Goetz's purpose of defending himself into their analysis of his intention under their various conceptions of intent. It would have been difficult to persuade Lesly, for example, that Goetz had a malicious motive to kill, for his apparent and presumptive motive was to ward off the attack. From Perlmuth's point of view, the motive of self-defense precluded a finding that Goetz desired the death of the victims as the "one thing . . . he wanted by shooting them." Thus considerations of self-defense came into the jury's deliberations by the back door— as a factor bearing on "intent to cause death."

As self-defense became an issue bearing on intention, the defense gained a conceptual advantage they thought they had lost. The District Attorney's office fought an appellate battle for nearly a year in order to establish the objective standard for assessing claims of self-defense. The fear and violent response of someone defending himself must be judged not solely by his own motives, but by the hypothetical fear and response of a reasonable person under the circumstances. But as the jury considered Goetz's motive to defend himself as a factor bearing on his intent to kill, they placed the entire burden of their analysis on his subjective perceptions and motives. It could only be these subjective motives—not the moral quality of his act as measured against the standard of reasonableness—that could influence the analysis whether he had a bad motive for shooting. Even an unreasonable belief in the necessity of self-defense was a good-faith belief, and if Goetz was acting in good faith, he did not have a criminal motive. Accordingly, if he desired to defend himself, he did not desire the death, in Perlmuth's words, as the "one thing . . . he wanted by shooting them."

The most carefully constructed legal edifices crumble at the touch of the jury's common sense. Their reasoning was not simply an expression of sympathy for Goetz. Their conception of the intention required for attempted murder is well grounded in the way ordinary people think about murder. The jurors interpreted the phrase "conscious aim or objective" differently from the way lawyers ordinarily understand its import.[34] But it makes sense to read this phrase as requiring that the defendant have intended death not as a means of defending himself but as an end in itself. It makes sense to require that the intent for attempting the heinous crime of murder be one that subjects the actor to censure and blame. As the jury viewed the problem, if Goetz had good motives, he could not be blamed for his shooting. Goetz may have thought he was a murderer in his heart, but according to the jury, he was not.

As a result of admitting a subjective theory of self-defense by the back door, the jury abandoned the task of judgment that the Court of Appeals had laid before it. They were supposed to consider not only whether Goetz had good motives, but whether he overreacted in formulating those motives. Their job was to get behind his intention and judge whether a reasonable person would have found shooting necessary under the circumstances. Yet they brought their common sense and their moral sensibilities to the instructions that Justice Crane gave them, and as a result they fashioned a mode of analysis that no one expected.

It is difficult to know how much of the instructions the jury could absorb simply by having the arcane and convoluted legal phrases read and reread to them. The jurors seem not to have noticed the subtle changes that were occurring in the instructions on self-defense each time they were read to them. In fact a controversy was raging in the courtroom about these instructions even as they were deliberating.

In the initial instruction defining the criteria and scope of self-defense, Justice Crane illustrated the principle that the defendant could not use more force than he reasonably believed necessary. He could not legitimately shoot, for example, if he "reasonably believed [i.e., should have believed] that he could have repelled any threat without firing his gun, for example, by drawing and displaying his weapon."[35] This example galvanized the defense into an unending campaign to modify the instructions and delete the suggestion that brandishing the pistol might have been sufficient to ward off the attack. They claimed that by introducing this example Crane was "marshalling the evidence," namely instructing the jury about the evidence supporting each side of an argument. Commenting on the evidence is considered inappropriate because the judge might thereby unwittingly lend his weight to a particular interpretation of the evidence.

The campaign to change the instructions began in earnest on Saturday afternoon, June 13, when the jury requested a reading of the attempted murder and justification charges. Slotnick and Baker pressed both for dropping the reference to "drawing and displaying his weapon" and for including a reference to Dr. Yudwitz's expert testimony that some people go on "automatic pilot" when they begin shooting under stress. There was no apparent theory under which they were entitled to both of these changes. If the reference to "drawing and displaying the weapon" was too detailed, if it veered too much in the direction of commenting on the evidence, then what possible justification could there be for singling out Dr. Yudwitz's testimony and signaling the jury that it was relevant to the question of reasonable self-defense? Yet the debate on the issue was one-sided. Waples said simply that he thought the original charge was correct; Slotnick and Baker tirelessly demanded the changes.

Crane then "capitulated"[36] to the defense's demand, as he later expressed it himself. He modified the charge on justification by dropping the language about "displaying the weapon" and twice repeating the following new instruction on the relevance of Dr. Yudwitz's testimony:[37]

> In assessing [the defendant's] belief and its reasonableness, you may consider the testimony of Dr. Bernard Yudwitz concerning the operation of the autonomic nervous system and its effect on the firing of a weapon in the circumstances you find were facing the defendant.

Justice Crane justified this change by claiming that it was merely "clarifying"[38] the charge and providing "an amplification of the passage talking about considering all the circumstances and facts."[39] He was, however, doing much more than that. Even apart from the signal implicit in making a change, the instruction on Yudwitz's testimony contained within it an unwarranted factual assumption, namely that Goetz was one of those people whose firing conformed to the pattern of automatic reaction about which Yudwitz had testi- fied. He had no basis for inferring that Goetz fit the general pattern he described, and yet the instruction informed the jury that anyone "in the circumstances you find were facing the defendant" was cov- ered by Yudwitz's testimony on the effect of the autonomic nervous system.

By agreeing to this change in the instructions, Justice Crane seemed to indicate a preference for the defense, which was probably not his intention. This generated an unfavorable image in the public mind—at worst of possible partiality toward the defense and at best of weakness and indecisiveness.[40] Most seriously, now that Slot- nick and Baker knew that they could get the judge to modify the instructions, they would press relentlessly for additional changes. Indeed as soon as Crane was done reading the modified instruction, they complained that he had not gone far enough: he should have referred specifically to their theory of "rapid succession" in explaining the relevance of Yudwitz's testimony.

On Monday morning, after a day of rest to ponder what had happened Saturday afternoon, everyone returned to court, steeled for further confrontation on the instructions. If Crane was inclined to recant his modified instructions, the defense would be sure to maintain pressure on him to go even further. In fact, they tried to persuade Justice Crane to call in the jury and read an additional instruction underscoring their theory of "rapid succession." Justice Crane, for his part, seemed chagrined that he had made any changes at all. He insisted that the original charge was fair and described his decision on Saturday as a response to Slotnick's "passionate"[41] demand. Then, he said, "I threw in the towel, so to speak."[42] Now, he indicated, he would be firm.

Yet the very next note from the jury reopened the wounds left by Waples's closing argument about the two bullet holes in Darrell Cabey's jacket. The jury wanted to see the jacket itself as well as the screwdrivers and hear the testimony reread about the bullet holes. It was clear that they were concentrating on the charge either of attempted murder or of assault against Cabey. The possibility that the jury might accept Waples's thesis that two bullets passed through the coat rekindled Slotnick's passions. And this time Justice Crane was more sympathetic. He too had come to believe that Waples's demonstration posed a problem of physics. It was hard for him to see that the same bullet could have passed through the left side of Cabey's coat while he was standing, crossed in front of Cabey's chest without grazing him, and then impacted flatly on the panel at the end of the car. This led him to fear that perhaps the jury would think a sixth shot was necessary to account for all the data—the two holes in the jacket as well as the flat impact on the cab wall.[43]

All the jury had requested was to see Cabey's jacket and hear the testimony pertaining to the jacket. Nonetheless, after calling the jury back into the courtroom, Justice Crane volunteered some gratuitous comments about the likelihood that Waples's thesis was correct. He stressed that there was no evidence to support Waples's demonstration, so that it "must rest on inferences from the facts in evidence principally the testimony of Detective Haase [that there were two bullet holes]."[44] And then he repeated a previous admonition:[45]

> where two inferences may reasonably be drawn, one consistent with innocence and the other consistent with guilt, the defendant is entitled to the inference of innocence.

He added similar warnings about not "speculating" that there were more than five bullets or making inferences that were physically impossible. It would have been difficult for the jury not to get the impression that Justice Crane was skeptical about Waples's entire demonstration. Waples himself was outraged by the relentless attack on his argument finally issuing in a victory for the defense. As soon as the jury left the room, he exploded:[46]

> I think what I just heard was the most one sided and most unwarranted instruction that I have ever heard given to a jury. It's completely unfair. I made a perfectly proper argument based on the evidence again repeated here, and I just cannot fathom how your Honor can give that instruction in good conscience to this jury.

The jury was indeed concerned at that moment about the Cabey count, and the exact manner of the shooting was high on the agenda of concerns. They had already reached a verdict of not guilty on the four counts of attempted murder and were now pondering the assault charge against Cabey. Significantly, they had concluded that Goetz's actions had not satisfied the elements of assault in the first degree,[47] including the required intent to cause serious physical injury.

It is not easy to explain why the arguments about intention that carried the day in the discussion of attempted murder did not lead to a similar conclusion in the analysis of assault. Logically, a good motive seems to preclude an intent to injure as an end in itself as much as it negates an intent to kill as an end in itself. But perhaps the intent to injure is morally more neutral and this made a difference in the jury's reasoning. Whatever the logic, the jury were not willing to think about intending to kill as a means of acting in self-defense; if they had, they would have found the intent and then turned to the issue of reasonable self-defense. But they were willing to contemplate intending to inflict serious physical injury as a step in the complex action of defending oneself. Thus they affirmed the intention and turned to the distinct problem of justification by self-defense.

In that context they had to ponder the mystery of how Goetz inflicted the damaging shot to Cabey's spinal cord. Was it the fourth or fifth shot? Was Cabey standing or sitting? Did Goetz pause and approach Cabey? As these questions would be resolved, so would the jury's judgment about the reasonableness of Goetz's response.

The juror Lesly had completely absorbed Waples's rapid, nervously executed demonstration of the claim that two bullets passed through Cabey's jacket. As he understood Waples's thesis, Cabey was standing facing the near wall of the train on the fourth shot and then spun around and sat down prior to the fifth shot. This may not be precisely the way Waples had intended the demonstration, but it made good sense of the physical fact that the bullet made a direct impact against the cab wall.[48] On the basis of this scenario of the shooting, Lesly reports, "I would have ruled against Goetz on the Cabey count."

Seeing Cabey's jacket in the jury room and hearing the testimony reread changed Lesly's mind. His understanding of Waples's thesis presupposed that the fourth shot passed through Cabey's jacket from inside to outside. But Detective Haase had testified that both entrance holes were on the outside of the jacket.[49] As soon as he learned of this during the reading, his view of the entire case was shaken:

> When I found out that according to the prosecution's expert that both of those bullets went from the outside of the jacket to the

inside, then that proved that what Waples said, could not have happened. Now I am not saying that we found him not guilty based on this alone.

The controlling point in Lesly's thinking was the angle of impact against the cab wall. If both bullets entered the jacket from the outside, that meant that Cabey must have been standing, with his back to the near wall, when the fourth shot went through the jacket without grazing him. But if his body was between the near wall and the bullet that missed him, that bullet could not, in Lesly's view, have impacted flatly against the cab wall. This was enough to convince him that "what Waples said could not have happened." We can be sure that Lesly pressed his change of heart on the jurors. He was so vocal in the deliberations that the other jurors dubbed him "Barry, Jr." after Barry Slotnick. In any event, with jurors of Lesly's sophistication and attention to detail, Justice Crane had no cause to worry that either Slotnick or Waples could confuse the 12 laypeople who had to decide the case.

The jurors Perlmuth and Lesly were fully aware of the tactical advantage of Waples's not having made his demonstration of the Cabey shots until his closing argument, thereby precluding a response from Slotnick. Perlmuth found the maneuver mildly improper. She was "kind of shocked" by a demonstration "when there was no evidence to support it." Lesly was fully aware that Waples had "obviously" made the demonstration "knowing that Slotnick would not be able to refute it."

Crane's final instruction on the two-bullet debate probably had less impact on this sophisticated jury than Waples feared. The jurors seemed to have a better grasp of the physical evidence and the logically possible inferences from the evidence than the judge and the defense team, who were still trying to figure out the point that Waples was trying to make. In fact, Waples had a limited point in mind. His purpose in the complicated demonstration was simply to refute Dr. Dimaio's scientific arguments and show that at least it was very likely that Cabey was sitting down at the time of the fifth shot.

But the jurors were much less impressed by Dimaio's dogmatic claims than Waples thought.[50] They were prepared to accept the fact that Cabey was sitting down and that he was critically injured by the fifth shot. But this did not settle anything in their mind. They were much more concerned by the root question whether Goetz actually paused, approached Cabey, and shot him at close range. That—and not whether one or two bullets passed through the jacket— was the heart of the problem of self-defense.

As the jury turned to this complex of problems, they had already generated a collective history of rejecting one witness almost entirely (Myra Friedman), cast serious doubts on the credibility of a police detective (Michael Clark), and reformulated the intention required for attempted murder. They had already unanimously voted not guilty nine times.[51] They were experiencing their intellectual independence. Even though the media had accepted the reliability of the confession for the last two years, they would have to think it through on their own. They would accept nothing at face value, and they would not limit themselves to the arguments they heard in court.

The anomalies in the evidence had already become so prominent in their thinking that they could not write them off as the normal discrepancies of different points of view. Carolyn Perlmuth was particularly impressed that no one heard the pause between the fourth and fifth shots. As Mark Lesly summed it up:

> We had eight other witnesses [on the train]. Nobody said that they heard a fifth separate shot. Everyone said it was four or five in rapid succession.

Lesly was aware that in this summary of the evidence he had adopted the slogan "rapid succession" that the defense used so cleverly to unite the witnesses under one label. In fact only one witness used those words himself, but all concurred in Slotnick's using that label to characterize their testimony. Lesly continued:

> I understood what Slotnick was trying to do [by imposing his label "rapid succession" on the testimony]. None of them heard any separation between the shots. . . . We had Armando Soler in the next car. It was loud enough for him to hear it in the next car. Josephine Holt and Mary Gant, lying on the floor of the subway car, did not hear any separation. Nobody but Boucher did.

Lesly was right. It all turned on Boucher. If he was believed, the jurors would have a basis for concluding that Goetz took the time to run over to Cabey and fire the last shot point-blank in his side. The problem with Boucher's testimony, however, was that he described Goetz shooting Cabey straight into the chest, not in his rear left side as the bullet wound indisputably showed. Perlmuth thought he was "sincere in what he said" but his testimony had "a lot of holes in it."

Mark Lesly was inclined to reject Boucher's story altogether. He began regarding Boucher as unreliable during his testimony when Boucher said that although his friend and longtime roommate Loren Michals had testified first, he had not discussed Michals's testimony with him; and then later, when asked how far away he was from the shooting, he came up with the figure 40 feet—the same distance that Michals specified but only after considerable uncertainty. If it was difficult for Michals to pinpoint the distance at 40 feet, Lesly could not accept, without at least a grain of salt, Boucher's unhesitatingly hitting upon the same number. In the same vein, Lesly was put off by Boucher's apparent certainty that Cabey did not jerk or move in the last second prior to the shot:

> He didn't even say, "I'm not sure." I believe that he was making this up. The reason he said that is that he didn't want there to be any question of his lunging for the gun or any dangerous movement. And that is why he said, "Oh no! he didn't twist, he didn't turn." He not only put Slotnick directly in front [in the courtroom reenactment], but he said, "He was in perfect profile."

Lesly's problem in thinking about Boucher's testimony was that he could not devise a motive for Boucher's lying on the stand. The general pattern for discrediting witnesses up to that point was to postulate a motive for not telling the truth. And the jury engaged in some wild speculation about why Boucher might have had it in for Goetz.[52] In fact, Boucher was an excellent witness—calm, consistent in his story,[53] and as Perlmuth inferred from his occupation as a store window designer, "he was probably an observant person." Nonetheless, Lesly concluded:

> My feeling is that Christopher Boucher made his story up. Why he did it, I don't know. But without any real knowledge of where the wounds were, he made his story up . . . with the intention of getting Goetz busted.

Standing alone, this conclusion leaves one nonplussed. The speculative imagination of this juror seems to have run away with him. But the fanciful suggestion that Boucher was acting maliciously toward Goetz has to be understood in the context of the jury's drive to explain everything, to account for every piece of evidence they did not accept. For a variety of reasons, neither Lesly nor the rest of the jury was inclined to accept Boucher's testimony as corroboration of the confession. But this left them with an anomaly: why did Boucher say what he said? In order to round off all the rough edges in the view of the case that was crystallizing in their minds, they had to explain away inconsistencies. Attributing bad motives to Boucher was Lesly's way of accounting for the anomaly.

In the early balloting on the Cabey count, eight jurors voted not guilty and four were undecided. The argument was not settled simply by generating serious doubts about whether there was a pause between the shots and by discrediting Boucher. In order to win over the undecided votes, the majority needed to provide an account of the anomalies generated by the alternative view that Goetz emptied his gun rapidly "on automatic pilot" without moving from his initial spot. Now the tables were turned: the confession was no longer the reigning hypothesis; it was the major anomaly generated by the new theory. How could the majority explain that away? There was no suggestion that Goetz was lying. They needed some account of how Goetz could have misperceived his final shot, how his memory could have distorted this detail and only this detail of the shooting.

Slotnick's argument in his summation was that Goetz recalled everything up to the "moment of fear." Then his perceptions went awry. Yet Waples had countered with 17 points on which the confession was seemingly accurate, including numerous details after the shooting began. The jury were impressed with Waples's effort to rescue the confession, but they cast about for some basis of "reasonable doubt" on the interaction with Cabey. The explanation that emerged was that Goetz was distraught and confused after nine days of being on the run and several hours of talking to the New Hampshire police before he put his confession on tape. Many jurors believed that Goetz, as well as Boucher, was influenced by what they mistakenly thought were early press reports that Goetz shot a fifth shot downward at someone sitting.[54] Their doubts were bolstered as well, Perlmuth reports, by Waples's having conceded in his summation that perhaps Goetz merely said, "You seem to be [doing] all right; here's another," in his mind. "It made everyone think," she says, "that these processes could have taken place mentally rather than actually."

These doubts were sufficient to bring the jury to a unanimous vote of not guilty on the charge of assault in the first degree. The standard of "reasonable doubt" provided them with a way out of their uncertainties about the conflicting evidence. It is not clear whether they would have voted the same way if Goetz had had the burden of proving self-defense by a preponderance of the evidence, as he does in the pending civil suits against him. When asked how they would have voted if Goetz had borne this additional burden to make his story plausible, most of the jurors balked. They were required to decide only whether the prosecution had proved the absence of self-defense beyond a reasonable doubt. And they had reasonable doubts. It does not follow, they insist, that they were convinced that Goetz did in fact act in reasonable self-defense, particularly on the Cabey shot.

One might be tempted to think that jurors had sympathy for Goetz as a person. There is no doubt that they identified with his situation at the time of the subway confrontation—as well they should have if the evidence brought them to that identification. But there is no evidence that they acted out of bias or personal rapport with the defendant. Indeed many of the jurors thought he was a bit odd. Perlmuth thought "that he was disturbed on the tape" and further that "it was obvious that he was kind of a quirky person beforehand also." Waples may have succeeded in convincing the jury that Goetz was not the ordinary reasonable person who rode the IRT downtown. But that was not enough for the jury to disregard the signs that his defensive response might have been reasonable under the circumstances.

After reaching a consensus on the general issue of justification, there was no serious disagreement. The jury disposed of the subsidiary charges of assault in the second degree and reckless endangerment in the first and second degree. Criminal possession of a weapon in the second degree also went quickly, for they had concluded that Goetz possessed the weapon solely for the purpose of self-defense. If that was his purpose in carrying a loaded gun on the subway, he could not have had an "unlawful purpose" in doing so. By Tuesday afternoon, June 16, the jury was ready to come in with the verdict.

A rush of whispers passed through the halls outside the courtroom. The journalists and other observers who had been there since the deliberations began on Friday hung on every hint that the two-and-a-half-year process of judgment had come to an end. Within minutes the observers, full of anticipation, seized every seat in the courtroom. The jury filed in, as they had numerous times with their questions for Justice Crane. They were stonefaced. No smiles, no glances toward the defendant. Their solemnity matched the intensity of everyone waiting for a verdict of one word or two, guilty or not guilty.

As he inquired every time the jury filed in with a question, the court clerk, Bob Hamkalo, asked them whether they had reached a verdict; this time the foreman, James Hurley, answered "yes." Mr. Hamkalo began reading off the charges. Mr. Hurley lifted the charge sheet to read off the jury's answers. Would the verdict be so complicated that he could not remember how the jury voted on each charge? Then the answers: guilty on the charge of criminal possession of a weapon in the third degree, but then, to everyone's surprise, not guilty on the two counts of criminal possession of a weapon in the fourth degree. At that point, Mark Baker said later, he knew he could relax. Goetz remained as impassive as he had been throughout the trial. The words "not guilty" resounded over and over again through the still, cavernous courtroom. Attempted murder against Darrell Cabey? At the momentous words "not guilty" a gasp welled up from the audience. It was all over. Journalists rushed for the phones. Mark Baker began to cry, and Goetz smiled, faintly.

11
Mixed Messages

IN the aftermath of the verdict came the rush to interpret its meaning. Black political leaders and black journalists protested the verdict as an expression of hostility against their race:[1]

> If Goetz was a black man who shot four white youths on a subway train, there would be no doubt about the verdict. The Goetz case is just more evidence that blacks are not safe in New York City.

Trying to defend the verdict the next day to an audience of black clergy, Mayor Koch encountered so much anger about the implications of racism that he had to beat a hasty retreat through a back door in the church.[2] The immediate reaction to a June verdict seemingly vindicating a white man's shooting four blacks was that everyone in the city, black and white, had reason to fear the tension that would emerge in the "long, hot" months of July and August.

The fact is that the vast majority of the city's residents supported the verdict. A Gallup poll indicated that the majority was significantly greater for non-Hispanic whites (83 percent) and Hispanics (78 percent) than among blacks (45 percent).[1] But among blacks who supported the verdict, the degree of support was often intense. On the day after the verdict, a black man called into the Sherrye Henry show with this gripping tale:

CALLER: I'm a New Yorker, black. Over the past seven years, three members, boys, in my family has been killed, the last one shot, with the killer that we see weekly—today—walking around. My wife has been mentally disturbed ever since this happened because no one is serving time for any of this. Members of my family have been robbed, two girls raped, no one is serving time for none of this. The question is: where is the justice? Cuomo said that he is against the death penalty. He said that what we should do is put the members away forever if they kill someone. My boys are dead. No one is serving any time. They knew who did it and they say, "not enough evidence" or for one reason or another, this is the case. My wife is crazy because she sees this guy on a daily basis. He spoke to her a few times. And this was the baby son . . . was the last one. And the question is: where is the justice? What do we do? Must we sit there to be robbed? sit there to be raped? sit there to be killed?

SHERRYE HENRY: Let me ask you, sir. I think I know the answer. How do you feel about the Goetz verdict?

CALLER: I think that Goetz did the right thing in defending himself.

SHERRYE HENRY: What a terribly tragic story. We know that the statistics tell us that black crime is usually committed against the black community. Here is a man who is living embodiment of that.

CALLER: You can't do anything until they do something to you. You must sit there and wait for them to attack you.

* Interviewer: Sir, can I ask you this question. I am very moved by your story. Why don't you sympathize with the four victims of Goetz's shooting on the subway? They're black kids who might have been your sons. Why don't you feel with them and their families?

CALLER: Well, as it was brought out in a couple of cases, one was on parole violation. He should never have been there to begin with. And the other one should have been in jail. In other words, this is "revolving door justice" and they are right back at our throat again. If the boys were where they were supposed to be, number one: they would never have been shot, and number two: they would never had in mind to do anything. The point is that the justice let them back out again and they were back at our throats again. . . . They admit they were going out to steal. . . .

As the primary victims of violence, blacks living in poverty have every reason to identify with Goetz's striking back against the sources of their fear. Victims and those who intensely fear violent crime have a distinctive posture on the Goetz case. Their starting point for discourse about the case is their recollection of fear, when the

---

* I was the additional interviewer on the show.

mugger pulls his knife or the burglar breaks the glass on the kitchen window. In that unexpected instant, human autonomy and self-worth become perverted by the rule of animal instinct. Individuals who normally carry themselves with dignity then cower before the brute force that thrives on disorder and the lawless search for advantage.

The elementary task of government is to protect us from these moments of fear. What we should gain from government by having surrendered our capacities for self-protection is, as Thomas Hobbes said in justifying the state's use of force, security in the war of "all against all." But it is clear that in contemporary urban America, the government has failed to fulfill its elementary function of securing the peace. Many middle-class residents of New York ignore the risks of criminal victimization, but others live in constant dread. The group that fears finally found its folk hero in Bernhard Goetz. He was everyman in a modern morality play in which right and order triumph over the forces of evil and disorder. Not only did he strike back against the elements that, in the view of many, terrorize the city, but Goetz demonstrated the impotency of law enforcement. A single individual, well armed and properly trained, can do a better job of thwarting crime than all the men in blue who, from time to time, patrol the subway cars.

The public mood was captured in the lyrics of a single, "Subway Vigilante," recorded by Ronny and the Urban Watchdogs:

> He's the subway vigilante
> The brave subway vigilante
> Where law and order can't
> he showed us how to take a stand
> He had enough and came out fightin'
> Drove the rats back into hidin'
> Let's cheer the subway vigilante
> He's one special kind of man

Would there other "special kind of men"? Would Goetz's deed draw imitators, as did the spate of political assassinations in the 1960s? Major Owens, a black Congressman from Brooklyn, thought the reaction of whites identifying with Goetz would be "Yeah, we were right, let's go get 'em."[4] Speaking for the Guardian Angels, Curtis Sliwa proudly reiterated this sentiment: "This has sent a message to all decent people that it's OK to fight back."[5]

Everyone was watching, but in the two and a half years between the shooting and the trial, there were no repetitions that the press could brand as Goetz-inspired, and in the summer following the verdict, life and crime continued as usual. The public retained its fascination with the moral drama of the subway shooting and of the process of judging Goetz, but his deed did not release a pent-up urge of the citizenry to arm itself and re-create his perceived victory over the muggers of the city.

Though Barry Slotnick himself tried to debunk the alleged racial overtones of the verdict, he did say publicly that the verdict stood for a "right" to defend oneself against the kind of the threat that Goetz faced.[6] This was an unfortunate interpretation of the jury's finding of not guilty on the shooting counts. The verdict simply expresses the jury's conclusion that the prosecution had not satisfied them beyond a reasonable doubt that Goetz did *not* act in reasonable self-defense.

Even if the verdict is taken to stand for the jury's conviction that Goetz acted justifiably under the New York statute, there is nothing in the language of the statute that identifies "justification" with a right to use force. The statutory defense applies with equal force even as to someone who is reasonably mistaken about whether he is about to be robbed. Being mistaken, even reasonably, does not generate a right to shoot and injure would-be aggressors. True, those faced with imminent actual aggression do have a right to avert the attack with the minimal force necessary under the circumstances. The right springs from the actual wrong committed by the aggressors. But where there is no wrong, no actual robbery, just a mistaken fear of robbery, there is no right to respond. The most we can say in a case of mistake is that the defender is *excused* for misperceiving the situation: we cannot properly blame him for his mistake. The New York statute collapses these dimensions of justification and excuse into one provision on "reasonably believing" in the necessity of self-defense. All we can say, therefore, is that if the jury finds that the mistake was reasonable under the circumstances (or has a reasonable doubt on the issue), it should not convict. To speak of a right to shoot someone who asks for or demands five dollars on the subway grossly misinterprets both the law and the jury's verdict of not guilty in Goetz's case.

Unfortunately, the public often interprets jury verdicts in cases of violence as judgments about the worth of the victims. In the prosecution of Dan White for killing the mayor and a county supervisor, George Moscone and Harvey Milk, in San Francisco, the jury returned a verdict of mitigated homicide based on White's mental condition at the time of the shooting. Because Harvey Milk was a highly visible gay activist, the public interpreted the verdict as a declaration that the life of gays is worth less than the lives of others. The same distortion seems inescapable in the Goetz case. Even if the jury based its decisions exclusively on the subjective circumstances of Goetz's shooting, on his reasonable mistake, on his personal fear, many segments of the public would invariably read the verdict as a public declaration on the moral value of the black victims.

The tangled insinuation of racism in the Goetz case—and generally in the American system of criminal justice—is not easily dismissed. Somehow it is not enough for jurors to declare publicly, as did the Goetz panel, that race was not a factor in their decision. They may not be aware of the racial factors that shape their intuitive judgments of the facts. And it is not enough to point to acquittal in cases where the color pattern is reversed. In Brooklyn, a year before the Goetz trial, a young black was acquitted on grounds of self-defense for shooting a white priest. In San Diego, California, a month after the Goetz verdict, a young black, Sagon Penn, was acquitted, also on grounds of self-defense, of killing a white police officer and injuring another white officer as well as a civilian riding along in the patrol car at the time of confrontation.[7] In the Howard Beach trial, resolved six months after the Goetz verdict, three white young men were convicted of manslaughter after they attacked several blacks passing through their neighborhood and fatally chased one of them into the path of an oncoming car.[8] But each of these cases arises on a unique set of facts. There is no way of establishing that any other trial posed exactly the same conflict as the Goetz case, only with racial identities reversed. That blacks are often acquitted of alleged crimes against whites and whites often convicted of crimes against blacks does not allay the anxieties of those who believe that racial factors informed the jury's verdict for Goetz.

It may well be true that racial fears invariably infuse routine judgments in American society about what kinds of acts constitute a serious danger or what kinds of violent responses should be regarded as reasonable acts of self-defense. Any jury of ordinary New Yorkers would be inescapably conscious of the skin color of Troy Canty, Barry Allen, James Ramseur, and Darrell Cabey. Given the tragic disproportion of crimes committed by black youth, ordinary sensible people cannot avoid considering race, along with youth, gender, dress, and apparent educational level, in making a judgment about whether a group of youths on the subway bespeaks danger. One might not call these kids "punks" as did the black witness Andrea Reid, but survival instincts in the city would unquestionably put one on guard.

This is, of course, a form of racial stereotyping, which implies that the innocent conforming to the stereotype of "black street toughs" are treated exactly the same as are the guilty. But the stereotyping is based no more on race than it is on youth, gender, dress, and the other cues that signal danger to urban dwellers. We might all be fairer to each other if there were no such cues based on generalized experience, but how much can we expect of the ordinary person when he picks his seat on the subway? There is no injustice to Troy Canty if a passenger decides not to sit next to him. Yet the rules of thumb that are appropriate for making judgments about one's personal safety don't hold up as guidelines for deciding in a court of law who is guilty or who should suffer punishment. If a judge or juror concludes, on the basis of even a partially racial profile, that Troy Canty must have intended to carry out a violent robbery, his rule of thumb would inflict a racially inspired injustice.

Criminal trials may not solve the problems of racial bias in our society, but at least they should not add to them. How should we judge the Goetz trial on that score? The remarkable fact about the Goetz proceedings is that on the verbal level at least, they were color-blind. Justice Crane did not allow the prosecution to bring into evidence a public statement that Goetz made a few years ago that reflected crass prejudice against blacks.[9] If this expression of prejudice was relevant at all, it was to demonstrate racial hostility as a motive for the shooting. Allowing the prosecution to bring in evidence of Goetz's racial bias would have invited the defense to produce witness after witness to testify that Goetz had a sound attitude toward blacks. The trial would have turned into a farcical battle between character witnesses for and against the subway gunman.

The four hours of taped confession provide as good an insight into Goetz's personality as any array of witnesses could produce by testifying to their observations of his behavior under normal conditions. One would expect that if Goetz had felt racial antagonism toward his perceived assailants, he would have let slip a racial remark in his agonized retelling of the story. Yet he says nothing about race. He does not even volunteer the racial identity of the four youths. Only after a New Hampshire policeman asks him directly does he say, in reply, that they were black. When he recalls his 1981 mugging by three blacks, he also omits the significant detail that they too were black youths. If the visual cues that Goetz picked up from his four feared assailants in 1984—youth, gender, race—reminded him of his painful beating in 1981, he says nothing in his confession to substantiate the connection.

According to one view, this systematic silence reveals how racially sensitive Goetz was and how much he tried to conceal it. It is simply not normal, the argument goes, for a white New Yorker fearful of violence on the streets to be as color-blind as is suggested by the image Goetz conveys in the taped confession. In two hours of unrecorded conversation with the New Hampshire police immediately prior to the taped conversation, he does remark in connection with the 1981 mugging (as recorded in the police report):[10]

> I think it's kind of ridiculous to consider that someone—let's say in my position—carrying things, would start up with three blacks alone, in the subway system.

In his videotaped confession, Goetz repeats essentially the same line but substitutes the word "people" for "blacks."[11] Perhaps he was sufficiently conscious of the image he was casting on tape that he carefully chose his words. But this interpretation strains the data. Goetz comes across as so disturbed and anguished in the course of the confession, particularly in his interactions with Assistant District Attorney Susan Braver, that it is hard to believe that he could choose his language to create a particular impression. We have to accept the implication that at the time of his confession, at least, racial consciousness and animosity did not weigh heavily in Goetz's mind.

The record of the defense on the racial issue is regrettably mixed. They made no systematic effort to keep blacks off the jury. Under New York and federal constitutional law as it stood at the time of trial, they could have used their peremptory challenges, as the defense tried to do in the Howard Beach trial, to insure a jury racially identical to the defendant.[12] Two blacks sat on the jury, and as the deliberations revealed, one of them proved to be a strong advocate for acquittal.[13]

There were moments in the trial when a racially motivated defense strategy would have dictated certain moves that Slotnick and Baker did not make. When the sanitation officer who came to Goetz's rescue during the 1981 mugging was on the stand, the defense could have tried to elicit from him the racial identity of Fred Clark and the two other youths responsible for Goetz's beating and the resulting permanent injuries. Yet they did not. So far as the jury could tell from the evidence introduced at the trial, the race of the prior assailants was either unknown or irrelevant.[14]

This silence about the race of the prior muggers is particularly striking, for a good case can be made for the legal relevance of all of Goetz's prior experiences that shaped his fears and his violent reaction when Troy Canty approached him on December 22, 1984. Does it not bear upon the reasonableness of his response that he was once mugged by youths who conformed in age, gender, and race to those whom he confronted the second time? Some judges interviewed respond that they would have regarded it as permissible for the witness to the prior mugging to disclose the race of the assailants to the jury.[15] Other lawyers active in civil rights causes insist that although Fred Clark's race was technically relevant to the responses of a reasonable person in Goetz's situation, the principle of color-blind justice would require suppression of all racial factors bearing on Goetz's acts.[16]

The question whether a reasonable person considers race in assessing the danger that four youths on the subway might represent goes to the heart of what the law demands of us. The statistically ordinary New Yorker would be more apprehensive of the "kind of people" who mugged him once, and it is difficult to expect the ordinary person in our time not to perceive race as one—just one—of the factors defining the "kind" of person who poses a danger. The law, however, may demand that we surmount racially based intuitions of danger. Though the question was not resolved in the Goetz case and there is no settled law on this issue, the standard of reasonableness may require us to be better than we really are.

Reading the record of the Goetz case, one hardly finds an explicit reference to the race of anyone. But indirectly and covertly, the defense played on the racial factor. Slotnick's strategy of relentlessly attacking the "gang of four," "the predators" on society, calling them "vultures" and "savages," carried undeniable racial undertones. These verbal attacks signaled a perception of the four youths as representing something more than four individuals committing an act of aggression against a defendant. That "something more" requires extrapolation from their characteristics to the class of individuals for which they stand. There is no doubt that one of the characteristics that figures in this implicit extrapolation is their blackness.

The covert appeal to racial bias came out most dramatically in the re-creation of the shooting, played out while Joseph Quirk was testifying. The defendant called in four props to stand in for the four victims Canty, Allen, Ramseur, and Cabey. The nominal purpose of the demonstration was to show the way in which each bullet entered the body of each victim. The defense's real purpose, however, was to re-create for the jury, as dramatically as possible, the scene that Goetz encountered when four young black passengers began to surround him. For that reason Barry Slotnick asked the Guardian Angels to send him four young black men to act as the props in the demonstration. In came the four young black Guardian Angels, fit and muscular, dressed in T-shirts, to play the parts of the four victims in a courtroom minidrama.[17]

Journalist observers of the trial had little inkling of the seriousness of this violation of fair procedure. It seemed natural that the four youths be played by four blacks. After all, when the television show "20/20" showed a re-creation of the shooting scene, they cast four black young men in the parts of the victims. Why should Barry Slotnick, as the director of this re-creation, not enjoy the same dramatic freedom? Most observers thought that he should, and Justice Crane temporarily concurred.[18]

One could imagine a system of trial in which each side produced a little play showing its version of the facts. But as a matter of fundamental principle, our system of justice rejects that mode of persuading the jury. True, our system of evidence permits scientific demonstration, showing the jury how something happened or could happen (Slotnick had Boucher guide his demonstration of how Goetz supposedly shot Cabey). But the American system of trial seeks, as far as possible, to eliminate modes of subverbal communication that elude cross-examination and rational evaluation by the jury.[19] The Berg case in New York advises trial judges not to test potentially rebellious witnesses like James Ramseur in front of the jury (they should not appear before the jury until their willingness to testify is established): the implications of a rebellious act of refusing to testify are not formulated as propositions subject to cross-examination.[20] The implication might be that the witness is afraid of the defendant, as the court suggested in the Berg case. Or the implication might be that the witness is simply a person of mean, rebellious character, as it was in the instance of James Ramseur's committing contempt in open court. Similarly, the implication arising from a dramatic re-creation of the Goetz shooting—the implication that anyone would have been afraid of being partially surrounded by four young black street toughs—was not subject to cross-examination and rational evaluation.

One effective test for assessing whether messages conveyed to the jury consist of propositions subject to cross-examination is whether these messages appear on the face of the trial transcript. There is no mention in the transcript that the human props were black. So far as the transcript is the best history of a trial, that critical fact will be invisible to researchers who will study the transcript a century from now.[21] The defense's covert message of racial fear came into the trial camouflaged as dramatic realism. Perhaps if Justice Crane had forced himself to articulate for the record what was going on as the defense called in four young black men as props, he would have realized the import of Slotnick's maneuver and refused to let him go forward.[22]

In the end, Slotnick's covert appeal to racial fear may have had more impact on the jury precisely because it remained hidden behind innuendo and suggestion. It spoke to that side of the jurors' personality that they could not confront directly. Paradoxically, Slotnick may have gained more from not inquiring about Fred Clark's race than from bringing the racial issue out into the open. Openly talking about racial fear in the courtroom might have helped the jury to deal more rationally with their own racial biases.

There is another racial dimension to the Goetz case that was never articulated in the trial and was hardly mentioned in the press reports of the subway encounter and the ensuing legal battle. It is difficult to ignore the strong connection between race and the background of poverty and deprivation that fathered four drifters like Troy Canty, Barry Allen, James Ramseur, and Darrell Cabey. These young men, with barely a grade school education, no future, and no reason to plan for the future, live in a present dominated by the temptations of drugs and easy, illegal gain. They are sophisticated enough, as Troy Canty told us compellingly from the stand, to plan their crimes to minimize the risk of serious jail time. Pilfering video games and petty larceny from grocery stores define their role in society.

The tragedy of this human loss should instill compassion and concern for correcting the structural problems in our society that deprive lower-class minorities of a stake in a system of secure property rights and peaceful public order. Lillian Rubin's book on the early phases of the Goetz proceedings[23] explores the social and family background of the four victims. The hostile public reaction to her plea for a broader view of the causes of crime by black youths reminds us, painfully, of the difference between the mentality of the 1960s and that of the 1980s.[24] Twenty years ago liberal intellectuals would have responded to her call for greater efforts to eliminate urban ghettos as the breeding ground of crime. A leading judge of the time, David Bazelon, argued that social deprivation should constitute an excuse for criminal conduct.[25] Today no one seriously considers Bazelon's argument that because social conditions account for criminal behavior as much as does mental condition, the two crimogenic factors should be treated similarly under the law. The dominant concern now seems to be how we can protect ourselves from the outcome of social forces that seem to be beyond our control.

Concern for correcting the root causes of crime reflects a liberal orientation toward social action that, alas, is no longer in keeping with the time. Liberals and conservatives have indeed arrayed themselves in contending camps on the Goetz prosecution. Yet the terms "liberal" and "conservative" carry connotations in this context that are just the opposite of their ordinary thrust. Conservatives typically side with the government in its efforts to suppress crime. But here we find conservatives standing squarely with a defendant charged with crimes of violence. Liberals ordinarily argue the side of the defense—the underdog seeking to protect himself against the overweening power of the state. But here we find liberals defending state power against the "anarchy" of packing guns and shooting in ambiguous situations.

William Kunstler, a well-known lawyer and political activist, is usually on the side of the defense resisting an oppressive government. Now, as the lawyer for Darrell Cabey in his multi-million-dollar tort suit against Goetz, he found himself strongly on the side of the prosecution, advocating conviction and imprisonment for Goetz, whom he called a "gunslinging avenger" prepared even after the trial, if need be, "particularly if members of minorities are involved, [to] pull another weapon from another fast draw holster, assume a combat stance, and shoot to kill once more."[26] For Kunstler, the consistent thread is protecting the rights of minorities. Sometimes this requires fighting, and sometimes supporting the prosecution.

The defense of Bernhard Goetz was strongly political in the sense that it rode a crest of popular enthusiasm for the symbolic significance of turning the tables on the youths who menace so many law-abiding citizens. The defense traded on the deep frustrations of those who, like the black man who called into the Sherrye Henry talk show, think of Goetz's victims as exemplary of the group repeatedly let out of jail in "revolving door justice" who constantly are "at our throats." The politics of the Goetz defense were popular, but they did not rise to the level of an issue of conscience or principle.

If the defense had attempted to build a case on a universal principle of human freedom, namely the right in special situations to bear the necessary means of self-defense, they would have fared better in their efforts both to address the jury on their innate power to vote their conscience and, if they had so chosen, to develop a convincing argument on behalf of the defense of necessity. Both arguments would have yielded an issue of principle on which the jury could have brought to bear its political and moral sensibilities. As the Goetz case actually unfolded, however, Slotnick and Baker thought they could appeal to "jury nullification" without developing a specific moral defect in the prevailing law. They had no complaint against the New York law of self-defense. True, they had fought and lost an appellate battle on the subjective versus the objective standard of self-defense, but this relatively esoteric question could hardly be the basis for the jury's defying the judge's instructions on the law.

The defense also had no apparent complaints against the law prohibiting the possession of a loaded gun, without a permit, in a public place. This was the charge on which Goetz was most vulnerable and on which he was eventually convicted and sentenced. But the defense had no brief against it. They raised no defense against it. They made no reference to the Second Amendment, to the right to bear arms, to the defense of necessity as recognized by New York law.[27] They seemed to think that the jury's sympathy for Goetz's deed would be a sufficiently strong sling for propelling their client around the strictures of guilt as defined in the judge's instructions.

Paradoxically, the general public generously construes the right of self-defense, both on the subway in Goetz's situation and in repelling burglars from one's home,[28] and at the same time, people fear the distribution of handguns and other firearms to enable more people effectively to realize their right of self-defense. These intersecting majorities make sense when viewed from the perspective of the pervasive, almost endemic fear that dominates urban life today. The ubiquitous fear of criminal assault generates support for someone like Goetz who fights back, but it also makes people afraid of the prospect that every stranger, particularly every minority stranger on the street, might be packing a loaded gun. Guns facilitate self-defense, but they also make it easier for criminals to intimidate victims of robbery and rape. In our time, the fear of what people will do with guns overshadows the value of guns in strengthening the ability of those attacked to defend themselves.

Given the deep aversion to the dissemination of guns, confirmed by many prospective jurors who said they could easily understand that Goetz might have been forced to shoot as a defensive measure but they nonetheless supported gun control, Slotnick and Baker may have made a sensible tactical decision not to profile the case as one posing the basic question of a right to bear arms. If the jurors had thought that more general issue was at stake, they might have reacted against Goetz and found that he was trigger-happy in overreacting to the cues of danger in the subway encounter; they might have convicted on some of the shooting charges as well as the single count of criminal possession.

It seems clear that since the drafting of the Second Amendment, a basic transformation has occurred in our thinking about arms and self-defense. The Second Amendment's right to "keep and bear" arms responds to fears of tyranny; it is clear we need a different philosophy to respond to the fears of the 1980s. We have faith today that the legal system can protect us from oppressive decisions of government more reliably than our ability to aim and shoot firearms. But we do not have the same faith in the legal system as a secure wall of defense against the criminal elements that roam the streets.

The value expressed in the Second Amendment has undergone a political metamorphosis—from a universal assertion of freedom on the left to a claim of class interest on the right. The alleged right to bear arms no longer expresses a universal concern about protecting a free society from the threat of tyranny; it has come to be attached in the public consciousness to the partisan objective of fighting off disenfranchised criminal elements. The left today, with some notable exceptions, stands on the side of gun control and the use of regulatory offenses[29] to prevent guns and other weapons from coming into the hands of the wrong people.

This political transformation teaches us how difficult it is to interpret the Second Amendment according to its framers' original intention. The dictates of reason in constitutional law require that we transcend the 18th-century origins of the right to bear arms and think about the right in the context of our present concerns and anxieties. Perhaps a well-trained citizenry's bearing arms would be no more harmful to the public interest than the widespread posses-

sion of another deadly weapon: the automobile. With adequate training, most people can become tolerably safe drivers. If as much time
and energy were devoted to training people how to use guns, we
would surely render negligible the risk of accidental firings.

Yet there remains a striking difference between automobiles and
guns. Except in rare cases, automobiles are not the vehicle of intimidation. They may make it easier to escape from the commission of a
crime, but they do not buttress the execution of violent crimes by
forcing the victim to submit. For this and other reasons, we downplay
the damage done by automobiles and overestimate, perhaps, the
danger posed by strangers possessing guns.

On this issue, as well as many others raised by the Goetz prosecution, the problems of modernity have fractured the voice of reason
in the law. A long appellate battle in the pretrial phase of the case
came to a clear legal conclusion: the objective standard requires
juries to make a moral judgment about whether the defendant's
actual fears and beliefs were reasonable under the circumstances.
Yet as the jury came to its own understanding of the law of the
intention required for attempted murder, the rejected subjective standard returned to rule the deliberations.* Many theories of self-defense
compete for supremacy—the punitive theory, the theory that someone
under attack has no choice, the "individualist" and "social" theories
of self-defense as a justification[30]—but none gained an upper hand
in the way the trial took its course. The first three fought for supremacy in the process leading to the jury's doubts about the prosecution's
case.

Modern legal thought is torn by the question whether harmful
consequences should aggravate an action of wicked intentions. As
the Goetz case was argued, the consequences to Darrell Cabey, in
particular, weighed heavily in the thinking of the lawyers. But as
the jury viewed the case, the primary question was Goetz's personal
view of what was going on and the intention on which he acted.
We were in conflict about these questions before the Goetz case,
and we are still in conflict.

The conflicting purposes of the law surfaced in the long-awaited
final stage of the Goetz proceeding, the sentencing decision by Justice
Crane. On the basic decision whether Goetz would go to jail, the
judge would stand alone. The jury's verdict would influence him
only so far as he subscribed to their judgment that there was a

---

* See Chapter Ten, pages 186–188, for details.

reasonable doubt about whether the consequences to the four victims of Goetz's carrying a gun were lawful or unlawful. The legislature has prescribed guidelines for the sentencing judge's determining the proper term of imprisonment. The complicated sentencing scheme for this offense requires that the judge set either an indeterminate term with a minimum of as much as two and one-third years in jail[31] or a fixed term of no less than one year[32] with the proviso that the judge can set a definite term lower than one year if, "having regard to the nature and circumstances of the offense and to the history and character of the defendant," he is "of the opinion" that a one-year sentence would be "unduly harsh."[33] In the end the sentencing options would turn on whether Justice Crane committed himself to a finding that the legislatively prescribed minimum of one year was too severe or harsh under the circumstances.

No field of law reveals our confusion of purpose more than sentencing. We would like to believe that sending people to jail could have the effect of reforming them and returning them to society as useful and productive citizens. At the height of this faith in rehabilitation, virtually every state introduced a scheme of individualized sentencing, buttressed by an apparatus of "mental health professionals" who would interview the defendant prior to sentencing and recommend the sentence that would be best for him. Sentencing ceased being a question of justice and became a process of administering the resources of the state for the benefit, supposedly, of the convicted offender. The faith in sentencing as an instrument of mental health has gone the way of other liberal causes of the last generation. We now know that sending convicted defendants to our overcrowded jails offers no therapeutic benefit. We have no more faith that we can change the basic value structure of criminals than that we can solve the social problems of poverty and desperation that generate crime in the first place.

The legal framework of indeterminate, individualized sentencing has remained in force in New York, but the system is now complicated by an overlay of renewed concern for protecting society and doing justice both to the victim and the offender. In 1982 the New York legislature amended its statement of purpose in the Penal Law to declare as one of its objectives "provid[ing] an appropriate public response to particular offenses."[34] The bureaucratic term "appropriate public response" is our current, embarrassed way of talking about just retribution, repaying the wrongdoer by making him suffer. The amendment reflects the wave of concern for justice to victims, who invariably feel mistreated when those who transgress against them escape their just deserts. The 1982 amendment stresses that the "appropriate" response must consider "the consequences of the offense for the victim, including the victim's family, and the community."[35]

The problem with applying this guideline to the offense of which Goetz was convicted is that his carrying the loaded weapon in public did not by itself claim a victim. The jury acquitted him of all charges that pertained to the specific victims. Due respect for the verdict of not guilty on all the shooting charges precluded Justice Crane from alluding to the consequences to the four youths in setting the sentence. In the public perception of the process, however, the consequences to the four victims were undeniable. As the New York Times noted, "But then not all [who illegally possess weapons] fire their illegal weapons or cause injuries, as Mr. Goetz did."[36] For many concerned citizens, the sentencing process offered an opportunity to reconsider whether the verdict did justice to the four black victims.

When every other purpose of punishment fails, legislatures and judges fall back on the logic of general deterrence. Sending offenders to jail may not reform them, but the example of their suffering will make others think twice about the risks they are taking in violating the law. The legislature stipulated a one-year penalty for the victimless, regulatory offense of carrying a weapon, thereby backing up the regulatory prohibition with force. If people do not see the fairness and moral necessity of the law's requiring them to give up their arms, they can at least understand that it is not in their advantage to act in ways that entail heavy penalties.

Ironically, as Goetz was engaged in systematically flouting the law suppressing guns in New York City, he thought that his would-be muggers would be deterred from violating the same law. He did not fear that they, as professional petty thieves, would be armed. He knew that they would ply their lawless trade without incurring the high costs of state prison. In his revealing testimony at the trial, Troy Canty confirmed the capacity that he and his friends had for engaging in rational calculation about the penal costs of particular crimes. If petty thieves are deterred and Goetz was sufficiently street-wise to realize this, why was he not deterred on December 22, 1984, and the innumerable occasions prior to that date that he left his apartment with a loaded gun in his quick-draw holster? The simple answer is that Goetz thought he was right. The four youths knew they were engaged in an illegal enterprise, and they saw no reason to take unnecessary risks. But Goetz believed firmly that the law as applied to him was wrong. The issue for him was not arming himself with an instrument of illegal gain, but equipping himself with a necessary means of self-protection.

The sentencing process itself more closely resembles a town meeting than a controlled legal proceeding, reeking of arcane ritual and stylized responses. In the three months between verdict and sentence, anyone could intervene in the proceeding and advise Justice Crane about the desired sentence. Thirty-six responses, some in the form of letters, others in the form of legal briefs, constituted the file on October 19, the day of judgment. Justice Crane announced that 25 were opposed to jail time for the defendant; 11 were in favor of incarceration. Various institutions had intervened and offered their services if the judge should decide on community service in lieu of imprisonment. Whatever the sentence would be, the voices of many communities would register in the judge's meditations on the right sentence.

The argument between Waples and Slotnick recapitulated many of the themes of the trial. Waples stressed Goetz's mental instability and dangerousness, his lack of remorse about his deed, and his unchanged conviction that he had a right to possess and carry guns. Justice Crane therefore had insufficient basis for deviating from the statutory minimum of one year in jail. Slotnick offered a number of contradictory arguments in favor of leniency. Justice Crane should treat Goetz as though he were indistinguishable from routine offenders with criminal records, roughly half of whom receive probation instead of imprisonment for their crime of gun possession. But, inconsistently, the judge should acknowledge that because of invasive publicity and the rigors of nearly three years of trial, Goetz had suffered enough. And if that did not persuade him, Justice Crane should respond to Goetz's popularity: a sentence of incarceration, Slotnick claimed, would "break the heart of New York."

The informality of the argument about sentencing was enough to instill nostalgia for the evidentiary formalities of the trial. Waples substantiated his claim about Goetz's dangerousness by citing various incidents of alleged violence in his neighborhood—burning down a newsstand, setting fire to the possessions of a homeless woman—and buttressed the claim by vouching that he had interviewed reliable witnesses to these events. Slotnick's claims were equally casual. He cited various experiences of diverse groups wishing him well in the defense. He seemed to think that it was a good argument that the teamsters or a group of students at a local law school expressed opposition to incarceration for their hero.

As soon as Slotnick finished, a young black man with dreadlocks rose at the back of the courtroom and screamed, "If I got the mandatory year, why shouldn't he?" Though obviously improper in the context of the proceedings, the remark underscored the necessity of equal justice that was on everyone's mind.

What Slotnick most obviously failed to do, at sentencing as well as during the trial, was argue the rights and wrongs of Goetz's walking the streets with a loaded handgun under his belt. During the trial, he had an opportunity to argue that Goetz's conduct was justified as matter of necessity, but he missed it and exposed his client to a virtually automatic conviction. During the sentencing proceedings, he had a chance to present a case that Goetz had recognized that his conduct was wrong and that he would not repeat the offense. But not a word was heard that could ease the judge's concerns that Goetz would simply return to his prior pattern of doing what he thought was right, the law be damned.

Goetz had the right to speak last. He had a chance to convince the court that he learned something in the process of his trial and judgment. He would accept the decision of the legislature and the jury and abide by the law on possessing and carrying weapons. But, still wearing his usual garb of blue jeans and a dress shirt open at the collar, he rose to his feet and said nothing. He would remain in the shadows of the moral struggle that his actions had bequeathed to the rest of us.

The path of least resistance for Justice Crane would have been to sentence Goetz to a number of hours of obligatory community service. The probation department had already submitted a presentencing report recommending a sentence other than incarceration. Resisting the popular clamor but also deviating from the legislative minimum, Justice Crane rendered a compromise decision. After delivering a detailed justification for his decision, stressing the importance of equality in sentencing and upholding the policy of the legislature to suppress the unlicensed possession of guns in New York City, he sentenced Goetz to six months in jail, a fine of $5,075, and an additional four and a half years of probation. While under the supervision of the probation department Goetz will have to serve 280 hours in community service with a medical-rehabilitation center and receive psychiatric counseling with a therapist of his choice.

The judge had declined to find that one year in prison would be too harsh, but he reasoned that the sentence he imposed would be just as onerous on Goetz as the legislative minimum. One implication of the split sentence—imprisonment plus probation—is that Goetz could be released, even if he received maximum credit for good behavior in prison, only after an actual minimum of four months behind bars. If he had been sentenced to one year, without subsequent probation, he could have received parole—or "conditional release" as it is called in New York—after serving only two months. Realizing this disadvantage to his client, Slotnick immediately approached the bench and asked the judge to replace the split sentence with the statutory minimum of one year. Justice Crane refused, and the defense declared its intention to appeal.

The defense indeed had good grounds for appealing Justice Crane's imposing a split sentence in place of the statutory minimum of one year. The statute provides that the only way around the minimum term is a finding that the penalty would be unduly harsh. Justice Crane proposed, in effect, that he and other judges should be able to decide when penalties were as onerous as one year in jail. If the Appellate Division upheld Crane's sentence, they would signal approval of this technique for undermining the legislatively mandated minimum jail term. As of late February 1988, when the briefs on the appeal were due to be filed, Goetz's fate was still uncertain. When and how long he would go to jail remained undecided; he was still free on bail, still plying his trade as an electronics repairman in his crammed apartment on 14th Street.

The legal aftermath of the trial would drag on for some time, but of more persistent duration will be the public debate initiated by the shooting of Troy Canty, Barry Allen, James Ramseur, and Darrell Cabey. The prosecution of Bernhard Goetz will remain with us as a focal point of our best efforts to find a just solution to the problem of defensive response to perceived dangers on the streets. The legal system succeeded in directing the public's energies away from retaliatory action and into legal argument. But the issues are too deep, the fears too great, to settle the argument with a verdict and a sentence. As long as we fear mugging on the subway, we will be engaged by the burdens of pondering when self-defense should be a crime.

Notes

Chapter 1: A Shooting in the Subway

1. In the first week after the shooting, the story was widely recounted that prior to the shooting, the gunman said, "I have five dollars for each of you." See *New York Times,* December 24, 1984, p. 1. In one of his confessions recorded on December 31, 1984, Goetz insisted that instead, he said, "I have five dollars for you." See transcript of the videotaped confession (hereafter referred to as video transcript), p. 38.

2. There are two confessions. On the audiotaped confession, given to the New Hampshire police in the early evening of December 31, he says, "You seem to be doing all right; here's another." On the videotaped confession, given later the same evening to New York authorities, he says, "You seem to be all right; here's another." This ambiguity is retained by indicating the word "doing" in brackets throughout the text.

3. Article by David Sanger, *New York Times,* December 30, 1984, section IV, p. 6. A reference to "sharpened screwdrivers" also appears the day before, December 29, 1984, in an Op-Ed piece, Schanberg, "A New Morality Play."

4. For coverage of the victims' side of the story, see the articles by Margot Hornblower, *Washington Post,* January 11, 1985, p. A3, and Jimmy Breslin, *New York Daily News,* December 30, 1984, p. 6.

5. Transcript of tape-recorded confession (hereafter referred to as audio transcript), p. 38.

6. For the best summary of Goetz's early years, see the article by Carol Agus, "Wimp or Wolf," *New York Newsday,* December 15, 1985, pp. 12–51.

7. Audio transcript, p. 38.

8. The first indictment contained two counts of criminal possession in the fourth degree, New York Penal Law (hereafter abbreviated NYPL) § 265.01(1), and one count of criminal possession in the third degree, NYPL § 265.02(4).

9. See supra note 2.

10. The decision to resubmit a charge to a grand jury rests in the discretion of the court. See New York Criminal Procedure Law § 190.75(3). The defense sought appellate review of Crane's decision but was rebuffed on the ground that the decision could be reviewed only by an appeal from a conviction on the indictment. See In the Matter of Application of Bernhard Goetz, 111 AD2d 729 (1985), affirmed 65 NY2d 609 (1985).

11. The ten new charges, with the sections of the New York Penal Law in parenthesis, are four counts of attempted murder in the second degree (§ 110, § 125.40), four counts of assault in the first degree (§ 120.10), one count of reckless endangerment in the first degree (§ 120.10), and one count of criminal possession of a weapon in the second degree (§ 265.03).

12. On so-called "affirmative defenses" like duress and extreme emotional disturbance, the defense must prove the issue by a preponderance of the evidence. See NYPL § 40.00 (duress) and § 125.20(2) (extreme emotional disturbance).

13. Today European legal systems, though often labeled inquisitorial, are properly called accusatorial, because the functions of accusing and prosecuting the suspect are carried out by a distinct branch of the executive, the public prosecutor. In the classical inquisitorial system, judges acted as both accusers and triers of fact. Also, many European systems today have lay persons (called lay assessors) sitting on the bench with the judge and deciding questions of law and fact with him.

14. The entourage typically included Mark Baker, who as the junior member of the team was in charge of legal questions, Frank King, Slotnick's investigator, and often Gillian Coulter, a paralegal in Slotnick's office.

15. This description obviously does not apply to those exchanges out of the presence of the jury in which Slotnick was angry or feigned anger. I don't recall Baker's ever speaking in anger or beneath his customary level of polite deference.

16. At the defense table, Slotnick typically sat at the far left, toward the center of the courtroom, then King, Goetz, sometimes Coulter, and then Baker. In the day-to-day conduct of the trial, Slotnick seemed to confer with King far more often than with Baker or Goetz.

17. Waples's parents came to hear him a few times; apparently no one close to Goetz ever came to the trial.

18. Both Slotnick and Baker are Orthodox or nearly Orthodox in their observance of Jewish law. Both requested and received a suspension of the trial during the two days of the Jewish holiday of Shevuot, which in 1987 fell on June 3 and 4.

19. As reported by Agus, supra note 6, at pp. 23–25.

20. See People v. Bernard W. Goetz, 12 NY2d 689 (1962) (reversing conviction for "endangering the life or health of a child").

21. Lillian Rubin attempts to give us a psychohistory of Goetz and his shooting in her book Quiet Rage: Bernie Goetz in a Time of Madness (Farrar, Straus & Giroux, 1986). For my critique of this approach and its irrelevance for the law, see Fletcher, "Goetz on Trial," New York Review of Books, vol. 34, no. 7, p. 22 (April 23, 1987).

22. Audio transcript, p. 10.

23. Id.

24. Id. at 12.

25. Id. at 8.

26. Id. at 44.

27. Id. Cf. video transcript, pp. 24–25.

28. Video transcript, p. 24.

29. Audio transcript, pp. 10–11.

30. There are two different versions of the statement that gave the verification he wanted. Compare audio transcript, p. 18 ("he said, 'Give me your money.' ") with video transcript, p. 38 ("but I needed verification and he said, 'give me five dollars.' ").

31. Goetz has recounted this rule to me numerous times in personal conversation.

32. That the prosecutor was female in the 1981 case may account for the extraordinary anger and hostility that Goetz expresses toward Assistant District Attorney Susan Braver, who was in charge of taking his confession on videotape.

33. Goetz's complaints about the workings of the system seem ill founded—at least in this case. Fred Clark was the only one of the three suspects apprehended. He was charged with criminal mischief in the fourth degree, NYPL § 145.00, and harassment, § 240.25. He was convicted of criminal assault in the third degree, NYPL § 120.00, and sentenced to six months in jail. So far as I know, he served the full term in jail.

34. This detail comes into focus on the videotape transcript, p. 21.

35. Audio transcript, p. 34.

36. Id. at 17.

37. Id. at 18.

38. Video transcript, p. 39 (answer in response to question about whether he thought he was "about to be robbed").

39. Id. at 11.

40. Id. at 46 ("But do you know, up here [New Hampshire] how, how nice the people are, how nice the children are? How safe it is up here?").

41. Hobbes attributes these words to a stand-in for Sir Edward Coke in his *Dialogue between a Philosopher and a Student of the Common Law* 55 (J. Crespy ed., 1971).

42. Video transcript, p. 22.

Chapter 2: Passion and Reason in Self-Defense

1. See NYPL § 35.15.

2. See NYPL § 35.05.

3. See NYPL § 35.30.

4. See NYPL § § 40.00; 30.05.

5. See, e.g., People v. Torres, 128 Misc. 2d 129 (1985), recognizing the admissibility of expert testimony on the "battered wife" syndrome.

6. NYPL § 160.00.

7. NYPL § 155.05(2)(e)(i).

8. Note that I am treating the question of actual necessity separately from the question of Goetz's mistaken belief in the necessity of using deadly physical force in response.

9. NYPL § 35.15 on self-defense does not distinguish between the defense of self and the defense of third parties.

10. NYPL § 35.15(2)(b) (robbery is among four enumerated crimes sufficiently serious to warrant a defense with deadly force; the others are kidnapping, forcible rape, and forcible sodomy).

11. NYPL § 35.15 ("if he knows he can [retreat] with complete safety as to himself and others").

12. The best explanation for this apparent contradiction (duty to retreat from the more, not the less serious attack) is that the statute combines two distinct traditions in the theory of using deadly force. One theory, generating a duty to retreat, is based on personal defense. The other, not requiring retreat, is based on the authority of every citizen to prevent the occurrence of a serious felony. See supra note 10.

13. Many of the academic commentators who have spoken or written about the Goetz case seem to lack expertise in New York law. They rely upon the general principles of law taught in our law schools and repeated in basic texts on criminal law. For example, Harvard professor Arthur Miller opined in the "20/20" show on the Goetz case, March 21, 1985, that legitimate self-defense presupposes a threat of deadly physical force. His colleague Alan Dershowitz wrote after the verdict, "Any person who is in immediate danger of death or serious bodily harm may use any means necessary to prevent the assault." *Los Angeles Times,* Op-Ed page, June 17, 1987. Both ignore the distinct ground in the New York statute that speaks directly to the prevention of a robbery.

14. See G. Williams, *Textbook of Criminal Law* 504 (2d ed., 1983) ("The law would be oppressive if it said: it is true that you took this action because you felt it in your bones that you were in peril, and it is true that you were right, but you cannot now assign reasonable grounds for your belief, so you were only right by a fluke and will be convicted"); 2 P. Robinson, *Defenses to Crime* 12–29 (1984).

15. For further elaboration of this distinction, see my article "The Right and the Reasonable," 98 *Harvard Law Review* 949 (1985), cited by the Court of Appeals in People v. Goetz, 68 NY2d 98, 112 (1987).

16. See Chapter Three.

17. In fact, he changed his instruction several times, but on relatively minor points. See Chapter Nine.

18. See Coker v. Georgia, 433 U.S. 584 (1977).

19. 1 Mathew Hale, *History of the Pleas of the Crown* 413 (1736).

20. W. Shakespeare, *Hamlet,* act V, scene 1 ("Universal" ed., 1893).

21. 3 E. Coke, *Third Institute* 55 (1644).

22. J. Locke, *Treatise of Civil Government* 14 (Sherman ed., 1937).

23. Record at 4888.

24. See I. Kant, *Metaphysical Elements of Justice* 41 (1797) (J. Ladd translation) ("for even in such a situation [i.e., "an unjust assailant on my own life"] the recommendation of moderation is not of [law], but belongs only to ethics").

25. 4 W. Blackstone, *Commentaries on the Laws of England* 181 (1765–69).

26. If there were any relationship between self-defense and punishment, you would think that less force would be tolerable in self-defense before trial than in punishing the convicted offender after trial; the trial reduces the risk of mistake in treating an ambiguous intrusion—like that of Troy Canty—as a punishable crime.

27. 116 Cal. Rptr. 233, 526 P2d 241, 12 C.3d 470 (1974).

28. Ill. Rev. Stat. § 38, § 7–1.

29. NYPL § 35.15(2) (c).

30. Colo. Rev. Stat. § 18–1–704.5 Cf. Cal. Penal Code § 198.5 (if an unlawful and forcible entry has occurred, an occupant who uses deadly force against the intruder "shall be presumed to have held a reasonable fear of imminent peril of death or great bodily harm"). Both statutes appear to be limited to cases in which the owner is on the premises, and therefore neither justifies the use of spring guns against burglars.

Chapter 3: Tolerant Reason

1. See Dr. Bonham's Case, 77 Eng. Rep. 646 (1670).

2. This finding is called a "directed verdict." In a civil case, either the plaintiff or the defendant can receive a directed verdict. In criminal cases, however, the right of a defendant to a jury trial under the Sixth Amendment precludes a directed verdict for the prosecution. The defendant is entitled to the equivalent, a dismissal of the charges by the judge, if there is not enough evidence to send the case to a jury.

3. People v. Gonzalez, 80 AD2d 543 (Supreme Court Appellate Division, 1st Dept., 1981).

4. So far as I can determine, the prosecutor's concession in this case was simply a thoughtless mistake.

5. See supra note 3.

6. People v. Desmond, 93 AD2d 822, 823 (2d Dept., 1983).

7. The court relied primarily on the Court of Appeals decision in People v. Miller, 39 NY2d 543 (1976), discussed below at notes 29–30, and a popular epigram from Brown v. United States, 256 U.S. 335, 343 (1921) ("Detached reflection cannot be demanded in the presence of an uplifted knife").

8. The most important of these are People v. Wagman, 99 AD2d 521 (1984), and People v. Long, 104 AD2d 902 (1984).

9. There is some dispute about whether the criminal courts in Manhattan are bound by the decisions of departments of the Appellate Division other than the First Department, to which appeals from their decisions run. Compare 1 Carmody-Wait, *Cyclopedia of New York Practice with Forms* § 2:63, p. 75 (2d ed., 1965) (decisions by all departments binding unless there is a decision by the local department to the contrary) with the comment by Justice Lang in People v. Waterman, 122 Misc. 489, 495 n.2 (Criminal Court, New York County, 1984) ("I subscribe to the view that a court is bound to follow the law as interpreted by courts which have appellate jurisdiction over it. . . . Other [departments of the Appellate Division] are entitled to have their rulings accorded great respect and weight but adhering to those rulings is not mandatory").

10. Susan Braver had instructed the first grand jury that they

> must examine the circumstances from defendant's viewpoint as it appeared reasonably to him at the time of each shot. The danger was not merely what defendant did in fact believe it was, but whether he had a right to believe, reasonably, under the circumstances. . . .

She avoided references to what a reasonable person under the circumstances would have believed. See Appendix (unpublished), Manuscript Opinion by Justice Crane, January 16, 1986.

11. Manuscript Opinion by Justice Crane (hereafter cited as Crane's opinion), p. 10; People v. Goetz, 131 Misc. 2d 1, 5 (1986).

12. According to Assistant District Attorney Robert Pittler, who was primarily responsible for the prosecution's argument on appeal, three factors inclined the second grand jury to indict when the first grand jury had not. One was the shift in public opinion against Goetz; the second was the testimony of Troy Canty and James Ramseur before the second grand jury; and the third was Waples's instruction on self-defense.

13. People v. Santiago, 110 AD2d 569 (1st Dept., April 1985).

14. The full instructions went like this:

> You should place yourselves figuratively in the shoes of the defendant and determine whether an ordinary reasonable man, knowing the facts and circumstances and observing the acts and conduct of the defendant as you found such circumstances and conduct to be, would be justified in reasonably believing that the decedent was using or about to use deadly physical force against him, and would be justified in reasonably believing that defensive deadly physical force was necessary to defend himself.
> If by applying such a test, you determine that an ordinary reasonable man would be justified in so reasonably believing, then you should find the defendant was justified in so reasonably believing. [Id. at 570.]

15. Id.

16. The grand jury is a throwback to the inquisitorial mode of procedure, in which the same person functions as both judge and prosecutor. As part of this combined function, the prosecutor instructs the grand jury on the law they should apply to the facts. The prosecutor functions, therefore, both as an advocate and as arbiter of the proceedings.

17. There is no doubt, however, that if Crane had truly wanted to uphold the indictment, he could have found a legal means to do so. Even if Waples had been wrong in his instruction on the "reasonable man" standard, it is not self-evident that this error had a critical influence on the grand jury's deliberations. Minor errors do not count. There is surprisingly little law on the question when an error before a grand jury is sufficiently grave to warrant reversal. It was significant in Justice Crane's thinking on this issue that the erroneous instruction was a response to a juror's question. Crane's opinion at 26; People v. Goetz, 131 Misc. 2d 1, 10 (1986).

18. Relying on the Appellate Division decision in People v. McManus, 108 AD2d 474 (1985), Justice Crane reasoned that self-defense was not a defense to the charge of reckless endangerment and therefore concluded that because Waples's error before the grand jury was immaterial, that charge of reckless endangerment could survive. By the time the Court of Appeals heard the appeal in *Goetz*, the Appellate Division decision in *McManus* had been reversed in People v. McManus, 67 NY2d 541 (1986). At the time of the *Goetz* appeal, therefore, the law was that self-defense applied to reckless endangerment as well as to the nine counts that Crane had dismissed.

19. There was another, independent ground for the dismissal, namely the likelihood that Troy Canty and James Ramseur had committed perjury in their testimony to the second grand jury. Evidence of their criminal intentions came out in November 1985 after the grand jury returned the indictment. The Court of Appeals rejected this prop for the dismissal on the ground that "there was no basis for the Criminal Term [i.e., Justice Crane] to speculate as to whether Canty's and Ramseur's testimony was perjurious." People v. Goetz, 68 NY2d 96, 116 (1986).

20. Crane's opinion at 19; 133 Misc. 2d at 6.

21. Id at 22; 133 Misc. 2d at 8.

22. Appellant's brief to the Court of Appeals at 59.

23. People v. Goetz, 116 AD2d 316 (April 17, 1986).

24. The list cited by the court omits *Gonzalez* and includes a few cases decided after *Santiago*, e.g., People v. Montanez, 118 AD2d 414 (1st Dept., 1986), and People v. Powell, 112 AD2d 450 (2d Dept., 1985).

25. People v. Goetz, 116 AD2d at 331.

26. 39 NY2d 543 (1976).

27. 39 NY2d at 552.

28. Id. at 551. See also id. at 548: "Thus, the perceptions, the state of mind, of the participants to the encounter are critical to a claim of justification."

29. Crane's opinion at 20; 133 Misc. 2d at 7.

30. 116 AD2d at 331.

31. 41 NY2d 906 (1977).

32. Id. at 907.

33. Crane's opinion at 21: 133 Misc. 2d at 7.

34. 116 AD2d at 331.

35. Appellant's brief at 56.

36. Id.

37. Id. at 57.

38. Lambert v. California, 355 U.S. 225 (1957).

39. New York law punishes negligent assault, NYPL § 120.00(3), and negligent homicide, NYPL § 125.10. Other crimes require more serious levels of personal culpability—e.g., NYPL § 150.05 (arson punished only if recklessly committed).

40. Instead of adopting a crime of negligent or reckless attempt, the Model Penal Code invented the crime of reckless endangerment. MPC § 211.2.

41. MPC § 3.04(1) (a).

42. MPC § 3.09(1).

43. At 116 AD2d 329, the majority of the Appellate Division reasoned,

> This change in language [from "believe" to "reasonably believe" in the New York code] is critical and must be viewed in light of the subjective standard in the Model Penal Code . . . which expressly affords a defense of justification to a defendant who honestly but unreasonably believes that he is acting in self-defense.

44. The defense could have countered this argument by claiming that the change in wording was merely cosmetic, that it was designed merely to unite the model code's two provisions—one providing the defense and the other cutting it back in cases of negligent mistakes—into one more efficient standard. There was no evidence that the New York legislature intended to depart from the model code in any significant respect, including the treatment of mistaken self-defense. This argument never came out in the appellate debate.

45. See "Drafting a New Penal Law for New York: An Interview with Richard Denzer," 18 *Buffalo Law Review* 251 (1969). The same issue of the *Buffalo Law Review* includes several other articles about the 1965 Penal Law, but none of them discusses the drafting of § 35.15.

46. People v. Goetz, 68 NY2d at 110.

47. Appellant's brief at 63.

48. A well-researched recent article—Richard Singer, "Resurgence of Mens Rea: II—Honest but Unreasonable Mistake of Fact in Self-Defense," 28 *Boston College Law Review* 459 (1987)—demonstrates that this provision of the MPC has had virtually no impact on the law of the fifty states. There is no evidence, for example, that any state court in the country would have instructed the jury to acquit Goetz

of attempted murder on the basis simply of a good-faith belief that he had to defend himself by shooting the four youths.

49. *New York Law Journal,* February 18, 1986, p. 1.

50. Id.

51. Id.

Chapter 4: The Significance of Suffering

1. I concede the contrary Christian tradition, expressed in Matthew 5:28, that takes the intent for the deed.

2. Bartlett identifies this saying as "epigram 32" in Paladas [fl. 400] in 10 *The Greek Anthology* (J. W. MacKail ed., 1906).

3. MPC § 5.05(1).

4. Record at 4762–63.

5. Record at 4773.

6. See Chapter One, note 2.

7. NYPL § § 120.05, 120.10.

8. NYPL § 120.00.

9. NYPL § 110.00.

10. NYPL § 265.00 (criminal possession in the fourth degree).

11. NYPL § § 265.02 (class D felony), and 70.00(2)(d) (criminal possession in the third degree).

12. NYPL § 400.00(2): "A license for a pistol or revolver shall be issued to . . . (f) have and carry concealed, without regard to employment or place of possession, by any person when proper cause exists for the issuance thereof."

13. NYPL § 400.00 (4-a).

14. This is Goetz's recollection of the reason given. See the video transcript, p. 24.

15. 68 NY2d 264, 501 NE2d 11, 508 NYS2d 403 (October 1986).

16. 68 NY2d at 267.

17. 68 NY2d at 268.

18. Today, so many constitutional problems attend the use of presumptions in criminal cases that it would seem sensible to avoid using presumptions altogether. See, e.g., County Court of Ulster County v. Allen, 442 U.S. 140 (1979) (five votes to four, Supreme Court upholds the New York presumption, permitting but not requiring the jury to infer from the fact of a gun in a car that all the passengers knowingly possessed it).

19. NYPL § 265.15(4).

20. Id.

21. NYPL § 265.02(4). The crime is defined as committed by anyone "who possesses any loaded firearm." But the same section provides there is no violation "if such possession takes place in such person's home or place of business."

22. NYPL § 125.15(1).

23. NYPL § 120.05(4) ("by means of a deadly weapon or a dangerous instrument").

24. Recklessness is conventionally distinguished from negligence, where the actor creates the risk but neither chooses it nor knows of it. See Model Penal Code § 2.02(2).

25. New York, NYPL § 15.05(3) (recklessness requires [1] that the risk be substantial and unjustifiable and [2] that choosing to run the risk "constitutes a gross deviation from the standard of conduct that a reasonable person would observe in the situation").

26. NYPL § 120.20.

27. See NYPL § 120.25 (requires "grave risk of death" rather than merely "substantial risk of serious physical injury").

28. NYPL § 125.15 (1).

29. The difference in punishment is worth noting. Manslaughter in the second degree is a class C felony, punished by a maximum term of 15 years, NYPL 70.00(2) (c); reckless endangerment in the second degree is a class A misdemeanor, punished by a maximum of one year, NYPL 70.15(1). The only difference between the two offenses is whether the reckless act results in death.

30. NYPL § 125.25(2) ("Under circumstances evincing a depraved indifference to human life, he recklessly engages in conduct which creates a grave risk of death . . . and thereby causes the death of another person").

31. NYPL § 120.25 (the wording is identical to NYPL § 125.25[3] except for the last clause on causing death). The fortuitous occurrence of death, a result beyond the actor's control, raises the penalty from a maximum of seven years to life imprisonment.

32. Victor Flores testified as follows (Record at 5887):

> WAPLES: Did you hear any other sounds when the shooting was going on?
> FLORES: There was the sound from ceiling of the car. I heard a sound.
> WAPLES: What sound did you hear?
> FLORES: Like something hit metal.
> WAPLES: And where was that in relation to where you were?
> FLORES: That was very close to where I was sitting.
> WAPLES: You're talking about the ceiling of the car now?
> FLORES: Ceiling.

33. Significantly, the Model Penal Code presumes recklessness where one person knowingly points a gun "at or in the direction of another." MPC § 211.1.

34. NYPL § 35.05.

35. Id.

36. If Justice Crane had been forced to decided the issue, he probably would have rejected Waples's argument on the basis of a footnote in the Court of Appeals opinion in People v. Goetz, 868 NY2d 96, 104 n.2, which says that "justification is a defense to [i.e., reckless endangerment]." The footnote does not distinguish, however, between different types of justification and is therefore consistent with Waples's contention that the proper justification for reckless endangerment is necessity rather than self-defense.

37. For further elaboration on this tactical issue, see Chapter Six, pp. 109–112.

38. Gregory Waples disclosed this to me in an interview on June 18, 1987. So far as I know, it has not been reported in the press.

39. Neither of these guilty pleas would have hurt Goetz in his defense against the civil tort actions brought by the shooting victims.

40. Oliver Wendell Holmes, Jr., *The Common Law* 1 (1881).

Chapter 5: People Matter

1. Record at 1071.

2. Record at 1190.

3. As an attractive young white woman, she might well sympathize more with the victims than with the perpetrators of street crime. Varinsky distinguished, interestingly, between married and unmarried women in their likely fear of violent attack, unmarried women being more vulnerable because they often travel alone. Perlmuth is married.

4. The prospective juror sitting next to the nun was in fact an orthodox Jew wearing a yarmulke. The defense also interposed a peremptory challenge against him, but the reasons for this decision were not clear.

5. Record at 4642.

6. Record at 4657.

7. Record at 4659.

8. Record at 980.

9. Record at 2956.

10. Record at 2944.

11. The 11 consisted of the 10 mentioned in the text plus Michael Axelrod, a 34-year-old white telephone technician.

12. Record at 2807.

13. Record at 4497.

14. Record at 785–86.

15. Record at 793.

16. This trend has been in reversed, at least in California, where the Supreme Court held that the standard of liability for a trespasser is, in principle, the same as for other potential victims. Rowland v. Christian, 69 Cal. 2d 108 (1968).

17. The problem is that the spring gun fires blind, without distinguishing between those who wander on the premises by mistake and those who are in fact burglars.

18. See G. Fletcher, *Rethinking Criminal Law* 274–321 (1978).

19. Record at 2767–68.

20. Record at 4120–21.

21. There remained only the task of selecting the four alternate jurors, who came as well from the third batch of 18. The four selected were Jon Patten, 50, a white male real estate executive; Dephine McFadden, 37, a black female bank clerk; Lou Vereen, 43, a black female warehouse employee; and Augustine Ayala, 33, a white male medical technician. The alternates would sit apart but next to the jury. In the order of their selection, they would replace jurors who could not complete their service in the trial.

22. Record at 4681.

Chapter 6: Trying the Truth

1. Record at 4768.

2. Record at 4776.

3. Record at 4787.

4. NYPL § 125.20(2) (the defense is applicable only in homicide cases).

5. Telephone interview, September 18, 1987.

6. Video transcript, pp. 23–24.

7. Record at 4875.

8. I witnessed this statement on the morning of Wednesday, April 29, the third day of the trial.

9. Record at 4836.

10. Record at 4889.

11. Record at 4854.

12. Record at 4855.

13. Record at 4857.

14. People v. Molineux, 168 NY 264 (1901).

15. See Record at 7287.

16. Crane ruled that the chain-snatching incident alleged against Barry Allen was too tangential to the issues under debate.

17. NYPL § 35.05.

18. See the discussion of the defense's effort to bring in witnesses who would testify, as reasonable people, about their response to threatened aggression. Record at 7394–7413.

19. Record at 6914.

20. Record at 8653–54.

Chapter 7: What the Jury Saw and Heard

1. Their role stops short of prompting their witnesses when they do not perform as expected. Prompting falls under the ban against asking "leading questions." A lawyer disappointed in his witness may not try to put words in his mouth. He cannot ask (assuming that the witness would be prepared to answer "yes"), "Isn't it true that you saw the gunman smiling as he was shooting?" He must try to elicit this testimony without giving away the script. But when they turn into critics on cross-examination, lawyers can ask all the leading questions they want and insist, often contemptuously, that the witness answer "yes" or "no." As one would expect, defense counsel tend to be stronger on cross than on direct examination; they spend most of their time counterpunching the prosecution's witnesses. This was the case with Waples and Slotnick. Waples was effective on direct examination and less so on cross-examination; Slotnick was skillful on cross-examination but ill at ease on direct examination.

2. Audio transcript, p. 8. Cf. the video transcript, p. 24 (Canty's line was "How are you doing?").

3. Audio transcript, p. 8.

4. Id. at 18. Cf. video transcript, p. 28 (Canty repeats his demand for five dollars).

5. According to the video transcript, p. 28 and p. 38, Goetz feels strongly that he said, "I'll give you five dollars" before he started shooting. He denies saying, as the papers reported, "I'll give each of you five dollars." He does not mention this response on the audiotape, and it would not fit with his saying there that Canty's second statement was "Give me your money."

6. Audio transcript, p. 25; cf. video transcript, p. 30 (the statement is "You seem to be doing all right; here's another").

7. Audio transcript, p. 12.

8. Id.

9. Video transcript, p. 11.

10. Video transcript, p. 27.

11. Audio transcript, p. 11.

12. Video transcript, p. 31.

13. Record at 5250.

14. As indicated in note 1 above, on direct examination lawyers are not allowed to ask leading questions, i.e., questions that put words into the witness's mouth. The witness is supposed to tell the story without guidance or suggestion from the lawyer examining him. On cross-examination, which is designed to test the veracity and accuracy of the testimony, the prohibition against leading questions is relaxed.

15. Record at 5924.

16. Record at 5926.

17. Record at 6215.

18. Record at 6330.

19. Record at 6337.

20. Record at 6834.

21. Record at 6840.

22. Record at 6840–41.

23. Record at 6856.

24. Record at 6864.

25. Record at 6063.

26. For further discussion of the relevance of actual harm, see Chapter Four.

27. For the full quote, see supra page 13.

28. Record at 7779–80.

29. A representative of the Guardian Angels told me this shortly after the incident.

30. Technically, everyone who testifies before a New York grand jury receives immunity unless he waives it. But the District Attorney will only call people to testify who waive their immunity or to whom he is prepared to "grant" immunity, i.e., allow the statutory grant of immunity to take effect. The immunity covers all crimes mentioned in testimony responsive to the questions asked in the grand jury proceeding. See Criminal Procedure Law § 190.40. The immunity extends to testimony at trial, but does not cover perjury, either before the grand jury or at trial.

31. The only other relevant exception would have been the privilege for material communicated in confidence to one's lawyer.

32. Record at 5931.

33. Id.

34. Id.

35. Record at 5934.

36. Record at 5935.

37. Record at 7251.

38. Record at 7279.

39. Record at 7252.

40. *New York Post,* May 21, 1987, p. 1 headline.

41. Id., p. 7.

42. On the day of the shoe incident, Ramseur had told court guard Dan Doelger in the elevator that he had a boil on his foot and that it was irritating him. Doelger was standing next to Ramseur at the time Ramseur took off his shoe. Doelger has repeatedly said that he was convinced that Ramseur's action in taking off the shoe was not hostile.

43. *New York Times,* May 24, 1987, p. 26.

44. Record at 7267–68.

45. *New York Times,* May 23, 1987, p. 31.

46. Darrell Cabey was not competent to testify, and Barry Allen, who had not received immunity at the grand jury stage, took the Fifth Amendment to virtually every question.

Chapter 8: What the Jury Did Not Know

1. Record at 8211.

2. Record at 7487.

3. This is the version that appears in the Record at 4942.

4. These two statements were sufficient to convince Justice Crane that Canty and Ramseur had committed perjury before the second grand jury. He cites this likelihood as an additional ground for dismissing the charges that would be defeated by a good claim of self-defense. See Crane's opinion at 26–28; People v. Goetz, 133 Misc. 2d 1, 11–12 (1986).

5. Slotnick said that he would produce an expert to show that the word did have a special, more incriminating meaning in context, but this never came to pass.

6. An additional requirement with this exception created a bind for the defense. The exception would apply only if Cabey was unavailable as a witness. If he was available as a witness, he could testify himself about what he told Filangeri and Breslin; there would be no need to hear the statement from the mouth of a person to whom the statement was made. Yet the defense wanted to preserve the possibility of calling Darrell Cabey as a witness themselves, in which case they might be able to introduce his inconsistent statements on the day of the shooting to impeach his testimony in court. They could not have it both ways. Either Cabey was available or he was not. If the defense sought to make him available, they could not rely on that particular exception to the hearsay rule (declaration against penal interest); if they declared him unavailable, they would forfeit the possibility of introducing the statement as a prior inconsistent statement by a witness.

7. The defense took note of Filangeri's having made a notation of the statement in the ambulance and then having submitted a report that he heard it. Because it is the duty of paramedics to report relevant statements made by crime victims to their superiors, the defense claimed that the statement (or the record of it?) should qualify for admission under the "business record exception" to the hearsay rule. Yet this exception only permits the admission of the record itself when the statements it contains are all independently admissible. If the statement itself is hearsay, as was Filangeri's statement of Cabey's statement, the business record exception does not cure the defect and make admissible something that would otherwise not come in. See *McCormick on Evidence* 912 (3d ed., 1984, by K. Broun, G. Dix, and others). Also, the defense claimed that Cabey's statement was a "false exculpatory statement." But this is not a recognized exception to the hearsay rule.

8. Later in the trial the defense made another effort to get Cabey's statements into evidence, this time relying again on the mysterious argument of a "false exculpatory statement." Apparently, this was another version of the argument that the statements would tend to prove Cabey's state of mind rather than the content of the statements.

9. Record at 6273.

10. Record at 6274.

11. Record at 6275–76.

12. Record at 6290.

13. Observing this episode at the trial, I had the distinct sense that Justice Crane's decision turned in large part on his assessment of the likelihood that these exculpatory statements were truthful. Crane had already gone on record as being highly skeptical of Canty's and Ramseur's testimony before the second grand jury that they intended no harm in the subway confrontation. When contradictory evidence emerged in November 1985 (Cabey's statement to Breslin and Canty's to Peter Smith), he was sufficiently convinced that they had committed perjury before the grand jury to dismiss the indictment partly on that ground. See supra note 2.

14. Record at 7008–10. This statement came in, technically, as a prior inconsistent statement used to impeach Andrea Reid's credibility. One of Slotnick's investigators had surreptitiously taped the statement in an interview with her at her home during the trial. When as a witness, she denied making the statement, Slotnick "refreshed her recollection" by having her listen to the tape, which led her to concede making the statement. And the tape was later admitted into evidence.

15. Record at 6177.

16. Record at 6187.

17. Record at 6188–89.

18. There were numerous problems with Slotnick's blurting out the statement in front of the jury. First, the statement was hearsay; second, it was obviously inflammatory and prejudicial to the prosecution; and third, as Crane points out, the statement was not yet in evidence.

19. Record at 6194.

20. Record at 6195.

21. Record at 6195–96.

22. 59 NY2d 300 (1983).

23. This point of New York law was challenged in the Howard Beach prosecution, but the matter has not yet been resolved by the Court of Appeals.

24. Crane relied on the case of People v. Thomas, 51 NY2d 466 (1980), which held that the defense could not have one of its own witnesses take the Fifth Amendment in the presence of the jury. Although Allen was a prosecution witness and not a defense witness, the case is good authority for Crane's decision. In *Thomas,* however, the court stressed that the decision to allow the witness to take the Fifth Amendment in the presence of the jury "rests within the sound discretion of the trial court." Id. at 472. This means that Crane could also have exercised his discretion to reach the opposite result.

25. In his closing argument Slotnick would tell the jurors that Allen was there.

26. 50 NY2d 747 (1980).

27. Kirk Johnson in the *New York Times,* May 11, 1987, p. B2.

28. Surprisingly, however, Crane repeats the defense's mistake of describing the issue as arising under the "confrontation clause" of the Sixth Amendment. See People v. Goetz, 135 Misc. 2d 888, 891 (1987). The relevant constitutional clause in disputes about granting immunity to a reluctant witness is not the confrontation clause, but the distinct clause of the Sixth Amendment that provides, "the accused shall enjoy the right . . . to have compulsory process for obtaining witnesses in his favor." Crane cites no case, nor does there seem to be a case that connects a dispute about immunity for a witness with the accused's right "to be confronted with the witnesses against him."

29. People v. Goetz, 135 Misc. 2d 888 (1987) (characterizing the decision not to grant immunity as a matter of "trial strategy"). So far as there is any case law authority on the question whether the "missing witness" charge should be granted in response to the prosecution's decision not to grant immunity, it seems all to be contrary to Crane's decision. See, e.g., United States v. Morrison, 365 F2d 521 (D.C. Cir., 1966); United States v. Flomenhoft, 714 F2d 708, 713 (7th Cir., 1983).

Chapter 9: Perfecting the Law

1. On the early history of legal controls over jury verdicts and in general on the themes of this chapter, see M. Kadish and S. Kadish, *Discretion to Disobey* 45–66 (1973).

2. See Bushnell's Case, 6 *Howell's State Trials* 999 (1670).

3. A tribute to the jurors in Old Bailey says that they established "the Right of the Juries to give their verdict according to their conviction." See Scheflin and Van Dyke, "Jury Nullification: The Contours of a Controversy," 43 *Law & Contemporary Problems* 51, 57 n.19 (Autumn 1980).

4. 1 Stat. 596 (1798) (the phrase omitted in the quote refers, with ambiguous implications for the authority of the jury, to their determining law and fact "under the direction of the court").

5. New York Constitution article I, § 8. See Scheflin, "Jury Nullification: The Right to Say No," 45 *Southern California Law Review* 168, 204 n.130 (1972).

6. Constitution of Maryland article XV, § 5. Compare Indiana Constitution article I, § 19 ("the jury shall have the right to determine the law and the facts").

7. Both aspects of nullification are grouped under the vague rationale of "doing justice" in the individual case. See, e.g., Wigmore, "A Program for the Trial of a Jury," 12 *American Judicature Society* 166 (1929).

8. See Kates, "Handgun Prohibition and the Original Meaning of the Second Amendment," 82 *Michigan Law Review* 204 (1983).

9. United States v. Anderson, Crim. No. 602–71 (D.N.J. 1973), Transcript at 8396–94, as cited in Scheflin and Van Dyke, supra note 3, at 53, n.2.

10. For an example of tight control over the jury's deliberations in a case of political conscience, see the prosecution of Benjamin Spock, William Sloane Coffin, Jr., Mitchell Goodman, and Michael Ferber for conspiracy to advocate violations of the Selective Service Law. The trial judge would not let the jury consider issues bearing on the motives of the defendants to protest the war in Vietnam. See J. Mitford, *The Trial of Dr. Spock* (1969). United States v. Spock, 416 F2d 165 (3d Cir., 1969).

11. If the defense is an affirmative defense, like duress, the appropriate finding is that the jury is convinced by a preponderance of the evidence; if the defense is an ordinary defense, the necessary conclusion is simply that the jury has at least a reasonable doubt about the defense.

12. Associated Press, April 16, 1987.

13. On the effort to invoke the necessity defense in this context, see United States v. Kabat, 797 F2d 580 (1986), *cert. denied,* 101 S. Ct. 1958 (1987).

14. For a history of the case from the perspective of the presiding judge, see H. Stern, *Judgment in Berlin* (1984). I was of counsel for the defense in this case and responsible for arguing the defense of necessity.

15. The defense of necessity would obviously not justify routine Arab hijacking and kidnapping of passengers. Factual differences in context and purpose distinguish Tiede's situation clearly from forcing a TWA airliner down in Beirut and holding its passengers as hostages for the demand of releasing Palestinian prisoners in Israeli jails. Tiede's intention was merely to secure passage to West Berlin, not to gain sufficient control over the airplane to make other demands. He had no intention of keeping the passengers and crew a moment longer than necessary to fly and land in West Berlin. Most significantly, however, he could assume that most of his victims would agree or at least sympathize with his personal political objective of escaping to the West.

16. NYPL § 25.05(2).

17. MPC § 3.02.

18. All of these provisions are contained in NYPL § 400.00(2).

19. See Kates, "The Battle over Gun Control," 84 *The Public Interest* 42, 45 (Summer 1986).

20. These figures were reported in a story in *USA Today,* October 20, 1987, p. 3A.

21. Sometimes the appeal to necessity is a bit farfetched, as, for example, in the trial of Susan (Katya) Komisaruk in San Francisco for destroying governmental property. She attacked the computer at Vandenberg Air Force Base in order to avert, as she said, the threat of nuclear war. Her defense was the higher law of necessity. See the report in the *Los Angeles Times,* November 14, 1987, p. 32.

22. MPC § 3.02(1)(c).

23. NYPL § 35.05(2).

24. The reference is to the "Sixth Avenue incident" described in the video transcript, pp. 23–24.

25. 60 NY2d 142 (1983).

26. 98 AD2d 908 (3d Dept., 1983).

27. People v. Moore, 42 AD2d 268 (2d Dept., 1973).

28. It is not clear to me either that (1) the arrest would be invalid if the driving was justified or (2) an invalid arrest would bear on the subsequent assault that the defendant allegedly committed against the officer.

29. People v. Beineck, 60 AD2d 718 (4th Dept., 1977).

30. 62 NY2d 126 (1984).

31. Id. at 130.

32. Id.

33. The use of the this phrase "justification may excuse" shows how confused the court is about the nature of justification and the distinction between justification and excuse.

34. The material quoted in the text continues at 62 NY2d 130–31: "Accordingly, the only charge defendant was entitled to on the fourth count of the indictment was temporary innocent possession; any benefit he was entitled to because of the claim of self-defense pertained to the use of a weapon and he received that when the court charged justification in connection with the counts of attempted murder and assault."

35. See People v. Pons, 68 NY2d 264 (1986).

36. In People v. Jose C., 127 Misc. 2d 689 (1985), Justice Crane interprets People v. Almodovar, discussed above, as prohibiting all forms of justification, including NYPL § 35.05 (necessity), in cases of criminal possession of a weapon in the third degree.

Chapter 10: Arguing Toward a Verdict

1. Record at 5207.

2. See Chapter Seven, note 42.

3. See T. Kuhn, *The Structure of Scientific Revolutions* 68–69 (2d ed., 1970).

4. It could not explain, for example, the elliptical orbits of the planets. See id. at 156.

5. As juror Carolyn Perlmuth described Slotnick's closing argument, "it [was] really rambling and kind of disorganized. And everyone was falling asleep. Mark Baker fell asleep during that, and some of the jurors. That is why the judge kept calling those breaks." All references to Carolyn Perlmuth's statements are based on a recorded interview conducted Friday, July 3, 1987.

6. Interview with Carolyn Perlmuth.

7. Record at 8825.

8. Id.

9. This is the full list of 17 factual components and the witnesses who corroborated Goetz's own version of what happened:
   1. Who was sitting where when he entered the train.
      —Confirmed by Troy Canty.
   2. Troy Canty and Barry Allen approached him.
      —Three witnesses—Josephine Holt, Garth Reid, and Mary Gant—said they saw only two people standing over him.
   3. Troy Canty asked him for five dollars.
      —Confirmed by Troy Canty.
   4. He stood up.
      —Confirmed by Troy Canty.
   5. He shot Canty first.
      —Also confirmed by Canty.
   6. The second person he shot was the second person who approached him.
      —It must have been Barry Allen.
   7. Barry Allen was running through the crowd when shot.
      —Confirmed by the witnesses Victor Flores and Andrea Reid and the medical testimony that Allen was shot in the back.
   8. After firing the first two shots, he pivoted to his right and fired two more.
      —Confirmed by Garth Reid.
   9. He fired the third shot at someone trying to "climb through the wall."
      —It must have been James Ramseur.
   10. He fired twice at Darrell Cabey.
       —Two bullet holes in Cabey's jacket, as pointed out by Detective Charles Haase.
   11. He fired the first shot at Cabey when the latter was standing up.
       —Confirmed by the defense expert Dominick Dimaio.
   12. He fired the second shot at Cabey when the latter was sitting down.
       —Confirmed by Christopher Boucher.

13. He fired five shots.

—Confirmed by police investigators who recovered the bullets.

14. After the shooting, he went over to Troy Canty and said something to him.

—Confirmed by Victor Flores.

15. After the shooting, he noticed two women kneeling on the floor of the car.

—Confirmed by the conductor Armando Soler and Mary Gant, one of the two women.

16. He told the conductor, "These guys tried to rob me."

—Confirmed by the conductor.

17. He left the train by jumping down to the tracks.

—Confirmed by Flores and the conductor Soler.

Record at 8856–64.

10. Record at 8893.

11. Goetz himself made a number of comments supporting the interpretation that he did not actually approach Cabey and speak to him. See the audio transcript, p. 26 ("Looking and acting are the same thing, virtually.")

12. Slotnick's cross-examination of Detective Haase generated the following exchange at pp. 5096–97 of the Record:

Q: Would you tell the jury and show them [the jacket] and you can stand up, exhibit it for the jury to see where the entrance wound [sic] is in that jacket.

A: Entrance hole.

Q: Entrance hole.

A: There are two entrance holes. There is this one here, which is the upper, left back; and there is one here, which is below the left armpit. . . .

Q: Now does that jacket have any other corresponding holes on the other side?

A: Yes.

Q: Okay. Can we turn it over and perhaps see the other holes?

A: They're marked with a tape.

Q: Okay. And I presume, since those are entrance holes, these would be exit holes, is that correct?

A: That's correct.

13. Record at 8872: "If Dominick Dimaio's hypothesis were correct that Darrell Cabey's spinal cord was severed by the first shot and that he fell into the seat and [he] was in that seat when the second shot was fired, then that would mean that the shot that missed Darrell Cabey passed through his jacket and struck this simulated panel right here, but that is impossible . . . the defendant was standing up and holding the gun above where the bullet entered the jacket, so it had to be going down. . . . There is no way in the world . . . that a bullet can [be] coming through this jacket on a downward trajectory and . . . miraculously make an angular turn and strike the wall in the subway car. . . ."

14. Record at 8875. The argument assumes that Goetz could not have fired the fifth shot at a sitting Cabey at a height and angle that would have enabled the

bullet to penetrate through the jacket, whiz by Cabey's chest, and make a direct impact on the cab wall.

15. This was a curious argument for Waples to make, for his general line in arguing against Dimaio, supported by Dr. Hirsch's testimony, was that any height and any angle of the gun were possible.

16. But note that the jurors were not necessarily bound by Haase's testimony. See Mark Leslie's theory developed on pages 192–193.

17. Record at 9120.

18. Record at 9127–28 [emphasis added].

19. The only case the defense cited on their behalf was People v. Griffin, 29 NY2d 91 (1971), in which the Court of Appeals did rule that it was error for the prosecution to say in its summation, without supportive evidence, that the defendant had inflicted a wound on himself that would distinguish his face from its appearance at the time of the crime. In the view of the high court, the trial court should have permitted the defense to reopen its case in order to rebut this statement. If Justice Crane had believed that Waples had indeed made a damaging factual claim unsupported by the evidence, he would have had a legal basis for granting the relief requested by the defense.

20. Record at 8938.

21. Record at 8977.

22. All references to Mark Leslie's views are based on a recorded interview conducted Thursday evening, July 2, 1987.

23. The recorded interviews with Carolyn Perlmuth and Mark Leslie in the week after the verdict generated about 80 pages of transcript.

24. The first indictment contained two counts of criminal possession of a weapon in the fourth degree and one count of the same crime in the third degree. The second indictment contained four counts of assault in the first degree and four counts of attempted murder (one of each for each of the victims), one count of reckless endangerment in the first degree, and one count of criminal possession of a weapon in the second degree.

25. If they voted not guilty of assault in the first degree, they were to consider, as to each of the victims, the lesser charge of reckless assault in the second degree. If they voted not guilty on reckless endangerment in the first degree, they were to consider the lesser charge of reckless endangerment in the second degree.

26. Criminal Procedure Law § 60.22.

27. Constructive possession is an extension of the actual physical control over an object. If someone has a right of access to guns, he has constructive possession over them wherever they happen to be.

28. The note read, "Third item, define corroboration (law), dominion, domain, construct: what constitutes these." Record at 9270.

29. For the same reasons, judges often sequester juries in hotels during their deliberations. This jury was sequestered from Wednesday, June 10, the beginning of final arguments, to June 16, the day of their verdict.

30. Record at 9282.

31. This was a motive that Leslie understood. He dictated notes on the trial every night and then sold his tapes to the *New York Post* for $4,000. The *Post* ran a series of three articles about Leslie's inside view of the trial.

32. Neither the story nor the tapes of the conversations with Goetz were admitted into evidence.

33. As quoted by Perlmuth.

34. Her theory does bear some resemblance, however, to the narrow theory of intention used in the doctrine of double effect. See the discussion in Chapter Four, pages 76–77.

35. Record at 9223.

36. Record at 9374.

37. Record at 9357–58.

38. Record at 9319.

39. Record at 9374.

40. See the comments by Benjamin Ward after the verdict came in, *New York Daily News,* June 18, 1987, p. 5.

41. Record at 9396.

42. Record at 9396–97.

43. Justice Crane did not seem to be concerned that the defense's alternative explanation, namely that one bullet made both holes, was not only unlikely, but clearly impossible under the constraints provided by the testimony, in particular Detective Haase's statement that both holes on the outside of the jacket were entrance holes. There is no way that a bullet can enter a jacket from the outside twice without passing through a fold in the jacket a third time. This hypothesis was not before the jury. If it was the only alternative explanation for the facts, however, it should have made Waples's theory seem less farfetched.

44. Record at 9412.

45. Id.

46. Record at 9416.

47. As Justice Crane laid them out, the five elements are: (1) the defendant shot the victim with a pistol, (2) intent to cause "serious physical injury," (3) the actual occurrence of "serious physical injury," (4) defendant "caused" the injury by means of a pistol, and (5) the pistol was a "deadly weapon." The terms in quotations are used in the statute defining the crime, NYPL § 120.10(1).

48. If the path of the bullet ran between Cabey's body and the near wall of the train, the angle of impact against the cab wall would be more consistent with the

physical evidence of a circular indentation on the wall, indicating a trajectory more or less perpendicular to the wall. If the bullet had to pass through the jacket on the other side of Cabey's body, it would have had an angular trajectory toward the same point on the cab wall. An angular impact would have been inconsistent with the physical evidence.

49. See supra note 12.

50. This is way Mark Lesly summed up his reactions to Dimaio's testimony and the battle of the experts: "You just can't say that it's impossible. But thank God, [Waples] brought in Dr. Hirsch who said, 'Of course, it's possible.' And then I say, 'O.K. Yeah. You just said what I had felt anyway.'"

51. They had voted not guilty on two counts of criminal possession of a weapon in the fourth degree, four counts of attempted murder, and three counts of assault in the first degree (as against Canty, Allen, and Ramseur).

52. Some jurors thought, as Perlmuth reports, "he did it in order to get a free trip to New York. . . . Or that he did it get attention." Another juror—not Lesly— came up with a farfetched theory based on the assumption that Michals and Boucher were gay. As Lesly reflected on the argument: "He's a gay and gays are a persecuted minority in this country, just like blacks. . . . perhaps, I'm speculating here, he identified with another minority group. Maybe it was much simpler than that. He was given a hell of a fright and he wanted to get back at him [Goetz]. I don't know. I didn't necessarily have to come to a conclusion as to motivation." Perlmuth said she thought this was "kind of tortuous." The speculations are significant as indication of the jurors' efforts to make sense of the witnesses' behavior and the testimony they were prepared to reject.

53. For further details on Slotnick's cross-examination, see Chapter Seven, pages 123–125.

54. So far as I can tell, there were no press reports about a fifth shot until January 3, when the Associated Press and the *New York Times* reported the comments Susan Braver made at the arraignment in New York.

Chapter 11: Mixed Messages

1. Representative Albert Vann from Brooklyn as quoted in the *New York Daily News,* June 18, 1987, p. 5.

2. Id.

3. The poll, based on 1,013 New York city residents 18 years and older, was published in *Newsday,* June 28, 1987, p. 6.

4. As quoted in the *New York Daily News,* June 18, 1987, p. 5.

5. Id.

6. Sherrye Henry show on WOR, June 17, 1987.

7. *Los Angeles Times,* July 17, 1987, p. 1.

8. *New York Times,* December 22, 1987, p. 1.

9. This is the statement at a block meeting circa 1981, as reported by Myra Friedman in her article in *New York* magazine, February 18, 1985, in which Goetz reportedly said, "The only way we're going to clean up this street is to get rid of the spics and niggers."

10. See *New York Daily News*, January 3, 1985, p. 30.

11. Video transcript, p. 21 ("is it conceivable that one person alone in the subway system, carrying a package, would start up with three people?")

12. The trial judge ruled that this use of the peremptory challenge was unconstitutional; the defense appealed to the Court of Appeals, but the matter remains unresolved. See *New York Times*, September 20, 1987, p. E6.

13. Robert Leach was instrumental in moving the jury toward an acquittal on the charges of criminal possession of a weapon in the fourth degree.

14. As revealed in his statements on the "Donahue" show a few days after the verdict, however, juror Mark Lesly was acutely aware that Fred Clark was black. Juror Carolyn Perlmuth said she was surprised by this revelation.

15. In an interview after the trial, Justice Crane took the position that he would not have permitted the witness to answer an inquiry about Fred Clark's race. Crane's judgment that race should not be discussed openly in the trial rests in part on the decision of the Appellate Division in People v. Dexter Thomas, *New York Law Journal*, April 18, 1987, a prosecution for criminal possession of a weapon, in which the defendant, black, said that he picked up the weapon when he saw two white men coming toward him in his black neighborhood. The men were undercover police. The prosecutor repeatedly referred to the officers' being white, thereby implying that the defendant's fear was unreasonable.

16. Jack Greenberg, former head of Legal Defense Fund, took this position.

17. For further details on this re-creation, see Chapter Seven.

18. After the trial recessed and then reconvened, Crane insisted that court guards play the parts of the four victims.

19. There are some inevitable exceptions to this general principle. Items of physical evidence, such as the two guns Myra Friedman turned over to the police, do not translate precisely into verbal propositions, but they are nonetheless admissible. Also, the jury evaluates the credibility of the witnesses on the basis of subverbal cues given off in the course of their testimony.

20. For further discussion of the *Berg* case and the way Justice Crane decided to let Ramseur be tested in front of the jury, see Chapter Eight.

21. Researchers will have to rely either on this account of the trial or, ironically, on the pro-Goetz *New York Post*, May 29, 1987, p. 13, which accurately reports the racial component of the demonstration.

22. Compare Justice Crane's description of the facial expressions of two women whom Slotnick brought into court in an effort to refute Troy Canty's claim that he did not know either of them: "In fairness, it should be noted that when the witness [Canty] disclaimed recognition of each of these witnesses [i.e., the two women, who were not technically witnesses], they visibly reacted in somewhat of an expression of disbelief." Record at 5773.

244 A Crime of Self-Defense

23. L. Rubin, *Quiet Rage: Bernie Goetz in a Time of Madness* (Farrar, Straus & Giroux, 1986).

24. My impression of a "hostile public reaction" is based largely on newspaper commentary and discussions with people who have read the book. Other aspects of the book may account for some of the unfavorable reaction. Rubin attempts to account for Goetz's acts by writing a psychohistory of his life. She digs up many interesting details, but the account reveals some of the excesses of a psychological-deterministic approach to criminal behavior. See my review, "Goetz on Trial," *New York Review of Books,* vol. 34, no. 7, p. 22 (April 23, 1987).

25. See Bazelon, "The Morality of the Criminal Law," 49 *Southern California Law Review* 385 (1976).

26. As quoted from supporting papers submitted to Justice Crane during his deliberations on sentencing.

27. The defense did assert the defense of necessity to the charge of criminal possession of a weapon in the second degree, which requires possession of a loaded weapon with "the intent to use it unlawfully." This was an instance in which necessity clearly could not apply. If the defendant had the intent to use the weapon for an unlawful purpose, he could not simultaneously have the good purpose required for the defense of necessity. That the defense urged necessity in this context suggests that they may not have had a good grasp of the theory behind the defense.

28. For notes on the expansion of the law of self-defense to include a right to shoot intruding burglars, see Chapter Two.

29. See the works of Donald Kates cited in notes 8 and 19 to Chapter Nine.

30. See Chapter Two for further elaboration.

31. Criminal possession of a weapon in the third degree is a class D felony, which means that the maximum term in jail is seven years. NYPL § 70.00(2)(d). It is also classified as a "violent felony offense," NYPL § 70.02(1)(c), which implies that the minimum term for an indeterminate sentence must be one third of the maximum, or two and one-third years. NYPL § 70.02(4).

32. NYPL § 70.02(c).

33. NYPL § 70.02(c)(i).

34. NYPL § 1.05(5).

35. Id.

36. *New York Times,* October 20, 1987, editorial page.

Index